Pitt Series in
Policy and Institutional Studies

The SEC and Capital Market Regulation

The Politics of Expertise

Anne M. Khademian

UNIVERSITY OF PITTSBURGH PRESS

Pittsburgh and London

Published by the University of Pittsburgh Press, Pittsburgh, Pa., 15260
Copyright © 1992, University of Pittsburgh Press
Manufactured in the United States of America

Khademian, Anne M., 1961–
    The SEC and capital market regulation : the politics of expertise /
Anne M. Khademian.
      p. cm. — (Pitt series in policy and institutional studies)
    Includes bibliographical references and index.
    ISBN 0-8229-3725-5 (cl)
    1. United States. Securities and Exchange Commission. 2. Capital
market—Law and Legislation—United States. 3. Securities—United
States. 4. Legislative oversight—United States. I. Title.
II. Series.
KF1444.K47   1992
363.0082′58—dc20   92-11577
                                                      CIP

A CIP catalogue record for this book is available from the British Library.
Eurospan, London

For Zarir

Contents

Acknowledgements

I have met and worked with many terrific people during the course of this study, and I am grateful for the contributions they each have made. The study is built upon countless hours of interviews with past and present staff and commissioners of the Securities and Exchange Commission, past and present staff members of the House and Senate, former members of Congress, and representatives of the securities industry. They each found time for me within their rigorous seventy-hour work weeks. The pledge of anonymity prevents me from identifying particular individuals I routinely called upon for clarification and information, and who allowed me to sound out my ideas with the benefit of their insight and experience. Please know that I am sincerely grateful.

In its various configurations, the manuscript has benefited from the thorough reading and thoughtful comments of Charles Franklin, Gary Miller, John Gilmour, William Lowry, Robert Katzmann, Bert Rockman, Donald Kettl, Nancy Davidson, Robert Johnson, Jack Knight, and two anonymous readers. I am especially grateful to Charles Franklin for his guidance, and to Gary Miller, whose teaching and research has most significantly influenced the way I think about bureaucratic politics.

For financial support, I thank the Brookings Institution, the University of Wisconsin Graduate School, and the Washington University Graduate School and Department of Political Science.

I am indebted to Jane Flanders, Frank Moone, and Bert Rockman of the University of Pittsburgh Press for their support of the study and their enormous help in bringing it to completion.

Finally, I am grateful for the support of my husband, my parents, my grandmother, and family, and my nieces and nephews—Ali, Alireza, Azadeh, Baharan, Caleb, Goli, Kamran, Kayhan, Kaveh, Kayvan, Madeline, Mohammadreza, Negin, Noah, and Richard.

The SEC and Capital Market Regulation

1 Introduction

*B*ureaucracies operate under constant outside pressure, which is sometimes more intense than at other times. When politicians have agendas, when constituents complain, or when catastrophes occur, hearings will be held, letters written, phone calls made, press coverage intensified, and (possibly) mandates created or radically amended. It is the American process of directing the bureaucracy and holding it accountable (Aberbach 1990; Derthick 1990). But bureaucracies also operate with a great deal of clout derived from their expertise. How we fight a war, explore space, fight disease, distribute agricultural aid, or regulate an industry is largely determined by a cadre of nonelected experts on whom politicians routinely rely for their policy options and to whom they often defer (Dexter 1969; Allison 1971; Lowi 1979; Dodd and Schott 1979).

In a democratic society bureaucrats are held accountable to elected officials for their actions and are bound by their legislative mandate. Yet when technically complex issues are involved, there is a need to delegate responsibility to experts who are independent of the political fray. This creates a tension between accountability and expertise, and the constant struggle to reconcile that tension is fundamental to the development of a government bureaucracy in the United States (Wilson 1887; Hyneman 1950; Kaufman 1956; Eisenstadt 1965; Rourke 1984; Waldo 1986; Gormley 1989). To understand why bureaucracies behave as they do, we must focus on and account for this tension.

The application of rational-choice theory to the study of bureaucratic behavior makes it possible to address this essential tension in an interesting way. This analytic approach has sparked a new insight into the institutional design of the bureaucracy as a composite of past struggles over the preferred approach to government policy making and, consequently, preferred policy outcomes. In very general terms, the theory of rational choice first assumes that political actors have objectives and that they act so as to maximize (or at least attain) those objectives. Applying the theory to a bureaucracy, we assume that an agency wants to maximize its annual budget (Fiorina and Noll 1978), or perhaps achieve stability in its relations with political overseers and consistency in implementing policy (Ferejohn 1987). In addition, elected officials are assumed to have objectives concerning an agency's behavior so as to promote their chances of reelection (Fiorina 1977).

Second, rational-choice theorists assume that the key to understanding goal-oriented behavior in the political world is to understand the rules of politics—the formal and informal structures or institutions[1] that define, constrain, and encourage particular types of behavior (Riker 1982, 1987). Again, applying this theory to a bureaucracy, we must consider the following: the political decision to delegate authority to an agency, its location in the government system, its mandate for action, as well as its internal structure—all are important to various political actors as ways of conditioning and regulating bureaucratic behavior and, consequently, policy outcomes (Knott and Miller 1987; Fiorina 1982, 1986).

The rational-choice literature offers useful approaches to studying the institutions that govern the bureaucracy. The institutional arrangements in Congress and the executive branch encourage their members to deal with the bureaucracy in ways that benefit their electoral interests and policy concerns. Further, the literature suggests why we should study bureaucratic rules, or institutions, as well as traditional battles over the rules. Decisions to establish a multiheaded commission, an agency's enforcement and rule-making authority, and how it reaches a decision—all represent the competing political interests that won or lost the battle to create the agency. These factors tell us much about the agency's behavior (Moe 1989).

To repeat, this approach can capture the dynamics of accountability and expertise as it relates to bureaucratic behavior. The battle over drawing the line between bureaucratic expertise (or the political independence of an agency) and accountability (or the accessibility of an agency to elected officials) is nowhere more clearly illustrated than in the design and development of bureaucratic institutions (Skowronek 1982). However, much of the rational-choice literature has been preoccupied with the question of accountability, or elected officials' motives and means of trying to control the bureaucracy. With important exceptions (to be discussed), the political significance of *expertise* in defining, developing, and changing a bureaucracy's structure and decision making, as well as how it develops a legislative agenda, is often given scant consideration.

Instead, an agency is typically treated as an agent to be controlled or manipulated by competing principals who define its mandate and structure (Ross 1973; McCubbins and Page 1987; see also Levinthal 1988; Moe 1984). The agency is important only insofar as its behavior reflects the preferences and priorities of outside principals— such as congressional committees and their constituents (Weingast 1984) or the president (Rothenberg 1987)—who have various tools of accountability with which to dominate agency behavior at strategic times. It is usually assumed that if the mechanisms for controlling the bureaucracy are working, an agency's preference for policy outcomes different from those of its principals are suppressed by a concern for maintaining or increasing congressional appropriations, or simply by a desire to avoid excessive oversight (Calvert, Moran, and Weingast 1987). Simply put, bureaucratic expertise is presumed to play no independent and significant role in determining the rules of policy making, or in ultimate policy outcomes.

While the attempt to demonstrate control may be attractive to those concerned about a "runaway" bureaucracy, this is not necessarily realistic. Indeed, the effort recalls early debates over the "dichotomy" between politics and administration. It was argued that an administrative apparatus could be constructed that was merely an apolitical mechanism for implementing decisions made by elected officials (Goodnow 1900; White 1926; but see Dahl 1947 and Appleby 1949; this subject is discussed in greater detail in chapter 8). Yet an agency's design and decision-making processes, as well as policy outcomes, are as critical to bureaucratic personnel as to any politician or interest group with a stake in policy outcomes, and bureaucracies have political resources of their own for expressing their preferences.

Most significantly, an agency's expertise is influential in defining options for policy making (Simon 1976; Rourke 1984; Kingdon

1984), and bureaucratic personnel have succeeded in institutionaliz-ing their expertise in the internal structures of agencies. Self-governing professions typically define personnel and quality of work standards independently of (or in place of) statutory guidelines, and as a profession's routine standards and procedures become institu-tional components of decision making, the autonomy of the profes-sion can become the agency's as well (Mosher 1982). Eventually, the very structures and procedures by which elected officials are thought to control the bureaucracy can prove to be an important source of bureaucratic clout. Specifically, the development of stan-dard operating procedures premised on bureaucratic expertise, an agency's gradual adaptation to its environment, and institutional iner-tia can all limit the politicians' ability to manipulate bureaucratic behavior (Allison 1971; March and Olsen 1989, 1984).

Further, as many scholars have clearly demonstrated, a complex bureaucracy is not easily reduced to the goals of budget maximiza-tion, or simply keeping oversight to a minimum (Wilson 1989). Motivations for behavior can vary from one professional group to another within an agency (Katzmann 1980), from political appoin-tees to career officials (Aberbach and Rockman 1976; Warwick 1975), and from the specialists (or professionals) to the manage-ment generalists (Janowitz 1960; Lipsky 1980).

Perhaps this very complexity motivates many of the rational-choice "principal-agent" analyses of bureaucracy. Rather than deal with diverse goals, the subtle clout of expertise, and the complicated relationships linking an agency, politicians, and interest groups, a bureaucracy is methodologically more accessible (particularly with respect to the application of formal mathematical models) if we assume that agencies—despite their complexity—respond to a few basic incentives. Given that assumption, it is not a leap to assume that actions taken by an agency represent the priorities and preferences of politicians having the means to hold agencies accountable.

There are, however, important exceptions to this limited princi-pal-agent perspective. Where many rational-choice scholars are preoccupied with the means of controlling the bureaucracy, sev-eral have begun to deal with the *limits* of such control. For exam-ple, Hill (1985, 1987) and Hammond, Hill, and Miller (1986) see strategies for bureaucratic decision making and implementation as playing a key role in determining policy outcomes; Bendor, Taylor, and van Gaalen (1987) address the role of expertise in conditioning a principal's ability to control an agent; and Knott and Miller (1987) examine the role of high- and low-level bureaucratic personnel as explicit political players with preferences for the design and maintenance of bureaucratic structure and process.[2] In dealing with the limits of outside control, these theorists are beginning to redress the importance of expertise and accountability in the study of the bureaucracy.

Both the political desire to control the bureaucracy and the need for reliable expertise influence the formal and informal structures that condition and create incentives for bureaucratic behavior. If we want to explain the behavior of the U.S. bureaucracy, we must examine how both motives have become institutionalized. The rational-choice premise—that in addition to representing political preferences for policy outcomes, the rules of politics condition behavior—offers a useful means to do just that.

This book attempts, first, to analyze the tension between expertise and accountability in the federal regulation of securities (stocks and bonds); second, to analyze how that tension has been captured institutionally; and third, to demonstrate the implications of that tension for the politics of federal securities policy. The study focuses on the Securities and Exchange Commission (SEC) and the longstanding battle over the rules that define its jurisdiction and its decision making, as well as its role in making federal securities policy. I seek to explain stability and change in the federal regulation of securities by examining the interaction of goal-oriented political actors with an interest in securities policy and their attempts to use institutional structure and procedure to influence and define the policy process.

In a very general sense, this study is in the rational-choice tradition by its recognition of goal-oriented behavior and the importance of institutional design in conditioning that behavior. I assume that both the SEC and elected officials (those with constituent interests in securities policy) seek particular outcomes, and that these actors struggle, from their various institutional bases, to generate the conditions necessary to realize those preferences. However, I deviate from much of the rational-choice literature in two important ways. First, I develop and analyze qualitatively, rather than with formal models, the structures and procedures of federal securities policy making. Second, I assume that the demand for expertise in the regulation of the securities markets, and the expertise provided by SEC personnel, are important *independent* factors in nurturing the formal and informal institutions guiding the SEC's behavior and federal securities policy.

The tension between accountability and expertise is most conspicuous in the SEC's interaction with its congressional legislative committees: the House Energy and Commerce Committee and the Senate Banking, Housing, and Urban Affairs Committee. These committees have jurisdiction over the SEC's mandate, and consequently are most frequently engaged in overseeing the agency and making it accountable. These committees are also key to the representation of powerful economic groups concerned with securities regulation. Consequently, the study focuses predominantly on relations between the SEC and these committees as central to the balance between accountability and expertise. However, I do not neglect the importance of other actors in shaping the politics of the SEC. The president is seen primarily as an influence who competes with the congressional legislative committees; I also address the role of Congress and of the courts in discussions concerning the SEC's internal decision making. Each of these "outside" forces has played an integral role from time to time in defining federal securities policy. The role of these actors is particularly important when there is disagreement over the direction of the agency.

Why the SEC?

In choosing to study the SEC, I was motivated by two concerns. First, as just discussed, was my intention to redress the analytical imbalance between expertise and accountability that has developed in recent studies. Many of the formal, rational-choice models of the bureaucracy are quite attractive in offering simple explanations for a wide range of behavior. If bureaucratic behavior appears discretionary, one can argue that given the mechanisms designed to control a bureaucracy, the policy options it chooses can be traced to the preferences of elected officials (Calvert, McCubbins, and Weingast 1989). If a bureau's behavior sparks oversight hearings or investigations, one can argue that the prestructured incentive system perhaps failed, but that nevertheless politicians had the means (such as hearings or new legislation) and the motive (responding to constituent "fire alarms") to bring the agency back into line

(McCubbins and Schwartz 1984). And if politicians threaten to pass legislation that will direct the behavior of an agency more explicitly, but fail to do so, one can argue that the politicians were merely posturing to get the agency to take a more moderate position (Ferejohn and Shipan 1988). But it is very troublesome that increasingly our "good" explanations for bureaucratic behavior are not concerned about an agency itself and the political clout of expertise—only how it responds to the machinations of competing politicians.

To examine the tension between accountability and expertise more clearly, and the impact of that tension on policy outcomes, I selected an agency with considerable technical expertise in the area it regulates and the qualifications of its staff. The SEC monitors the world of investment and high finance. This is a highly specialized and sensitive responsibility because of the close connection between capital flow and the performance of the national economy. In addition, significant numbers of the SEC staff responsible for regulating the markets are attorneys who specialize in corporate and securities law, financial accountants, and, increasingly, professional economists with Ph.D.s.

A second reason for choosing the SEC was the dramatic changes that have taken place in the capital markets in recent years and the significance of those changes for the U.S. economy. The 1980s saw an explosion in investment product innovation, computerized trading, and intensified competition for investment capital. These changes have redefined the roles of investment banking firms, promoted the development of sophisticated intermarket investment strategies, speeded dramatic increases and declines in the Dow Jones industrial average, blurred distinctions between commercial bank activities and the securities industry, given aggressive entrepreneurs leverage over corporate giants, and linked the markets in Hong Kong, Tokyo, and London with the stock and futures markets in New York and Chicago.

Attempts to regulate this complicated transformation have been much publicized and highly controversial. What changes, if any, should be made in the regulation of securities markets and the futures markets—especially the buying and selling of stock index futures?[3] What constraints, if any, should be placed on stock market activities when prices rise and fall precipitously? What limits should be placed on the use of leverage for corporate takeovers, and what should be done to establish equity between the rights of shareholders and the responsibilities of corporate management? And how do we redefine existing legislation to deal with elaborate, yet elusive, forms of fraud and market manipulation such as insider trading?

Answers to these and other policy questions are critical to the interests of all investors, large and small, as well as to maintaining a sound capital flow and a healthy economy. Specifically, new regulations may affect shareholders' rights, investment strategies, and investor profits, and new regulations may attract or discourage investment in the U.S. economy. Yet the central player in these unfolding debates, the SEC, has remained relatively unexamined.

As regulator of the markets for the distribution, sale, and trading of stocks, bonds, and other securities, the SEC has significant enforcement and rule-making authority. SEC proposals for regulating stock index futures, for example, have been the subject of extensive hearings in Congress, and the SEC could receive authority over these investment instruments—as of 1990 under the jurisdiction of another agency.[4] The SEC's opposition to takeover legislation (particularly proposals that favor corporate management at the expense of investors) has been critical to maintaining the legislative status quo.[5] And it is largely up to the discretion of the SEC to determine how far it will prosecute cases of investor fraud and market manipulation—such as the string of insider-trading cases that culminated in charges against Drexel Burnham Lambert and Drexel executive Michael Milken in the 1980s.

Because of its importance, the SEC has been the target of criticism among academic and legal scholars specializing in securities law. Some have charged the SEC with a heavy-handed use of its enforcement and rule-making authority, and they claim that the results do not necessarily protect investors or allocate capital efficiently (Freeman 1976; Kripke 1979; Karmel 1981). Other critics charge that the SEC should promote these ends more aggressively (Poser 1981; Macey and Haddock 1985; Seligman 1985), and they raise important concerns about the SEC's role in regulating the increasingly complex markets for securities. However, before we can adequately assess the SEC's performance as a regulator, we must understand the agency's political context. How does the agency make its decisions, and why? Why do we expect the SEC to play a key advisory role in determining the regulation of stock index futures, and why should the SEC have jurisdiction over these products over the opposition of the futures industry? Why was the SEC influential in preventing the passage of antitakeover legislation? And why does the agency act with so much discretion in its enforcement activities?

These are interesting questions because of their implications for theory—how significant is bureaucratic expertise as an independent influence on policy outcomes?—and for policy. This study attempts to address these questions by examining the preferences and priorities of interests inside and outside the SEC regarding the regulation of securities, the use of expertise and the tools of accountability for shaping outcomes, and how existing institutional structures—formal and informal—condition the policy debate.

The Political Context of the SEC

The balance between expertise and accountability in the making of federal securities policy is determined by three factors that define the resources, or clout, of the SEC in dealing with its legislative committees, other elected officials, and regulated interests. These factors are (1) the technical and uncertain nature of securities policy; (2) the diversity of interests regulated by the SEC; and (3) the degree to which Congress (and to some extent, the president) is sensitive to policies that affects constituents and the public: SEC enforcement activities.

The Technical and Uncertain Nature of Securities Policy

Members of the House Energy and Commerce Committee and the Senate Banking Committee could be interested in the SEC's activities for various reasons. They may represent economically powerful constituents with strong preferences for particular policy outcomes. They may also want to be associated with maintaining market integrity for the broader interests of the public and for the nation's economic well-being. Further, these representatives and senators have powerful ways of influencing securities policy through the SEC. The House Energy and Commerce Committee and Senate Banking Committee authorize the agency's annual appropriation; they have authority over its legislative mandate; they oversee and investigate its activities; and the Senate Banking Committee has the authority to approve presidential appointees to the five-member commission.

However, the power of committee members is limited partly by the technical and uncertain nature of securities policy. The success of the nation's capital markets rests, to a great degree, on investor confidence. Confidence is high when investors believe that the capital markets will give them competitive returns and that the securities markets professionals will fulfill their fiduciary responsibilities in handling investor capital. Consequently, policy makers face ticklish trade-offs between regulating the primary markets (the sale of initial distributions) and secondary (exchange) markets for securities. Maintaining investor confidence requires that regulators keep the markets as free of fraud and manipulation as possible, but policies intended to achieve those purposes may dampen investors' trust and drive investment capital overseas.

For members of Congress, it is risky to mandate legislation or try to influence decisions by the SEC that could be blamed for reducing investor confidence. No politician wants to be associated with a downturn in the markets or, worse, a downturn in the economy. In the securities industry, economic fortunes ride on the psychology of investor confidence, and misstatements or inexperienced ventures into policy making could spell election-time disaster for committee members. Therefore, to the extent that issues are technical (dealing with the fine points of securities law or operations of the capital markets) and the outcome of a policy is uncertain,[6] any attempt by committee members to influence or dictate agency decision making is checked by the need to defer to the "experts" at the SEC.

Other factors are obviously important, but the technical and unpredictable nature of securities policy gives the SEC influence over the legislative process as well as over its own rule-making activities. The comment of a former SEC staffer illustrates the impact of such technicality and uncertainty on the relations between the SEC and its congressional committees. He was asked how dependent the legislative committees were on SEC cooperation in getting securities-related statutes passed:

> Extremely dependent! I don't know of a single time when the SEC opposed something that got enacted. Too many people in Congress are not closely involved in the area and feel they have to defer to the SEC. Not many would profess a working knowledge of securities law.[7]

Similar comments by a former congressional staffer specializing in securities regulation refer to the same need to defer to the SEC:

> No one wants to be blamed for a catastrophe. Answers are not clear in this area, particularly in the modern financial world. The markets are delicate and there is a precarious balance. Certain moves could have unintended consequences, and no one wants to be blamed for that.

Legislation considered by the House Ways and Means Committee just before the 1987 stock market crash provides a good example. At the height of activity in leveraged buyouts, the staff of Chairman Dan Rostenkowski (D-Ill.) began looking at alternate tax treatments for debt, versus equity, on corporate balance sheets. It was believed that the tax law encouraged leveraged buyouts by giving corporations a break on debt. In a leveraged buyout, a public company is made private by purchasing publicly held shares at a value higher than the market price. The shares are typically purchased by an investment group (such as company management) that pays for the transaction by issuing high-yield bonds to investors. Debt on the bonds is then paid for by sale of the assets of the acquired company. Given the favorable tax treatment of debt, this transaction was attractive for corporate managers wanting to retain control of a company, and the above-market prices for outstanding shares also fueled the rising New York stock markets. Reports of the Rostenkowski legislation reached Wall Street days before the worst market crash in history, and many were quick to blame the representative, in part, for the 508-point slide in the Dow during one week in October (*National Journal* 1/9/88, 79; *Presidential Task Force on Market Mechanisms* 1988, I-13). In other words, the legislation was seen as a disincentive to investment.

The Diversity of Regulated Interests

Another factor adding to the clout of SEC expertise in determining securities policy is the diversity among regulated interests. Again, other factors are important, but diversity contributes to the SEC's role as an influential decision maker, as well as to Congress's tendency to defer to the agency on legislation. Members of Congress will typically respond to constituents' preferences—particularly if they are economically powerful. When constituents are united for or against a particular policy, congressional committee members are more likely to intervene in an agency's decision making to push for rulings favoring those preferences.[8] However, a lack of consensus among powerful constituent groups may discourage intervention on behalf of any particular interest—that is, if support for one group might antagonize another.[9]

There is considerable diversity among the powerful economic interests regulated by the SEC. First, because of the structure of the securities industry, strong producer interests oppose strong consumer interests. The power of brokerage firms, stock exchange markets, and investment bankers that sell and trade securities is counterbalanced by the interests of the institutional investor, as well as the corporate issuer. Institutional investors—for example, mutual funds, trust funds, pension funds, and insurance companies—prefer low brokerage fees on large-volume transactions. This contrasts with the preferences of the brokerage industry and the exchanges that benefit from high commissions for large-volume trades.[10] In addition, as investment bankers begin to participate more in the trading of securities—an activity traditionally scorned for the more "dignified" practice of underwriting (Brooks 1987, 5– 18)—they now compete with the institutions in buying and selling large blocks of stock. The different preferences between corporations that issue stock and the investment bankers who facilitate the process (that is, suppliers) are not quite so stark: both are interested in the successful distribution of an issue. However, in the most basic sense, they do have different preferences regarding fees charged to the corporate issuer for the advice, underwriting, and distribution services provided by investment bankers and brokerage firms.

Second, such diversity pits brokerage house against brokerage house. Specialized firms that serve the institutional investor have different preferences from brokers who serve primarily individual investors. This division, long manifested in the politics of the New York Stock Exchange (Loomis 1969), has recently arisen concerning the efficacy of program trading and its role in destabilizing the markets. Program trading is a method for implementing various investment strategies through rapid (usually computerized) executions of orders to buy and sell large quantities of stock and futures contracts based on stock indexes. Many brokerage firms use the practice to trade shares for their institutional customers as well as for their own account. Firms serving individual investors, however, want the practice restricted. They argue that program trading exacerbates market volatility and keeps the small public investor from entering the market (*New York Times* 2/5/88, 1; *Washington Post* 11/10/89, F 1; *Congressional Quarterly Weekly*, 3/10/90, 728–31).

Third, there is a competitive division between the secondary markets for trading securities: the over-the-counter market[11] and the stock exchanges. In 1971, the National Association of Securities Dealers (NASD) implemented a computerized quotation system for stocks traded over-the-counter. The NASD automatic quotation system (NASDAQ) gives brokers and dealers up-to-the-minute quotes on securities traded over-the-counter, nationwide. In 1982, the NASD initiated a program within NASDAQ for the system's most frequently traded securities. Stocks traded in this upper tier must meet higher quality standards than stocks traded in the broader NASDAQ, and investors are given more information about trading activity and stock price in these higher-tier shares (Teweles and Bradley 1987, 191–92). As a result, over-the-counter trading has become more competitive with the exchange markets by offering investors some of the stock-quality benefits of the exchange markets. The over-the-counter system of competing market makers (firms willing to buy and sell a particular security) also offers competitive advantages over the structural limitations of a stock exchange: whereas the stock exchanges are somewhat structurally bound by the traditional provision of a market for small "round lot" (100-share) orders, the over-the-counter market offers greater flexibility in handling large "block orders" of stock (10,000 shares or more).

Finally, the industry's interests are divided by size. Large brokerage firms have different interests from small, regional firms; large investment banking concerns have different interests from smaller underwriters; and the small regional stock exchanges have different needs from the New York Stock Exchange (NYSE) and the American Stock Exchange (AMEX). However, in an industry where technological change and competition have blurred the lines between underwriting, the trading of securities, and banking, and where innovation in investment vehicles and trading techniques is a constant threat to any firm's economic niche, large and small participants have an interest in a regulatory process that is not biased in favor of one group, will give careful and knowledgeable consideration to regulatory change, and cannot be swayed by congressional strong-arm tactics.

When a policy issue highlights this diversity between the regulated interests, the role of the SEC in determining policy outcomes is strengthened. Further, as I will contend in chapter 4, this diversity among interests has helped to promote a particular type of nominee to the SEC. This type, or profile, is also supported by the SEC's professional staff. To the extent that a president's selection of a commissioner is constrained by these expectations, the diversity of interests also enables the SEC to maintain its role as the securities "expert."

Congressional Caution and SEC Enforcement Activities

Much of the SEC's regulatory activity is police work. The agency patrols the markets to prevent and prosecute market fraud and manipulation. In this realm of regulatory activity, the SEC exercises significant discretion, free of congressional (and most of the time, presidential) intervention. This is partly owing to the traditionally strong bipartisan support for the agency's Division of Enforcement, as well as Congress's hesitation to intervene in enforcement activities.

On the one hand, the SEC's enforcement of the law is a tangible and popular public policy that members of the House Energy and Commerce Committee and the Senate Banking Committee can easily promote. The SEC has earned a reputation for rigorous enforcement of the securities laws. The agency has shown time and again that prominent individuals and Wall Street firms engaged in fraud or manipulation can be targets of an SEC investigation as readily as lesser known individuals and firms. In 1962 the agency brought a case against two prominent members of the American Stock Exchange that led to a reorganization of that exchange's governance system (Seligman 1982, 307). In the early 1970s the SEC investigation of financier Robert Vesco, who stole millions from investors through fraudulent shell corporations and mutual funds, revealed contributions he made to President Nixon's 1972 reelection campaign (*New York Times* 5/23/73, 14). In the late 1970s the SEC brought enforcement actions against the well-known corporations of Exxon, Lockheed Aerospace, and Gulf Oil for "questionable" overseas payments and also forced the companies to make changes in corporate governance (*Securities Regulation and Law Report* 10/5/77, A20; ibid. 4/21/76, A3; 3/19/75, ibid. A23–24). It was the SEC that charged the Carter administration's budget director, Burt Lance, with violations of the antifraud, reporting, and proxy solicitation provisions of the securities acts (SEC, *Annual Report* 1978, 35); and the SEC's cases against Drexel Burnham Lambert and Michael Milken also give credence to its reputation for tough enforcement against powerful firms and individuals.

These highly visible cases give the SEC, an agency with limited resources, additional leverage in preempting future fraud and manipulation. They have also made the agency enormously popular in Congress. When the SEC exposes the insider trading activities of an Ivan Boesky, who bilked individual investors out of millions of dollars, or points out the misdeeds of a huge defense contractor, both Democratic and Republican committee members have wanted to be associated with the campaign to protect the interests of investors. Further, they can easily demonstrate their support for these activities by authorizing more money for the Division of Enforcement, whose effectiveness is measured by the number of cases brought and prosecuted. The comments of a former House staff member capture this interest in a strong enforcement program:

> There is a consensus that the markets should be fair, and that the individual investor should have confidence to invest. That's not a partisan issue. Everyone sympathizes with the investor who does not want to be out technologied, or who doesn't want to play with a stacked deck. . . . Bottom line is, it's good politics to catch the rich crooks. The Ivan Boeskys . . . the rich inside trader who manipulated the market, epitomizes the evil character.

The comments of a former member of the Senate Banking Committee also reveal the logic behind congressional support for enforcement. He argues that it is a visible way to defend the integrity of the markets and the interests of investors—constituents who vote:

> There is a great feeling [in Congress] that the SEC represents the investors, and every congressman and senator has investors in their constitu-

encies. It is important to be protected, and the SEC is seen as the policeman that provides disclosure and prosecutes fraud. It keeps the markets honest, respected, effective.

On the other hand, it is precisely because of the SEC's wide range of popular and successful police work that the agency can preempt congressional intervention in its enforcement activities. This is not to say that members of Congress, in general, and the legislative committees, in particular, do not inquire about the status of a case. Indeed, a quick letter or phone call to the SEC for a constituent who has been defrauded, or who is the target of an investigation, is quite common. But the "service" is typically limited to an inquiry, and the agency's Division of Enforcement treats the inquiry as it would any other. When asked whether members of Congress had any impact on the decision making of the Enforcement Division, a staff member of that division replied:

> Only . . . if a congressman sends a letter it is looked at and reviewed like all letters [that we get]. . . . But I can't recall any time when there has been political interference. We get calls about the need to be more aggressive or effective, but no congressman or senator has ever thumped across the table and told us to do X, Y, and Z. We independently make decisions as to who or what we will investigate.

Congress's reluctance to intervene in SEC enforcement actions was also confirmed by former members of the legislative committees. When asked about possible congressional influence over the SEC's enforcement activities, a former representative made the distinction between enforcement policy in a "generic" sense, where congressional debate was appropriate, and specific enforcement actions, where it was not:

> I felt that as long as they had something under consideration, we should be careful. . . . To interfere with the SEC would be to politicize the agency. Now, I think it is legitimate for Congress to set policy changes in the law, to discuss whether policy in generic type cases is appropriate, but on a specific level when the SEC is dealing with certain cases, you had better not get them to prejudge the issue. . . . Now, I was very much a casework congressman, but when I made an inquiry at the SEC I was very careful to put in my request, to put into words that I was interested in information on the status of a case, and that I was not involved on the substance.

As these remarks indicate, to inquire on behalf of a constituent can be dangerous for a member of Congress who does not want to risk being associated with fraud. The implication of five senators who intervened in the ongoing investigation of a California savings and loan institution by banking regulators is indicative of the dangerous taint of fraud. Following the recent failure of that same institution (one of the most costly for taxpayers) as well as charges that the bank sold junk bonds to unknowing depositors, each of the five senators had to campaign rigorously in an attempt to clear his name of any wrongdoing (*Congressional Quarterly Weekly* 11/11/89, 3029–35). The success of the SEC's enforcement program makes it an especially dangerous agency for Congress to tamper with. Any attempt to preempt an ongoing investigation potentially leading to a criminal indictment could be politically disastrous.[12]

The result is that Congress depends on the SEC somewhat to make popular public policy: members of the SEC's legislative committees want to be seen as supporting an activity aimed at protecting the interests of investors—constituents—as well as the integrity of the capital markets; yet the relative success of the SEC's enforcement program and the possibility of being associated with fraudulent activities prevents them from intervening in enforcement endeavors.

No doubt the danger of being associated with fraudulent activities also makes the president sensitive to SEC enforcement cases. As mentioned above, an SEC investigation into the activities of a financier named Vesco discovered contributions he made to the Nixon campaign committee. Efforts by the Nixon administration to have the reference deleted from the enforcement report resulted in scandal for the administration, and the SEC pursued the case, nevertheless (see chapter 5).

This sensitivity to enforcement is a prominent feature of the SEC's regulatory environment. Along with the technicality and uncertainty of securities policy and the diversity of regulated interests, this factor creates a distinctive balance between the role of expertise and the tools of accountability in the battle to shape federal securities policy. Within this context, the SEC plays a clear and independent role in determining federal securities policy. This study examines that role and the agency's impact on policy.

Some Additional Thoughts and the Study Design

Before proceeding, I should define *formal* and *informal institutions*.[13] Formal institutions are explicit structures and procedures provided for in the Constitution or through statute. The statutory design and mandate of the SEC, for example, make it a formal institution. Informal institutions are primarily procedures that become standard through consensus and use—procedures that act as rules to guide behavior. How the SEC interprets and implements its mandate, the "acceptable" qualifications for appointed SEC officials, or how decisions are reached within the SEC, constitute informal institutions.

The politics of capital market regulation takes place within a regulatory framework that is a combination of formal and informal institutions. While the law has broadly defined the SEC's regulatory role, much of its framework consists of interpretations that are commonly accepted among those involved in securities regulation. This framework will be referred to as *disclosure-enforcement*. As the term denotes, regulation of the securities markets focuses on the disclosure of material information (that is, information relevant to an investment decision) and enforcement actions taken against market fraud and manipulation. The framework is as much a product of the preferences of SEC personnel and decisions made by the agency as of the preferences and priorities of the agency's legislative committees. It also reflects the preferences and priorities expressed by the president in a more random, but at times more dramatic fashion. What changes periodically is how the agency interprets material information and the SEC's priorities in pursuing its mandate to police the securities markets.

The development, institutionalization, and maintenance of this regulatory framework are covered in chapters 2, 3, and 4. Each chapter argues that the system is the product of an ongoing interaction between SEC expertise and efforts by elected officials to influence or control the agency. On the one hand, the House and Senate legislative committees have had to rely on the SEC's expertise to initiate, implement, and enforce the securities laws. On the other hand, the SEC has had to rely on the committees for fundamentals: the ultimate passage of legislation and the agency's reauthorization. Further, both the SEC and its legislative committees depend somewhat on the president to appoint nominees to the commission who support the disclosure-enforcement framework. However, regarding technical policy with uncertain outcomes, the diversity of regulated interests, and the success and popularity of enforcement as a public policy, both the SEC and its legislative committees have incentives to maintain disclosure-enforcement as the best possible means to implement the securities laws and achieve their various objectives. Further, given the degree of support, when making appointments presidents rarely deviate from what is considered an acceptable nominee.

Chapters 5, 6, and 7 examine the role of disclosure-enforcement during a decade of intense dispute over securities policy and attempts by interested political actors to alter the framework so as to produce different policy outcomes. Arguably, one of the most dramatic shifts in the SEC's interpretation of material information and in its enforcement approach took place in the early 1980s. During the 1970s the SEC's stance on mandatory disclosure and its enforcement procedures followed the preferences of the agency's legislative committees and were rarely challenged by various administrations. However, political changes in the 1980s were translated into different agendas for the SEC, for Congress, and for the Reagan administration—and harmony turned to conflict over the agency's activities.

Efforts to change the behavior of the agency were directed at the disclosure-enforcement framework—the rules of securities regulation. This was evident primarily in the Reagan administration's attempts to alter the agency's decision making by appointing personnel from outside the traditional pool of appointees and by encouraging a greater role for economists—at the expense of attorneys—in the SEC. Chapter 5 addresses the regulatory activities of the SEC just before Reagan came into office and how the disclosure-enforcement framework conditioned that effort. Chapter 6 then discusses the challenges to disclosure-enforcement put forth at the close of the 1970s. Finally, chapter 7 examines the conflicts between members of the SEC and its legislative committees brought on by the Reagan agenda, and the impact of conflict on the disclosure-enforcement framework.

The eventual resolution of these debates again reflects the significance of the technical and uncertain character of securities policy, of the diversity of interests, and Congress's usual caution toward

SEC enforcement activities. Just as these features of the regulatory environment affected the initiation, institutionalization, and maintenance of the disclosure-enforcement framework, they also condition the politicking within that framework.

Despite the long stability of the disclosure-enforcement system, chapter 8 examines potential destabilizing forces and in particular the role of SEC personnel in effecting any alteration. Central to the discussion is the competition between economists and attorneys in defining securities policy and how that tension within the agency might alter the rules of disclosure-enforcement. The chapter contrasts the situation to similar tensions in other agencies. Finally, I will address broader theoretical questions concerning the tension between expertise and accountability and the reasons for acknowledging that tension in our studies of the bureaucracy.

Rational-choice analysis of bureaucracy has renewed our interest in institutional design. The formal and informal structures and procedural rules that guide bureaucratic behavior are critical to policy outcomes because they create incentives for action. If political actors care about policy outcomes, then they will also care about these formal and informal institutions. This premise allows us to explain the selection, design, and mandate of a wide variety of agencies, as well as the behavior of many.

However, excessive emphasis on control of the bureaucracy has drawn attention away from the independence of the bureaucracy (or its personnel) in maintaining the structures that condition behavior. Politicians' control over a bureaucracy is often limited by a traditional dependence on expertise and its entrenchment in bureaucratic structures and processes. It is my purpose to illustrate some of those limitations by closely analyzing one regulatory agency and the politicians who seek to influence it; to establish the importance of formal and informal institutions in determining federal securities policy; and to demonstrate the SEC's role as a player with political clout in the struggle over the political rules.

2 A Regulatory Framework

*T*he SEC was created in the early thirties when the demand for expertise in government was on the rise. Scholars of public administration routinely wrote of the need to bring greater expertise, or professionalism, into government to counter the influence of dominant economic interests (Landis 1938), as well as to enhance the efficiency of government activities (Mosher and Kingsley 1936). In addition, President Roosevelt's New Deal thrust the federal government into the regulation of complex economic activity that required legal and industrial specialists, or experts, to develop and oversee its policies (McCraw 1984).

An increasingly prominent role for experts was foretold in the political battles over the design and mandates of the new regulatory agencies set up to implement New Deal policies (Knott and Miller 1987). Debates over whether to create a new agency rather than use an existing one, over the number of commissioners appointed to an agency and partisan appointment criteria, as well as over its rule-making and enforcement authority reflected not only questions about an agency's direction and political control, but also how expertise should be incorporated in its work. Like other New Deal agencies, the SEC was a product of these two competing questions.

There was a widely shared public demand for the federal government to regulate Wall Street after the stock market crash of 1929. Members of Congress, pressured by constituents directly affected by the crash, supported this popular sentiment. But legislators were also concerned about the country's depressed economy as a whole and the need to restore robust participation in the capital markets to fuel economic recovery. If Wall Street saw new regulations as too restrictive or "hands-on," legislators might very well face a Wall Street backlash—a cessation of stock market activity. Bills would have to be skillfully drafted to balance the interests of the "investing public" with those of Wall Street interests who could dictate capital flow.

A contingent of Harvard lawyers drafted the expert legislation that balanced these concerns, but their work also revealed the lawyers' preference for regulation. These young professionals wanted to see the success of administrative government in general, and of New Deal policies in particular. Consequently, legislative and administrative preferences were compatible in many respects: regulation that would not cause an economic backlash was as important to members of Congress concerned about their constituents as to the professionals who wanted the administrative experiment and the New Deal to succeed.

These concerns and interests produced the Securities Act of 1933 and the Securities Exchange Act of 1934. The two laws gave the Securities and Exchange Commission (SEC) authority to prosecute fraud and manipulation of the markets and to regulate the issue, purchase, and sale of securities in the public interest. By examining the historical interaction among members of Congress, those who drafted and implemented the new statutes, and the president, we can better understand why these laws were passed, why the SEC was created, and how the disclosure-enforcement framework for regulating the capital markets came about. Together, the priorities of all these groups shaped the federal government's first cut at capital market regulation.

Regulation Before 1933

Prior to 1933, the securities markets were regulated by an assortment of state laws and by a system of self-governance by the industry. This patchwork of regulation covered the issue of securities by a company; information contained in a prospectus (a statement about the issuing firm, usually intended to promote the sale of an issue); and the buying and selling of securities in an initial distribution and in secondary trading on the exchanges. However, these regulations provided inadequate protection for the investor because of variations from state to state and within the industry.

Laws to protect the individual investor from fraudulent sales of stock, collectively known as "blue sky" laws, originated in the states. They were intended to shield the investing public from securities dealers who would sell shares of anything—including the sky (de Bedts 1964, 4; Parrish 1970, 5, 5n). The quality of protection and the level of enforcement varied from one state to another, but even the most effective antifraud statutes did not regulate interstate trafficking in securities (Parrish 1970, 29).

The securities industry had a system of internal regulation. The constitutions of many exchanges—primarily the New York Stock Exchange (NYSE) and the New York Curb Exchange (later the American Stock Exchange or AMEX)—regulated trading practices in a particular exchange market; they established qualifications for membership (a seat on an exchange) and stipulations for corporations listing their stock with the exchange (Bernheim and Schneider 1935, 757–63).[1] But as the stock market crash of 1929 and financial scandals of the early 1930s demonstrated, these highly touted systems were designed to protect the exchanges and their members, not necessarily investors (Parrish 1970, 39; McCraw 1984, 164).

Early attempts to pass federal securities legislation had always been opposed by Wall Street. Efforts to rein in the capital markets in the early 1920s were also stymied by a tremendous national economic expansion (de Bedts 1964, 4–6; Parrish 1970, 21–22). The stock market was booming, and small and large investors alike wanted a chance to profit. In the months before the October 1929 crash, activity in the financial markets was at an all-time high: in 1929, 1.125 billion shares of stock were traded on the New York Stock Exchange alone (Bernheim and Schneider 1935, 748).

Much of the volume in 1929 was accounted for by the $10.2 billion worth of new corporate securities that flooded the primary market—the market for the initial distribution of securities issues—in that year (ibid. 1935, 66). New issues were snatched up in the frenzy to invest, and speculative interest often sent the prices of unknown securities skyrocketing. Yet the sheer volume of issues allowed the fraudulent to be sold as readily as legitimate ones. Uninformed investors incurred tremendous losses when early prices of new issues tumbled in secondary market trading—the buying and selling of stocks after distribution in the primary market. The 1929 crash served to magnify the corrupt environment surrounding these "hot" issues, as well as the vulnerability of the public investor.

Just as fraudulent issues were overlooked before the crash, so too were the often manipulative practices of market professionals. Collusive buying and selling, in tandem with unfounded "leaks" about particular stocks, allowed members of the financial community to drive securities prices up and down at the expense of the investing public. These techniques, known as "pooling" and "bear raids," went on unabashedly throughout the 1920s. As in the case of fraudulent issues, the crash and subsequent investigations of the securities industry highlighted the magnitude of the problem (de Bedts 1964, 8–10).

President Roosevelt took office in 1933 with an agenda that mandated federal securities legislation. First, he wanted to prevent the fraudulent issue of new stock. Second, he wanted to place particular restrictions on the trading practices of exchange members to make the markets more accountable to the public (Roosevelt 1938, 1:653, 682). He satisfied the first objective with legislation that was written, introduced to Congress, and approved within the first hundred days of his administration—the Securities Act of 1933.

Weakness on Wall Street

In contrast to the previous decade, after the onset of the Depression Wall Street had neither the economic stamina nor the political clout to prevent the passage of the Securities Act of 1933. Economic repercussions of the stock market crash were as evident on Wall Street as in any other industry. Trading on the New York Stock Exchange dropped from a high of 1.125 billion shares in 1929 to .425 billion in 1932 (Bernheim and Schneider 1935, 748). A lower volume of trade meant decreased incomes for brokers, dealers, and the stock exchanges. In 1929, a seat (or membership) on the New York Stock Exchange was worth $625,000, a dramatic increase over the past decade; by 1932, the price had fallen to between $185,000 and $65,000 (ibid. 753). Also hit were the financial underwriters for corporate issues. By 1932 new issues dwindled to $1.2 billion, down from the $10.2 billion level of 1929 (ibid. 66). The speculative fever that drew investors to the markets in the late twenties was cooled by the market crash.

Amid the economic fallout there was political capital to be gained. New Deal Democrats were in control of Congress, and the time was right to rake the failures of a Republican administration and its Wall Street constituency over the coals. The crash provided the content, and a series of dramatic and well-publicized congressional hearings provided the means (de Bedts 1964, 40–41).

In 1932 the Senate Banking and Currency Committee initiated hearings to investigate the causes of the 1929 crash and to find ways to prevent such a market failure in the future. When the committee hired Ferdinand Pecora as chief counsel, the tough New York prosecutor went after Wall Street with a vengeance. He transformed the hearings from an inquiry into the market failure into a public display of Wall Street's dirtiest dealings. One by one, members of the nation's most prestigious financial houses were subjected to Pecora's questioning, which revealed illicit trading practices, market manipulations, and preferential treatment for the insiders of the financial world (Ritchie 1975, 2555–78).

Wall Street was in a weakened condition, and the Pecora hearings dealt blow after blow to the reputation of New York financiers. The widely publicized hearings served to identify the Democratic party as concerned with protecting the small investor from Wall Street fraud. A semblance of organized opposition by Wall Street was easily overwhelmed by the momentum of FDR's regulatory agenda, with skilled legislative guidance provided by his ally, Representative Sam Rayburn (D-Tex.), and a bill so skillfully drafted that every House member supported the measure.

Roosevelt and Rayburn

Franklin Roosevelt made securities regulation part of his campaign in 1932, and, once in office, took quick actions to formulate a bill. In the wake of the first revelations made public in the Pecora hearings (February 1933), Roosevelt commissioned Houston Thompson—a former chairman of the Federal Trade Commission (FTC) and author of the 1932 Democratic platform on securities regulation—to draft the initial legislation (Ritchie 1980, 44). The bill that Thompson produced drew fire in Senate hearings for its lack of clarity and for its provision that the FTC, charged with implementing the legislation, should judge the solvency of corporations issuing stock (Parrish 1970, 51–56).

Sam Rayburn, chairman of the House Interstate Commerce Committee, supported Roosevelt's determination to regulate securities, but knew that the shortcomings in Thompson's bill could jeopardize the effort. Rayburn recommended that the bill be redrafted and submitted as amendments to Thompson's measure (Parrish 1970, 56–57). Taking the cue from Rayburn, Roosevelt called on Felix Frankfurter, a Harvard law professor and a longtime friend and associate. Frankfurter responded by coming to Washington with three former students to redraft the bill: James Landis, Benjamin Cohen, and Thomas Corcoran. Together they provided a blend of expertise in securities law, legislative draftsmanship, and insight into the securities industry. After several days of intense marathon sessions, the new draft was ready, and Sam Rayburn introduced the "amendments" to the House (Ritchie 1980, 45–46).

Under Rayburn's guidance, the bill passed in committee unanimously and, one month later, in the full House. Rayburn was impressed by the careful writing of the Frankfurter team and later commented that he "did not know whether the bill passed so readily because it was so damned good or so damned incomprehensible" (Parrish 1970, 70; Seligman 1982, 66–67). Still, the Landis-Cohen-Corcoran draft had to be reconciled with the Senate's amended version of the Thompson bill. As chairman of the conference committee, Rayburn immediately called a vote on the Senate version—producing, as he had anticipated, a tie. He then declared the House version the winner by default. Following minor modifications in the full Senate, the federal Securities Act was enacted in May 1933 (Ritchie 1980, 48).

Both Roosevelt and Rayburn provided essential leadership for the passage of the bill, and the Harvard contingent provided the drafting expertise that gained congressional consensus. Roosevelt took the initiative by selecting Thompson to draft the first version and kept the legislation alive by soliciting Frankfurter's aid when the original bill received a beating in Congress. Both expertise and presidential support were critical, but without a strong congressional sponsor, the bill could have been rejected or heavily amended. Sam Rayburn proved to be a valuable ally of the New Deal, carefully guiding the bill toward final enactment.

The efforts of both politicians were facilitated, primarily, by the public's receptivity to securities regulation. Given popular support for the measure (reflected during the Pecora hearings), legislators had an incentive to see the bill enacted. The efforts of Roosevelt and Rayburn were also aided by Wall Street's inability to mount a campaign in opposition. The "villains" on Wall Street were being exposed daily by the Pecora hearings, and the proximity of the crash to the Depression was as good an argument as any for making market professionals accountable to the public.

A Disclosure Statute

Underlying the Securities Act was the premise that an *informed* investor was an investor protected from the fraudulent sale of new securities. The act required companies issuing new securities for public sale to register the issue with the Federal Trade Commission (FTC). Registration documents were to disclose detailed financial data that was "material," or relevant to making an investment decision. It was not the FTC's job to rule on the quality of a stock issue, but simply to give the investor a public record from which to make an informed decision (Roosevelt 1938, 2:96).

In drafting the legislation, James Landis, in particular, gave special attention to the FTC's ability to enforce disclosure (Landis 1938, 107–09). Two aspects of the act gave the agency some leverage. First, Landis capitalized on the importance of the timing of a securities issue. The act gave the FTC a twenty-day period to review disclosed documents. If there were no irregularities in the content or reporting of the information, the issue was registered and selling could begin on the twentieth day after filing. However, if the filing was incomplete or incorrect, the agency could prevent the issue from being sold by placing a stop order on the sale of the stock (Schwartz 1973, 2556–58).

The impact of a halt was twofold. First, a delay in issuing securities meant a delay in raising capital for the issuer, a delay in underwriting fees for an investment banker, and a delay in selling and trading new stock for brokers and dealers. Second, when—or if—the issue was later registered, the stop order could perhaps tarnish the issue for the investing public. Time was money, and Landis used the economic interests of the industry to encourage accurate disclosure (McCraw 1984, 174–75).

The act also addressed compliance after an issue was sold. A liability provision held accountable to the investing public corporate directors, accountants, underwriters, and any other person who contributed to developing a prospectus, on two grounds: (1) if material information in the document was found to be untrue; and (2) if a material fact had been omitted. Investors could sue if they purchased stock based on false or incomplete information (Schwartz 1973, 2559–62).

For accountants and their corporate clients, the liability provisions were particularly objectionable. The Securities Act gave the FTC the authority to set general accounting standards for reporting financial data (ibid., 2563–64). Theoretically, the agency could impose standards on an accounting profession that thrived on the "flexibility" it gave corporate clients (Chatov 1975, 283). On the one hand, standardized reporting would limit the liability of accountants; in certifying a disclosure document, they would be assured that the reporting technique was acceptable to the FTC. If, however, accountants were allowed to continue their "flexible" practices—that is, if the FTC did not set general standards—they risked being held liable for prospectus information based on questionable reporting techniques. Faced with a choice between continued flexibility but potential liability, and the end of flexible reporting, both the corporate sector and accountants focused on reducing the act's liability provisions through amendment. Both groups also resisted the FTC's (and later the SEC's) attempts to impose accounting standards (ibid., 68–70).

Wall Street was uniformly opposed to the liability provisions (Seligman 1982, 72). In July 1933 the Pecora hearings went into recess, and the financial community used the brief respite to galvanize support for weakening the Securities Act provisions. Editorials and articles by corporate directors, brokers, underwriters, and their lawyers called the provisions a burden too costly for the industry to bear. No sooner did the FTC begin operating its new securities division than a campaign to amend the 1933 act and to prevent passage of Roosevelt's next objective—regulation of the stock exchange markets—was in full swing (McCraw 1984, 177–78; Ritchie 1980, 56).

Whereas opponents of the 1933 act thought it was too oppressive, supporters—in particular, Roosevelt, Rayburn, Frankfurter, and Landis—felt it was only a first step toward necessary federal regulation of the markets. For example, the 1933 act required disclosure from corporations issuing new stock. Exempt from the act were securities sold intrastate; corporations with issues of securities already in the market; securities issued by government entities (federal, state and local); issues by railroads; issues that were guaranteed by national or state banks as well as building and loan associations; insurance annuity contracts; issues that would be repaid in less than nine months; and issues worth less than $100,000, if the FTC approved (Schwartz 1973, 2552–54). In a private meeting with Roosevelt, Landis spoke of the need to impose disclosure requirements on more issuers, and on a routine basis (Seligman 1982, 82–83).

In addition to expanding the disclosure requirements of the 1933 act, Landis and other supporters wanted to bring the stock exchanges under government supervision. They wanted to limit the amount of money a customer could borrow from a broker to purchase stock (the "margin"); they sought to eliminate floor traders on the exchanges—members who could trade for their own account, rather than a customer's, while remaining privy to information available on the exchange floor; and they supported the proscription of trading practices such as the "short sale" and "pooling" used by members of an exchange to manipulate stock prices (Seligman 1982, 83–86).

Once enacted, the liability provisions in the Securities Act rallied Wall Street opposition to any further attempts to regulate the financial markets. For its New Deal supporters, on the other hand, the 1933 act was only the beginning of a much larger plan to make the financial community accountable to the public. With an organized Wall Street lobbying effort well under way, and growing divisions within Congress and in the administration about the impact of additional legislation on capital formation—and, therefore, economic recovery—enactment of a new bill was questionable.

The Securities Exchange Act of 1934

When Roosevelt introduced the Securities Act to Congress in 1933, he announced his intention to bring the exchange markets under federal supervision. A high priority for the president was to have the new legislation establish minimum "margin" requirements for the purchase of stocks by brokers and investors (Roosevelt 1938, 3:90–93; Parrish 1970, 128–29). Much of the speculative buying and selling that precipitated the market crash was brought on by stock purchases backed by minimal collateral. Brokers extended credit to their customers that amounted to as much as 90 percent of the value of the stock, allowing customers to purchase stock with as little as 10 percent down. Banks extended similarly exorbitant amounts of credit to brokers. When the market tumbled in October 1929, so did the highly leveraged positions of brokers and investors (Gujarati 1984, 355–56; McCraw 1984, 179–80). Therefore, many argued that the regulation of margin levels might be one way to curb future speculative sprees.

Benjamin Cohen and Thomas Corcoran, two of the three drafters of the 1933 act, were commissioned by the Senate Banking Committee in early 1934 to draw up legislation for regulating the exchanges (Ritchie 1975, 2575). They worked under the pressures of diametrically opposed interests: Wall Street's attempts to prevent any legislation from passing and its efforts to dilute the liability provisions of the 1933 act, versus supporters of rigorous exchange regulation—primarily the Senate Banking Committee's chief counsel, Ferdinand Pecora, and his staff.

The resulting draft bore the mark of Pecora (who was in the midst of his Wall Street investigation and hearings) and his staff. Minimum margin requirements were specified in the legislation, and the FTC was given the authority to increase the levels if necessary; floor trading was to be abolished; specific trading practices were made illegal; and the disclosure requirements of the 1933 act were extended to all corporations that listed stock on an exchange (Ritchie 1975, 2575; Parrish 1970, 116–20). Wall Street went on the defensive, and the bill became the target of a powerful lobbying campaign.

Wall Street opposition was led by the president of the New York Stock Exchange, Richard Whitney, who enlisted the support of groups and interests representing a cross section of the financial community. Twenty-four of the nation's thirty-two stock exchanges were represented in testimony against the exchange bill before the House Interstate and Foreign Commerce Committee and the Senate Banking and Currency Committee. Also present at the hearings were delegates from the National Association of Manufacturers, the Investment Bankers' Association, the United States Chamber of Commerce, and numerous investment banking houses. Each witness testified to the burdens that the 1933 act had already imposed on their activities and predicted a paralysis of the nation's capital-raising mechanisms if the exchange legislation was passed.[2]

In tandem with the opposition's participation in the hearings, Congress was pressured by a letter-writing campaign orchestrated by Whitney. The letters—which originated, many held, in the offices of the New York Stock Exchange (de Bedts 1964, 73; Roosevelt 1938, 3:169–70)—all carried the same message: do not allow the federal government to take over the stock exchanges and destroy the workings of the free enterprise system. Why tamper, Whitney had argued, with a "perfect institution"? (Seligman 1982, 73).

The campaign was successful in postponing legislation. Without the momentum of the administration's first hundred days, members of Congress relented under the pressures of the financial community. By the end of February 1934, the first attempt at exchange regulation was stalled in committee, and Senate leaders announced that the debate over the bill would not be settled during the current session of Congress (ibid., 93). If a bill were to pass both houses, it would have to balance legislators' concerns for the public investor with their fears over a backlash from Wall Street.

New Deal Support and Political Compromise

Countering Wall Street's economic clout was the political power of the bill's supporters. Legislation to supervise the exchanges had the support of Sam Rayburn in the House of Representatives, and Senator Duncan Fletcher (D-Fla.), chairman of the Senate Banking Committee (Chatov 1975, 81).

The legislation had strong support from the administrators of the Securities Act, as well. In 1933 Roosevelt asked Landis to supervise the organization of the FTC's new securities division and during that year filled an unexpected vacancy by appointing Landis to be a commissioner in the agency. In his new role, Landis continued to push for strong legislation, and he enjoyed access to the office of the president to express his views (Ritchie 1980, 53). Together with Commissioner George Mathews, a La Follette Progressive from Wisconsin, and FTC General Counsel Robert Healy, the Federal Trade Commission was a powerful and active agency behind the New Deal agenda (McCraw 1984, 176; de Bedts 1964, 91–94).

Despite divisions in his administration over the efficacy of the legislation and its projected impact on the nation's economic recovery (Ritchie 1980, 52–55), Roosevelt continued to support it. The president's plan for reviving the national economy was at stake, and to let the legislation die would have signaled a defeat for the New Deal. To salvage his regulatory agenda, FDR remobilized a drafting team to come up with a compromise version of the Cohen-Corcoran bill that the Congress could support.

The redraft took only twelve days to complete. However, it struck three fundamental compromises—among members of the administration, Wall Street, and their representatives in Congress—that made the legislation viable. Most important was the provision that gave the Federal Reserve Board, rather than the FTC, discretionary authority to alter minimum margin requirements. The move allowed both members of the Treasury Department and the Federal Reserve (originally opposed to giving an agency outside of the administration authority over credit) to support the measure.

Second, the new draft did not abolish the practice of floor trading on the stock exchanges. Rather, the FTC was to study the practice and recommend changes. Members of the exchanges reeled in opposition to provisions in the original bill that proscribed one of their fundamental and privileged practices. A study left the door open for negotiation and compromise.

Finally, FDR asked Landis to draft amendments to the 1933 act to ease the liability provisions. The amendments specifically limited the liability of underwriters and were acceptable to representatives of the Investment Bankers Association—a key support group (Seligman 1982, 93–94).

Additional Compromise and the SEC

Rayburn and Fletcher quickly introduced the new draft in March 1934 (Ritchie 1980, 56, 58). The move signaled Wall Street that some form of stock exchange legislation was inevitable. Rather than continue to oppose the measure altogether, the Whitney campaign shifted its emphasis toward transforming the bill. Whitney pushed for removing the FTC as the enforcing agency and establishing a stock exchange authority with heavy industry representation (Parrish 1970, 124).

Two political facts might explain Wall Street's support for a new regulatory entity. First, Wall Street did not want the FTC supervising the practices of the exchanges. With commissioners Landis and Mathews, the agency was a strong ally of the New Deal, and it proved to be rigorous in its enforcement of the 1933 Securities Act (Chatov 1975, 83).

Second, the securities industry was one of many constituencies over which the FTC had some regulatory authority. To try to influence the composition of the agency through presidential appointments would be to compete with numerous other groups with their own economic interests. Rather than spend time and resources trying to influence an already competitive political decision process, Wall Street sought to soften the impact of stock exchange regulation by authorizing a new board—one whose sole constituency would be the securities industry and whose commissioners would have a securities industry background. Such a board might be more readily influenced by the needs and concerns of Wall Street.

Wall Street had an ally in Senator Carter Glass (D-Va.) for congressional support of a new stock exchange authority, but for a mixture of reasons. Glass, known as the father of the Federal Reserve System, had long opposed any intermixing of the speculative business of securities with the stability of the Federal Reserve (Ritchie 1980, 57). He was therefore firmly opposed to the Federal Reserve Board's participation in setting margins for stock purchases.

Glass's ear was also bent by constituents opposed to the FTC's policies. He shared their aversion to the agency's rigorous support for the New Deal agenda, as well as to the New Deal itself (Patterson 1967, 13–22; Seligman 1982, 97). If margin authority was not placed with the Federal Reserve Board or with the dreaded FTC, a likely compromise would give the authority to a new stock exchange commission (Parrish 1970, 133–34).

In the Senate, the bill was guided through debate by Duncan Fletcher. It passed 62 to 13 (Schwartz 1973, 2680), with the Glass

amendment calling for the creation of a new stock exchange authority. Rayburn led the debates in the House, where the vote was 282
to 84, and the authority of the FTC was left intact (ibid., 2679).

The final bill that emerged from the conference committee included concessions for both Wall Street and the New Deal contin-
gents. First, it created the Securities and Exchange Commission
(SEC) to enforce the Securities Act of 1933 and the Securities
Exchange Act of 1934. Wall Street got its new commission, but the
New Dealers won on its composition: five commissioners were to
be appointed by the president to five-year terms; no more than
three could be from the same political party as the president; and,
most important, there were no stipulations that members had to
have a securities industry background (Schwartz 1973, 2684). Second, the reformers succeeded in giving the Federal Reserve Board
authority over margin requirements. However, rather than impose
minimum standards that the Federal Reserve Board would have to
enforce, the act gave the central bank discretionary authority to
change margin levels as necessary (ibid., 2686–87).

Proponents of a strong exchange bill were disappointed that a
new, untested agency would be responsible for regulating the powerful stock exchanges (Ritchie 1980, 59). But three other aspects of
the new act were definite victories for the New Deal. First, the act
required exchanges to register with the SEC and empowered the
agency to "alter or supplement" exchange rules for the "proper
protection of investors" and to "maintain fair and orderly markets"
(Schwartz 1973, 2685–86, 2699). Second, it proscribed particular
trading practices such as the short sale and pooling under specified
conditions (ibid., 2690–91). Third, it extended the disclosure requirements of the 1933 act to all companies that listed their stock
with an exchange and required regular filings with the SEC throughout the year (ibid., 2692–94).

Initiation of the "Disclosure-Enforcement" Framework

Under the Securities Exchange Act (1934), responsibility for the
1933 Securities Act was transferred from the FTC to the Securities
and Exchange Commission (Schwartz 1970, 2710). Combined, the

two acts empowered the new commission to force the disclosure of financial data from every company that issued securities, with three exceptions: companies that did not issue new stock; companies that did not list their existing stock with an exchange, but traded it in the over-the-counter market (see chapter 3); and companies whose stock was not issued or traded publicly, but sold and traded in private distributions.

The acquisition of the FTC's rule-making authority gave the SEC a mandate to make sweeping changes in the reporting of financial data, the structure of the markets, and trading practices. First, the SEC assumed the responsibility for determining general accounting standards (Schwartz 1973, 2598, 2710). Second, section 15 of the Securities Exchange Act gave the SEC license to set rules for the regulation of the over-the-counter market, so long as investors were afforded the same protections as they received trading on a registered exchange (ibid., 2696). Third, as mentioned earlier, the SEC was authorized to "alter or supplement" the rules of an exchange (ibid., 2698–99). However, in a precedent set by the first members of the agency, the SEC chose to use its rule-making authority sparingly, to *structure* the reporting of data and to *structure* the trading activities on an exchange.[3] Instead, the enforcement of disclosure became its central objective. This approach was determined as much by the commissioners' desire to see the agency and the New Deal succeed as by congressional and presidential concerns that the agency maintain a balance between the interests of public investors and those of Wall Street.

Specifically, the SEC's disclosure-enforcement strategy—as initiated by the first commissioners—consisted of a cooperative use of its rule-making authority with the securities industry, but with aggressive enforcement of disclosure and the securities laws in general.

In exercising its rule-making authority over market structure and participation, the SEC took a cooperative stance vis-à-vis the securities industry. The agency sought to smooth the transition to bring the securities markets, corporate issuers, and accountants into compliance with the 1933 and 1934 legislation. In its early regulatory initiatives—registering the exchanges; formulating disclosure documents; reviewing exchange rules for listing stocks and its members' trading practices; determining acceptable accounting procedures; and bringing the over-the-counter market under its jurisdiction—

the SEC incorporated the stock exchanges and other industry organizations into its decision making and implementation of the law (Chatov 1975, 100, 98; Ritchie 1980, 65; McCraw 1984, 193).

This cooperative approach to implementation did not, however, indicate that this was a new agency to be easily captured by its clientele. The SEC early earned a reputation for vigorous enforcement of disclosure and other aspects of the new statutes (Seligman 1982, 112–13, 149–51; Ritchie 1980, 70–71). The enforcement of full disclosure, in tandem with effective policing of the financial markets, became the defining characteristics of a successful regulatory effort. Attempts by the agency to expand its future mandate, therefore, focused on increasing the number of financial entities subject to disclosure requirements and the necessary means to bring about compliance.

Two significant factors within the SEC helped to implement the disclosure-enforcement strategy. First, Roosevelt's nomination of Joseph Kennedy as chairman, as well as James Landis, George Mathews, Robert Healy, and Ferdinand Pecora (three of whom were formerly with the FTC), reflected the president's efforts to balance reform with recovery. The new agency's majority position set precedents for its later pursuit of its regulatory responsibilities.

Second, during the early years of the SEC, the Supreme Court struck down FDR's National Recovery Act as unconstitutional. The ruling dampened some of the activist spirit of the SEC, which was most clearly reflected during the Landis chairmanship.

The First Commissioners: Recovery and Reform

Perhaps the most significant factor that influenced the SEC's regulatory strategy was Roosevelt's selection of Joseph Kennedy as the agency's first chairman. Avid New Deal reformers reacted to the Kennedy appointment with disbelief. As an investment banker, Kennedy had made a fortune on the stock market, often by employing techniques the SEC was created to prevent. It was as if the president placed a "wolf in the henhouse." Many saw the choice as a political payoff to a longtime friend and heavy contributor to FDR's 1932 presidential campaign (McCraw 1984, 182; de Bedts 1964, 88–89).

However, FDR attached strategic significance to the appointment (Seligman 1982, 103–04; de Bedts 1964, 94). If his program for economic relief were to succeed, the cooperation of Wall Street was essential. Kennedy's chairmanship sent a signal to the financial industry: the administration sought to work with Wall Street to restore investor confidence in the market and to speed economic recovery. Kennedy served as a liaison between the New Deal's regulatory efforts and his former associates on Wall Street (Chatov 1975, 105–06; de Bedts 1964, 96–97; Seligman 1982, 111–12). Had Roosevelt selected a chairman with a strong interest in reforming the markets, Wall Street might have reacted adversely, and the New Deal recovery plan could have fizzled as public issues of securities dwindled.

Kennedy's efforts to cooperate with Wall Street were supported by commissioners Landis and Mathews (Chatov 1975, 106–07; Ritchie 1980, 62–63), both of whom Roosevelt reappointed from the FTC to the SEC in 1934. Commissioner Mathews, himself a certified public accountant, particularly endorsed the agency's decision to work with accountants in developing general standards. As a former practitioner, he sympathized with accountants in their objections to the new guidelines for financial reporting (Chatov 1975, 64, 165).

The support of Landis is more difficult to comprehend. As Roosevelt said, Landis's drafting expertise put "teeth" into both of the SEC's enabling statutes. Yet perhaps more important than his desire to see strong securities regulation implemented was Landis's hope that administrative government could be effective and that the New Deal agenda would succeed.

As a Harvard law professor, Landis wrote about the necessary features of a successful regulatory agency. He focused in particular on an enabling statute that allowed regulators to enforce compliance (Landis 1938, 89–122). In addition to giving the agency effective enforcement powers—such as the stop order, available to the SEC as a legislative sanction—Landis believed that the regulated interests should have an incentive to comply with the law (McCraw 1984, 172).

His willingness to work with the securities industry in developing a regulatory framework reflected a twofold strategy. First, he believed that if market participants contributed to developing a regulatory scheme (establishing and implementing rules and overseeing market activities), they would have a stake in the policy's success (ibid., 188). Second, and more important, cooperation was a means to enhance the agency's regulatory reach. If the SEC were to rely on its own staff for developing standards—exchange rules, disclosure forms, and listing requirements, for example—its achievements would have been severely limited by the constraints of its annual appropriation. By giving the industry a role in oversight and enforcement, the SEC could oversee a much broader regulatory effort (ibid., 186–87).

Support for this cooperative approach was not shared by all commissioners. Commissioners Pecora (general counsel for the Senate Banking Committee's hearings on the 1929 stock market crash) and Healy (former general counsel of the FTC) often felt that the approach was an abdication of the SEC's regulatory responsibilities. Healy, in particular, wanted the SEC to take a more proactive role in setting accounting standards (Chatov 1975, 106–09). His efforts were frustrated by the majority's acceptance of disclosure documents heavily footnoted to justify the use of a questionable accounting technique. For Kennedy, Landis, and Mathews, *compliance* with disclosure came first; how the information was reported was secondary (ibid., 110–11).

Commissioner Pecora opposed the cooperative approach because of his work on the Senate hearings, as well as his discontent with the limitations of his SEC appointment. First, he found it difficult to begin cooperating with the same Wall Street malefactors that he had spent two years exposing as criminals. Pecora's aggressive style was cramped by the agency's cooperative stance (McCraw 1984, 188; de Bedts 1964, 104–05).

Second, Pecora had set his sights on the chairmanship of the new agency, but was passed over by the president (Ritchie 1975, 2577–78). Officially, Roosevelt could not name a chairman to the Securities and Exchange Commission; the five commissioners voted among themselves for the position. However, by appointing his choice for chairman to the longest of the five available terms, FDR signaled his endorsement. Every year a seat on the SEC was to open for a new appointment. Members of the first commission, therefore, served for one, two, three, four, and five years. Roosevelt not only failed to endorse Pecora for the chairmanship, but also gave the New York prosecutor the shortest of the five terms. Landis's efforts at shuttle diplomacy between Pecora and Chairman Kennedy initially brought some unity to the agency. Six months later, however, Pecora left the SEC to take a position on the New York State Supreme Court (Ritchie 1980, 66–67; Seligman 1982, 106–08; de Bedts 1964, 105).

The selection of both Pecora and Kennedy reflected the balance that Roosevelt attempted to achieve between reforming the markets and stimulating economic recovery. His well-publicized findings through the Senate hearings made Pecora a representative of the reformers. On the other side, Kennedy's connections on Wall Street signaled Roosevelt's intention of revitalizing the markets.

The first agency had to maintain this balance. Specifically, Kennedy's efforts to cooperate with Wall Street in developing a regulatory framework had to be tempered. Balance was achieved by the agency's emphasis on full disclosure and its oversight of the securities industry to catch violations of the new federal laws. The SEC's vigorous enforcement actions during its early years earned it the name "watchdog of Wall Street" (Seligman 1982, 150). Its actions also set a precedent for the agency's regulatory role in later years.

Technical Expertise under Landis

Beyond symbolizing the president's need to balance recovery with reform, the appointment of Landis in 1935 was important to initiating the disclosure-enforcement approach. Under Landis's leadership the SEC's disclosure-enforcement focus took shape. To reconcile the conflicting forces of reform and recovery both inside and outside the agency, Landis adopted a neutral goal for the SEC: technical expertise. First, before the SEC made a regulatory initiative, the issue was thoroughly researched. The Landis commission did not exercise its rule-making authority unless the implications of the regulation for the structure and practices of the markets were understood. Second, any proposed regulatory initiative was analyzed in terms of the enabling statutes to ensure that it could stand up to judicial scrutiny (Seligman 1982, 126). The cautious approach of the agency's second chairman focused the SEC's regulatory strategy on compliance with existing law (the enforcement of disclosure) rather than on a willingness to test the limits of its mandate.

Landis's caution reflected both his legal background as well as his concern for the long-term stability of the SEC as an effective regulatory agency. In its 1935 *Schecter* decision, the Supreme Court ruled the National Industrial Recovery Act unconstitutional—a decision that dealt a direct blow to what many considered one of the New Deal's most effective programs. On a broader scale, the decision threatened other New Deal statutes (such as the Securities Act and the Securities Exchange Act) with a similar fate (Ritchie 1980, 83). As one of the "founders" of the federal securities laws, Landis had a vested interest in the SEC's efforts to establish a regulatory framework for the buying and selling of securities. As a lawyer, the new chairman understood the implications of judicial review for the reach and effectiveness of an administrative agency's policies.

During Landis's tenure, the SEC staff initiated numerous studies. Many dealt with controversial issues such as the segregation of brokers and dealers on an exchange floor and the proscription of unlisted trading (the trading of securities on an exchange that were not listed with that exchange). Critics argued that studies were simply a means of avoiding direct action, but the comprehensive analyses provided the basis for well-researched SEC initiatives in later years (Parrish 1970, 209–13).

It was also during Landis's tenure that the SEC began to attract high-quality lawyers to the staff (Seligman 1982, 126). The attraction was twofold. First, Landis's insistence on rigorous statutory interpretation set standards of legal expertise few agencies could match. The agency developed an impeccable record in court, with few of its enforcement or rule-making actions overturned on review (SEC, *Annual Report* 1936, 50–51).

Second, though the agency made few controversial initiatives dealing with either market structure or trading practices under its rule-making authority, it was vigorous in enforcement. Rather than develop its regulatory policy by making rules, the SEC took a reactive posture: it used its enforcement capability as both prosecutor and administrative judge to interpret and apply the federal statutes (Ritchie 1980, 66, 70–72; Seligman 1982, 151–52). The approach opened the door for young lawyers seeking court experience and an inside understanding of the federal securities laws as applied by the SEC. Because the agency became the established technical expert in securities law, legal experience with the SEC was in high demand in the financial community. (This is discussed in detail in chapter 4.)

To enforce disclosure was to compel compliance with existing law. The policy was basically nonthreatening to the stability of the SEC. First, the agency did not have to test the limits of its statutory authority by initiating and imposing controversial rules on the securities industry. Its willingness to work with the securities industry, when rule making was necessary, perhaps made it less likely that the financial community would contest the constitutionality of the SEC's actions. Second, the policy allowed the SEC to remain independent of the industry by concentrating its regulatory efforts on vigorous enforcement. As Landis himself described it, the SEC became "both a crackdown and a cooperating agency, depending on circumstances" (de Bedts 1964, 110).

Debating the Formal and Informal Rules of Securities Regulation

The creation of the SEC and the initial implementation of its mandate were the products of decisions made by various parties. Experts and eventual regulators, legislators and their constituents, and the administration—all had preferences and political priorities regarding the regulation of securities, and all had various means of influencing outcomes.

The debate over securities policy focused on the formal and informal rules of regulation. Regarding the formal rules, the various political actors contested the design and powers of a bureaucratic structure set up to regulate securities transactions. Whether the FTC or a new SEC enforced the law made a difference for those who would carry out the policy, for politicians with Wall Street constituents, and for an administration concerned about balancing recovery and reform. Regarding the informal rules, the same political actors differed on the implementation strategy within the formal framework. How the SEC interpreted and fulfilled its mandate was as critical to policy outcomes as the formal mandate itself. The disclosure-enforcement approach represented an acceptable balance between competing political interests.

Though concerns for checking and limiting the agency's behavior were present from the beginning, a deference toward expertise was also incorporated in the SEC. Consider once again the possible political objectives of members of the House Interstate and Foreign Commerce Committee, of the Senate Banking and Currency Committee, and of the president in the early 1930s. Following the stock market crash, there was popular support for protecting the public investor from fraud and manipulation in the purchase and sale of securities. If they could tame the economic clout of Wall Street, both members of Congress and the new president could glean political benefits. However, if any legislation was to pass, it had to balance reform with the need to revive the economy; a backlash from Wall Street could jeopardize recovery.

These political objectives were largely met by the drafting expertise of Landis, Cohen, and Corcoran in the 1933 act, and in the compromise version of 1934. In the 1933 act, the Harvard contingent produced legislation so exacting that—unlike Thompson's initial draft—it sailed through the House without debate. Apparently they struck a balance between reform and recovery that members of Congress could accept. The emphasis on government enforcement of disclosure, rather than a government ruling on the merit of a securities issue, was no doubt key to the legislators' acceptance. Without such drafting expertise, it is doubtful that lawmakers could have capitalized on the popular sentiment for reform of the capital markets.

As the momentum behind FDR's legislative agenda waned, the need for carefully drafted legislation became more obvious. When the president introduced legislation to regulate the exchange markets in 1934, Congress no longer unanimously supported a drive to rein in Wall Street. An organized campaign by the New York Stock Exchange's President Whitney bolstered Wall Street's political clout. This was reflected in the willingness of Senate leaders to let the first Cohen-Corcoran draft of the Securities Exchange Act drop until the next session. For exchange regulation to pass, recovery and reform had to be more carefully balanced than they were in 1933.

Again, the drafting expertise of Landis and his cohorts put together an agreeable compromise package. Wall Street's supporters in Congress were looking for legislation to reduce the liability provisions in the 1933 act, and legislators supporting the New Deal were seeking further regulation of the exchanges. To serve their constituents, both groups needed a compromise upon which they could agree. The 1934 Securities Exchange Act gave the supporters of administrative reform—the drafters—as well as opponents, some victories.

Congress clearly relied on the new agency's expertise to implement the new legislation. Though disclosure was central to its mandate, the SEC was given a wide range of rule-making and enforcement powers to do its job. How these authorities were employed was left to the SEC to define, with congressional oversight. As a result, the professional and political objectives of the SEC's staff and commissioners dominated the agency's initial regulatory strategy.

First, there were the concerns of political appointees such as Chairman Kennedy for reviving investment through Wall Street, rather than smothering investment with too stringent reforms. The cooperative oversight and rule-making efforts between the SEC and the exchanges reflected this objective. Second, there were the concerns of the legal profession for rule making that was above judicial reproach, policy making through enforcement, and an emphasis on disclosure so as not to challenge the statutory boundaries of the agency's mandate.

However, reliance ran both ways. Without the SEC's wide range of authority—sanctioned by Congress and the administration—the politicians and professionals within the agency would have faced constraints in shaping a regulatory framework for the securities industry. Further, the SEC's ability to set up the disclosure-enforcement framework was contingent on Congress giving it sufficient enforcement authority to remain independent from the industry.

The agency also depended on its legislative committees for any expansion or reduction of its initial mandate. Throughout the New Deal period, Congress moved to extend the agency's mandate by amendment and with new legislation. However, by 1940, Congress rejected actions taken by the SEC that were beyond the realm of disclosure and enforcement, and construed as "merit-based." Instead, legislators argued that the agency's mandate should be a strict representation of the initially employed disclosure-enforcement framework. Legislative activity in 1964 and 1975 confirmed the framework. Chapter 3 discusses the statutory delineation of the agency's regulatory strategy, and the eventual institutionalization of the regulatory framework.

3 Expansion, Delineation, and Institutionalization

*T*he disclosure-enforcement framework served as a blueprint for implementing the new securities acts. It represented a balance between the concerns of a variety of political actors, each working from a different base of power. This chapter discusses the transformation of that framework from a blueprint to an institutionalized set of rules that even today guide the SEC. Just as the development of disclosure-enforcement was the product of competing priorities, the transformation of the framework into a stable means of capital market regulation represented a balance between the expert advice of the SEC, and the political clout derived from that expertise, against the concerns of elected officials and their constituent groups for accountability and control of the agency.

The Public Utility Holding Company Act of 1935

The first expansion of the SEC's authority, the Public Utility Holding Company Act (PUHCA), was particularly ambitious. By the early 1930s, 80 percent of the nation's electrical energy production was controlled by fifteen holding companies; 98.5 percent of the interstate transmission of electricity was controlled by twenty holding companies; and 80 percent of all natural gas pipelines were secured by eleven companies (SEC, *Annual Report* 1952, 83).

Built from pyramids of securities issues, these sprawling companies often deceived the public investor in utility stocks and overcharged energy consumers. The unknowing investor could purchase what were ostensibly shares in a public utility but which were in fact shares in a subsidiary that existed on paper alone. The accumulation of capital and subsidiaries under the name of one parent company created an oligopoly in the provision of electricity and, as a result, high rates for consumers (Parrish 1970, 144–45).

As governor of New York in 1930, Franklin Roosevelt drew national attention for his Progressive-style attacks on this concentration of capital and the high energy costs they caused (de Bedts 1964, 112–16; Roosevelt 1938, 1:77–79, 91–92, 106– 08, 122–23, 229–63). Once in the White House, FDR made regulation of the holding companies a legislative priority. He had three different bills drafted, one of which was introduced by Commerce Committee Chairman Sam Rayburn (D-Tex.) in the House, and Burton Wheeler (D-Mont.) in the Senate (de Bedts 1964, 119– 20). The bill that emerged in August 1935 required public utility holding companies to register with the SEC and to disclose their financial activities and securities issues. It simplified the provision of energy by limiting the holdings of companies to a geographic rationale—that is, holdings were restricted to intrastate locations or to adjacent states for efficient energy distribution (Patterson 1967, 37–42; Seligman 1982, 130–32).

This last requirement, known as the "death sentence," gave the SEC authority to break up and reorganize companies that did not meet the law's stipulations. Whereas the agency cooperated with industry organizations to oversee the exchange markets, it used its authority aggressively to intervene in and restructure holding companies. Initially, numerous court battles challenged the constitutionality of the PUHCA (Ritchie 1980, 69–70). However, seventeen years after the law was passed, the SEC's campaign to streamline the public utility industry was complete (Seligman 1982, 247). By 1952, electric utilities owned by registered holding companies accounted for only 30 percent of the value of all private utility companies. Similarly, registered holding companies owned only 28 percent of the nation's aggregate suppliers and producers of natural gas (SEC, *Annual Report* 1952, 83).

Implementation of the PUHCA "death sentence" was unique in two respects. First, just as the SEC's cooperation with the exchange markets coincided with the president's plan for economic recovery (see chapter 2), there was a clear presidential mandate for SEC activism toward the public utility industry. Roosevelt's national political career was launched by his opposition to the public utility oligopoly, and he gave top priority to the regulation of utility holding companies. This was evident both in his early appointments to the SEC and in his public advocacy of the Public Utility Holding Company Act during congressional hearings on the bill.

Two SEC commissioners appointed by Roosevelt were active supporters of reform in the utilities industry. Robert Healy, named in 1934, led an investigation of public utilities as general counsel for the FTC. His study concluded with recommendations for drastic changes in the structure and functioning of the industry and its enormous holding companies (Parrish 1970, 153). J. D. Ross, appointed to fill a seat vacated by Ferdinand Pecora, had previously headed Seattle's municipally owned utility—considered to be an exemplary operation in the Pacific Northwest (de Bedts 1964, 183–85). With strong support within the SEC for restructuring, Roosevelt concentrated on galvanizing outside endorsement for the legislation as well. FDR's numerous radio broadcasts and statements to the press drew public favor for the bill and sent a clear message to Congress about his intentions (ibid., 128–30; Roosevelt 1938, 4:98–103, 138–39, 268–70).

Second, SEC activism in implementing the Public Utility Holding Company Act (PUHCA) was unique in that it was limited to regulating public utility holding companies and ended when its task was complete. After a seventeen-year struggle with companies that failed to meet the intrastate or adjacent state test, the SEC narrowed its regulatory focus: specifically, regulation of holding companies was limited to enforcing the disclosure of a utility company's holdings and acquisitions; disclosure for issues of securities; and disclosure of the logistics of energy provision—both electric and gas (SEC, *Annual Report* 1952, 111).

Perhaps more significant than the agency's initial implementation of the "death sentence" was the prominence of disclosure in the agency's continuing regulation of holding companies. The nationwide support generated by Roosevelt was no doubt significant for congressional sanction of the bill and for the SEC's rigorous enforcement. However, once the breakup of holding companies was accomplished, the SEC's approach to regulating holding companies became the enforcement of disclosure. For members of Congress who went through a heated legislative battle over the "death sentence" clause, disclosure of a holding company's activities was a relatively noncontroversial means to continue regulating the industry. For the SEC, the enforcement of disclosure was a natural extension of the agency's existing approach.

Expansion to the
Over-the-Counter Market

Congress expanded the SEC's jurisdiction again in 1938. The Maloney Act (named after its Democratic sponsor, Senator Francis Maloney of Connecticut) established SEC oversight of the trading activities and qualifications of market professionals in the over-the-counter market (to be discussed later). The provisions paralleled the SEC's oversight of the stock exchanges. Where the far-reaching PUHCA was initiated by the president, the more modest Maloney Act was initiated as a legislative proposal by the SEC after it had completed studies of the over-the-counter market. I will address the role of the SEC and its legislative committees in bringing about the legislation after briefly describing the differences between the OTC and exchange markets.

Over-the-Counter Markets Versus Exchanges[1]

The over-the-counter market differs from stock exchange markets in three basic respects. First, it has no specific location. Instead, the market is as vast as the number of over-the-counter dealers across the country. Trading takes place through a network of telephones, telegraphs, and computers. A stock exchange, on the other hand, offers a single, central location for the trading of securities.

The over-the-counter and exchange markets also differ in the way markets are "made," or the means by which buyers and sellers are brought together to make trades. A market is made over the counter by dealers who buy and sell stock for their own accounts. Dealers compete for market making on the basis of the markup they charge the investing public and other dealers: purchasers of stock are charged an increment above the current market value (what the dealers recognize as the value of the stock), while sellers are given an increment below current value. Trading continues as long as dealers are willing to buy and sell, or as long as the competitive markup is profitable.

In contrast, markets are made on an exchange by brokers and specialists who are members of that exchange. Where over-the-counter dealers make a profit by charging a markup on transactions for their own accounts, brokers earn commissions by trading shares for customers' accounts. A member broker with an order to buy or sell shares of stock goes to the specialist who makes a market in that particular stock. The specialist maintains a book of orders to buy and sell shares of stock. Trades are executed by the specialist by matching book orders with new orders sent to the floor, or through a bidding process in which the specialist acts as an auctioneer for the purchase and sale of a broker's orders.[2] The specialist system, therefore, provides a central market location for the execution of trades.

A third difference between the two markets lies in the trading responsibilities of the market professionals. The specialist on an exchange has an obligation to sell in a rising market (when heavy buying activity pushes share prices higher) and to buy in a falling market (when heavy selling activity pushes share prices lower). This offers both investors and companies that issue stock continuous trading in a central market location and some assurance of relatively low spreads between the bid and the asking price of a security—the difference between what buyers are willing to pay and the solicited price. The cost of these benefits, however, is reflected on an exchange in two ways: first, in the commission investors pay to brokers for executing their trades in the exchange market; second, in the qualifications companies must meet to list their securities with an exchange and in annual listing fees.

In contrast, over-the-counter dealers have no obligation to buy and sell with their own account. Without similar assurances for market continuity and liquidity, the cost of transacting in the over-the-counter market is lower for investors and traders than transacting through an exchange. Low costs have made the over-the-counter market attractive to companies issuing new securities as an opening for trade; to issuers who cannot meet the capital requirements of an exchange; to issuers who do not want to pay a listing fee; and to investors and other dealers who do not want to pay a brokerage fee, which is often less competitive than a markup.

The Maloney Act

At the outset, the SEC recognized trading in the over-the-counter market as a likely location for fraudulent dealings. Trading was geographically dispersed, the market was attractive to undercapitalized firms and new issues of stock, and dealers could make a market without any obligation to investors for a "fair" markup, as on an exchange.

Under the 1934 act, the SEC was given the authority to oversee the trading practices of a registered exchange market and the qualifications of its members, but the professional dealers in the high-volume over-the-counter market were unorganized and unregulated. As early as 1935, Chairman Landis proposed to bring the over-the-counter market under the SEC's purview by organizing a "self-disciplinary agency of dealers." As was typical under Landis, the agency negotiated with the industry and conducted studies before recommending legislation (SEC, *Annual Report* 1935, 18–19; McCraw 1984, 198–99; Seligman 1982, 143, 183).

The SEC initiative was prompted by an earlier effort by Wall Street investment bankers to bring some trading standards and professional accountability to the over-the-counter market. Public exposure of fraudulent issues and manipulative practices tainted the reputations of many securities firms, and the public was wary about investing. When sales were low, underwriters (investment bankers who back issues of securities) did not make a profit. It was hoped that if the over-the-counter market were cleaned up, the industry would rebound with the restoration of investor confidence.

The Investment Bankers' Conference (IBC)—the industry's trade group—went so far as to draft a code of fair practice to govern trading and participation in the over-the-counter market. The code received the approval of Roosevelt's National Recovery Administration (NRA). However, when the NRA was declared unconstitutional in 1935, the code's legitimacy also faltered. With the support of the IBC, the SEC under Landis invoked its rule-making authority in the 1934 act to develop a regulatory system for the over-the-counter market (Robbins 1966, 111).

In 1938, Chairman William Douglas (the SEC's third chairman and later a Supreme Court justice) proposed legislation for over-the-counter regulation that drew heavily on the work conducted under Landis. The proposal extended the SEC policy toward the exchange markets by calling for industry cooperation in the regulatory effort. Specifically, Douglas proposed market oversight based on the formation of professional associations of brokers and dealers that would, in turn, provide for the internal governance of their members. Such governance was to include rules for fair dealing, prohibition of fixed rates, membership qualifications, and democratic means for electing association leaders and establishing rules (Seligman 1982, 185–86). A similar system of internal governance was already in place on the stock exchanges.

As with the exchanges, the SEC had rule-making authority in the over-the-counter market that could be used, as Chairman Douglas once said, as a "shotgun, so to speak, behind the door" (Robbins 1966, 85). In other words, rather than use its authority to impose changes on the industry, the agency could threaten to prompt solutions from within the industry. Under section 15 of the Securities Exchange Act, the agency was given the authority to approve or disapprove any rule or decision passed by an over-the-counter association, as well as impose its own rules (Schwartz 1973, 2696). If an over-the-counter association were slow to act, or did not take actions acceptable to the SEC, the agency could preempt or halt the governance process within these industry organizations. However, this authority—to approve rules before they were enacted in the over-the-counter market—surpassed the SEC's rule-making authority over the exchanges, where the agency's authority was limited to the abrogation or supplement of existing rules (Jennings 1964, 676). Since passage of the Maloney Act in 1938, only one such professional organization has been founded for the over-the-counter market: the National Association of Securities Dealers (NASD), to which all participants in the market are required to belong.

This 1938 initiative, designed to further incorporate the securities industry in its regulatory strategy, was conditioned as much by SEC precedent as by the difficulties of regulating a geographically disperse entity. The SEC did not have the staff or resources for direct oversight of the nation's over-the-counter firms and dealers (Seligman 1982, 185). By forming an organization of brokers and dealers, the SEC could oversee the overseers: the industry had an incentive to polish its image (to increase investor confidence), and the SEC's authority to rule on market structure and market behavior provided a stimulus for the industry to police its own activities.

Yet the SEC's ability to extend its regulatory authority through legislative initiative required congressional approval. The Maloney Act extended only one aspect of the SEC's regulatory framework to the over-the-counter market: the use of its rule-making authority as a means to prompt industry cooperation in overseeing the actions of market professionals. In 1938, Chairman Douglas also recommended the full disclosure of material information relating to securities issues traded over the counter—the equivalent of disclosure provisions for securities listed on an exchange (ibid., 246). The recommendation was not part of the final legislation. In fact, Congress did not extend that authority to the SEC until it passed amendments to the Securities Exchange Act in 1964.

The delay in bringing about full disclosure for the over-the-counter market indicates the possible significance of presidential priorities for securing ambitious legislation. Despite tremendous controversy over the PUHCA "death sentence" in Congress and among holding companies, the measure was partly sustained by the strong popular support for the measure represented by the president. Over-the-counter legislation had its genesis in the meticulous studies and negotiations with the industry, conducted by the SEC under Landis, and had as its sponsors the agency and the investment banking community. The issue was neither urgent nor emotional, a fact reflected in Congress's reluctance to extend the SEC's authority. Further, the reaction of an important interest group (the IBC) to the legislation may have accounted for the limited expansion that Congress did enact. Interestingly, when Congress did enact full disclosure for over-the-counter issues (1964), the bill received President Johnson's endorsement (Cary 1967, 111–12). (This will be discussed later.) Nevertheless, the agency's authority was extended on the agency's own recommendation, and the legislation was enacted.

Expansion of the SEC's authority in 1938 set a long-term pattern for the agency's market oversight activities by building upon its cooperative approach with the industry. Though the Maloney Act did not insist on it, full disclosure was reemphasized as central to the agency's mandate by legislation passed in 1940. The agency rarely initiated changes in the *structure* of markets and market behavior, as in the restructuring of holding companies. However, the SEC's rigorous prosecutorial efforts and technical competence served to maintain its distance from the regulated interests.

Regulating Investment Companies

Rounding out the New Deal legislation were two acts that were again motivated by an SEC study, this time an investigation of the mutual fund industry. Findings of embezzlement and the personal aggrandizement of fund managers, at the expense of investors, resulted in the Investment Company Act of 1940 and its companion, the Investment Company Advisers' Act of 1940 (SEC, *Annual Report* 1939, 121–23; ibid. 1940, 176–78). The former required investment companies to register with the SEC, regulated the practices of investment advisors, and required the disclosure of any possible conflict of interest an advisor may have when initiating transactions for the public. The second act required the registration of advisors with the SEC (Gujarati 1984, 359–60).

Even among the SEC's most conservative members, the 1940 legislation was considered modest (SEC, *Annual Report* 1941, 2). The initial SEC proposal for regulating investment companies provided two layers of protection for investors in mutual funds. First, as specified in the final bill, investment companies were to register with the SEC, and to disclose investment relevant information to the agency such as company balance sheets, the company's investment portfolio, income earned, salaries paid to directors and officers of the company, and buying and selling activities in the company's portfolio (Bullock 1959, 94; Wexler 1975, 22–34). Second, although the request was eliminated from the final draft of the legislation, the SEC sought authority to enforce a standard of fairness for shareholders regarding the structure and operation of investment companies (Seligman 1982, 229–30).

Development and enactment of the Investment Company Acts proved the significance of both the SEC and its legislative committees in further delineating the disclosure-enforcement framework. On the one hand, the SEC had wide discretion to make proposals for regulating investment company activities. The agency's exhaustive study of investment companies—known as the *Investment Trust Study*—defined and documented the industry's failings vis-à-vis shareholders. Further, because the agency proposed the legislation to the committees, it set the agenda and its study shaped the debate. Yet legislative committee members could endorse agency proposals or develop their own ways of protecting shareholders. They chose to support not the fairness provision but the agency's proposal for full disclosure—that investment company shareholders would be protected to the extent that all relevant information concerning the company was divulged.

Enforcing investment company disclosure was a predictable outcome, given the professional and political incentives driving both the SEC and congressional committee members. First, it complemented the agency's established emphasis on prosecution of disclosure violations that was fostered by the interests of lawyers within the SEC. (See chapter 4.) Second, it allowed legislators to assuage investment company fears that the SEC might rule on the fairness of their structure and activities, yet it provided some form of regulation that could enhance the industry's public image. It also reaffirmed an earlier congressional decision: in 1933 Congress rejected the first draft of the Securities Act partly because the draft made the FTC responsible for judging the merits of a securities issue.

In tandem with the Maloney Act, the Investment Company Acts extended the disclosure-enforcement framework to the over-the-counter market and to investment company activity. To sum up, the framework for regulating the securities markets was based on the following: (1) enforcement of full disclosure of investment-relevant information for securities traded on an exchange (and later, over the counter); (2) use of the agency's authority to initiate changes in market structure or in the practices of industry organizations (such as the exchanges and the NASD), more as a means to prod industry solutions than as a means of intervention; and (3) formulation of reactive regulatory policy through actions taken against violations of the federal securities laws—administrative, civil, and criminal.

Explaining Variation in the Early SEC Mandate

To explain the statutory development of disclosure-enforcement throughout the New Deal, we must examine the competing priorities and concerns of the SEC and its legislative committees. The committee members' desire to serve their constituents was a defining feature of the new legislation. They were able to capitalize on popular sentiment for reform, in the case of PUHCA, and to acquiesce in the concerns of investment bankers and investment companies, with the Maloney and Investment Company acts. The professional ambitions of the SEC's legal staff, tempered by the president's agenda for economic recovery, guided the initial implementation of the laws and continued to shape the agency's preferences for New Deal legislation. The SEC's research and reports set the agenda for reforming the over-the-counter market and regulating the investment companies. Further, its recommendations for regulation of the over-the-counter market and investment companies were an extension of the agency's early regulatory strategy. However, political and economic conditions exogenous to the immediate relationship between Congress and the SEC also helped to shape the 1935, 1938, and 1940 acts, as well as the SEC's ability to enforce them.

Economic recovery was essential for the success of FDR's political agenda in 1934. This significantly affected how the original commission implemented its mandate. Roosevelt's endorsement of Kennedy for chairman set in motion cooperative oversight: the SEC's reliance on industry self-governance for some of its oversight activities and a reluctance to impose change on market structures and behavior. Rigorous enforcement efforts, instead, became the focus of its regulatory activities and its means of maintaining its independence from the industry.

The SEC had the green light in 1935 from all three branches of government to restructure the public utility industry. President Roosevelt took a personal interest in utility reform, and his early appointments to the SEC and public statements made his intentions clear to Congress. For its part, Congress acquiesced by leaving the PUHCA "death sentence" in the legislation, and the courts upheld the constitutionality of the act and the authority of the SEC (Parrish, 1970, 220).

An SEC study put over-the-counter legislation into play, but its passage required the industry's consent. The proposal reflected Landis's cautious use of regulatory initiatives. His concern for the agency's stability, as well as the ever present threat of judicial review, led him to recommend reliance on the industry's self-organization with SEC oversight. The decision did not commit the SEC to a policy that could become a drain on resources and impair the agency's administrative capabilities. Rather, the vast over-the-counter market was centralized by a professional organization that the SEC could easily oversee. Further, the cooperative approach had the industry's support and therefore was less vulnerable to court attacks.

Despite the Maloney Act's noncontroversial nature, it was perhaps a Wall Street scandal that finally pushed it through Congress. Chairman Douglas made strategic use of Richard Whitney's conviction for embezzlement (Whitney was president of the New York Stock Exchange) to propose expanded regulation over the financial community (Ritchie 1980, 78).

Finally, passage of the 1940 acts was conditioned by a Congress hostile to the New Deal. The momentum behind FDR's regulatory agenda in the administration's first hundred days and beyond showed signs of waning by 1938; recall that disclosure for over-the-counter issues had been left on the back burner. By 1940, opposition to the discretion of Roosevelt's "alphabet" agencies hardened among some members of Congress (Bernstein 1955, 134–37; Seligman 1982, 152). A request by the SEC to rule on the "fairness" of investment company operations (as they affected the investor) was therefore unwelcome. Instead, disclosure by investment companies was an acceptable alternative to Congress and had the support of investment company managers as well; an SEC study of investment companies revealed numerous abuses amid the somewhat chaotic rebuilding of the industry after the 1929 crash. Mild legislation would help to bolster the fiduciary image of companies for the investing public and to halt future, possibly more restrictive, legislation.

In each case, the interaction of congressional, SEC, and (occasionally) presidential objectives helped to shape the legislation that emerged. After 1940, the workability of the agency's regulatory framework was obvious: the SEC did not make overtures for additional legislation for nearly twenty years, and Congress did not address the SEC mandate again until it amended the Securities Act in 1964.

A Twenty-Four-Year Gap in Securities Legislation

Just as the priorities and concerns of the SEC, its legislative committees, and to some degree the administration shaped the New Deal expansion of the agency's mandate, each had a role to play in maintaining a legislative status quo from 1940 until 1964. Moreover, just as the New Deal legislation must be considered in the context of economic malaise and the 1929 stock market crash, the void in securities legislation is not surprising in a country at war. A wartime economy hampered the SEC's ability to initiate new legislation for several reasons.

The massive demands of World War II, as well as the Korean War, took a significant toll on the SEC's resources. This strain prevented the SEC from initiating and researching new legislation. For example, more than a third of the agency's staff was drafted during World War II, and staff reductions occurred during the Korean War, too. Further, the SEC's budget was cut during the period of U.S. involvement in both wars (SEC, *Annual Report* 1944, iv–v; ibid. 1945, 94–95; ibid. 1952, 195; ibid. 1953, 118).

The agency suffered in quality as well as quantity. Roosevelt made an effort to nominate well-qualified commissioners during the early years of the war (Seligman 1982, 238). But military service and wartime demands for high-caliber leadership elsewhere severely limited the selection pool for commissioners and SEC staff. Despite a handful of legislative initiatives between 1941 and 1955, such as several proposals to bring issues in the over-the-counter market under full disclosure,[3] the scarcity of talent, time, and manpower limited SEC activities to maintaining its basic oversight and enforcement activities.

The war also affected the location of the agency. During the United States' involvement in World War II, the significance of federal spending in the domestic economy overshadowed the activities of private finance. Wall Street was not inactive, but it did reflect a shift in national priorities and, consequently, the national interest for regulating private finance. Symbolic of this shift was the SEC's move from Washington to Philadelphia for the duration of the war (SEC, *Annual Report* 1942, Letter of Transmittal). The agency's distance from Washington hampered its ability to work with Congress for new legislation.

However, even if the SEC had remained in Washington at full funding levels, the agency would not necessarily have expanded its mandate during this twenty-four-year period, particularly during the Eisenhower administration. President Eisenhower took office with a charge to balance the federal budget by cutting back government spending and to encourage economic expansion by reducing the burdens of regulation (Eisenhower 1960, 1:19–24). For the most part, SEC Chairman Ralph Demmler, nominated by Eisenhower in 1953, shared the administration's agenda, as was reflected in the agency's priorities during his chairmanship.

First, in 1952, 1953, and 1955, the Budget Bureau recommended reductions in the SEC's budget. Demmler debated the proposed cuts because of already low staff levels and enforcement difficulties, but the priorities of the Eisenhower Budget Bureau prevailed (Seligman 1982, 268). Second, the Demmler SEC did not seek to expand the agency's mandate. Rather, legislative initiatives under Demmler consisted of technical adjustments to the securities acts (SEC, *Annual Report* 1953, 117) and recommendations to reduce the regulatory burdens on businesses (ibid. 1954, 1–3). Third, in contrast to the SEC's more rigorous enforcement endeavors throughout the 1930s and early 1940s, activity under Demmler dropped precipitously, particularly by 1955 (ibid. 1966, 168).

Demmler's priorities met strenuous opposition from Democrats on the SEC's legislative committees who tried to exploit what they saw as an increasingly fraudulent securities environment under a Republican administration. They latched onto Demmler's deregulatory agenda and feeble enforcement as violations of the agency's mandate (Senate Banking Committee, *Stock Market Study Report* 1955). Interestingly, enforcement actions were the target of congressional criticism. SEC police work was becoming popular among members of the House and Senate legislative committees. As SEC enforcement activities took on an increasingly high profile in following decades, congressional support became stronger and more vocal. (See chapter 5). It is also interesting that committee Democrats were not alone in supporting a more visible SEC to oversee the markets. By the early 1950s, members of the securities industry recognized the SEC's enforcement programs, in particular, as necessary to restore investor confidence in Wall Street (Seligman 1982, 266).

What is significant is that the legislative gap resulted from a combination of factors. Despite the SEC's interest in expanding its statutory authority during the war years (before and after Demmler), as shown in a few initiatives, the drain on the agency's budget and on the quality and quantity of its personnel prevented the agency from proposing new legislation. Reduced resources were obviously the result of diminished congressional appropriations.

However, dependency went both ways. When a Democratic Congress wanted to challenge the enforcement policies of a Republican administration, the lack of cooperation from the SEC stymied that effort. Without SEC initiatives for expanding its mandate during the

Demmler years (1953–1955), and because the SEC failed to embark on a more rigorous enforcement program, the Congress could criticize, but not determine, the agency's activities. Congress apparently relied on initiatives from the SEC to bring about change in the laws regulating securities.[4] Instead, it took a Wall Street scandal, the rapid growth of fraud and abuse, and a stock market crash to alarm both Congress and the SEC regarding the adequacy of securities regulation. Perhaps indicating Congress's reliance on the agency to address these problems, the next legislative response (in 1964), premised on an exhaustive 1962 study of the markets conducted by the SEC, was to expand the existing disclosure-enforcement framework.

The Special Study of 1961–1963

By 1960 the postwar securities markets were bursting out of the old regulatory structure. Growth in the securities industry exploded throughout the 1950s. For example, in 1950 the dollar volume on all of the nation's exchanges was $21 billion; by 1960, it more than doubled to $45 billion (SEC, *Annual Report* 1961, 220). In 1950, there were 3,930 brokers and dealers registered with the SEC; by 1961 there were 5,500. And in 1950 firms with membership in the New York Stock Exchange had 1,661 branch offices; by 1960, that number had nearly doubled to 3,166 (ibid., 1–3).

Growth in market volume also meant a strain on the SEC's enforcement and oversight capabilities. The agency confronted dramatic increases in brokerage fraud, mismanagement, and "failures" in the clearance of brokered orders to buy and sell securities (Cary 1967, 71). In 1961, the problem was vividly demonstrated by an SEC investigation of a specialist firm on the American Stock Exchange owned by the Re brothers. The brothers had engaged in insider trading, distributed fraudulent shares, manipulated trading on the exchange floor, circulated false information about various securities, and, needless to say, violated their responsibilities as a specialist firm to maintain fair and orderly markets (*New York Times* 4/29/61, 26; ibid. 5/11/61, 36; ibid. 5/26/61, 18). Further investigation by the SEC revealed widespread failings of internal governance, hitherto undetected, throughout the entire exchange. A former SEC staff member who had been involved in the AMEX investigation described the conditions on Wall Street in the early 1960s, and what the agency saw as gaps in its regulatory capabilities, as follows:

> As the stock market revived, the SEC was not prepared to deal with the increase in activity. Enforcement problems came behind unresolved regulatory problems that we didn't know that we had. The first focal point was the AMEX investigation involving the second biggest specialist firm on the exchange, Re and Re.... They were manipulating the prices of securities to assist corporate insiders.... The investigation showed that there was a fundamental failure in supervision by the self-regulating organization [the exchange] charged with regulating the activity of its own floor.

Enforcement and regulatory problems, combined with the agenda of a new SEC chairman, prompted the agency to seek congressional funding for a comprehensive study of the markets. In 1961 President Kennedy nominated William Cary to head the commission. Cary, a Columbia University professor of law, was described by former staff members of the SEC as having "a 1933 act background" and as determined to expand the disclosure requirements of the 1933 and 1934 acts to the over-the-counter market. The comments of a former staff member who worked with Cary illustrate the chairman's concerns for substantiating the SEC's enforcement and disclosure authority and his efforts to secure congressional funding for a comprehensive study:

> Chairman Cary ... decided early on that the SEC was woefully behind in its awareness of what was going on in the securities markets. He lobbied the House Commerce Committee and the Senate Banking Committee intensively for the funding [to do a study]. He literally went to every member on those committees, something that no one had done before.

The committees responded by authorizing the special study to examine the securities markets and the SEC's regulation of the markets that Cary had demanded. However, it was not just Cary's lobbying efforts and the commission's concerns that moved the House Commerce and Senate Banking committees to authorize the inquiry. First, the AMEX scandal received enormous press coverage, and the committees wanted further investigation of the exchange and the role of the SEC (*Congressional Quarterly Almanac* 1961, 501; ibid. 1962, 566). Second, regulatory issues were complicated when the Dow Jones industrial average fell by 27 percent in 1962 (Robbins 1966, 135). The crash affected investors and brokerage firms alike, and committee members (who represented constituent interests) were spurred to question the regulatory status quo.

The study was to be conducted primarily by investigators from outside the SEC because Congress also wanted to examine the agency's regulatory activities. Yet several staff members hired to conduct the study were already working for the SEC at the time, and many stayed on after its completion. According to these former staffers, there was regular cooperation and communication between the commission and the study staff. As one stated: "In the letter of transmittal [to Congress], it said that the staff was responsible for the contents [of the study], but there was actually a lot of consultation with the commission. [One study member] even acted as the staff liaison with the commission."

The study, which lasted two years, covered a wide range of topics, and its conclusions and recommendations had immediate as well as long-range significance for regulatory reform. The staff investigated not only market fraud, manipulation, and disclosure, but also questions of fundamental market structure. Among the topics addressed were standards for market professionals and the adequacy of controls on their behavior; the functions of the stock exchanges and over-the-counter market, their structures, problems, and interrelationships; the legal requirements and disclosure standards for stocks traded over the counter as well as stocks that were listed, and recommendations to expand disclosure requirements to the over-the-counter market; the implications of a fixed commission fee for brokerage in markets increasingly dominated by institutional investors; the growth and regulation of open-end investment companies (mutual funds); and the effectiveness of industry self-regulation (internal policing) with SEC oversight (SEC, *Annual Report* 1963, 1–3). Just as studies carried out under Chairman Landis provided the initiative for legislation to regulate the over-the-counter market, the SEC used the special study's findings to support legislative recommendations—the first being the Securities Acts amendments of 1964.

The 1964 Amendments

Given Chairman Cary's experience with the Securities Act of 1933, one of the commission's first priorities was to close the disclosure gaps in that act relating to new issues and gaps in the 1934 act relating to continuous reporting. Using the study's findings, the SEC recommended amending the securities acts to extend the disclosure-enforcement framework to the over-the-counter market. Whereas the Maloney Act had extended the agency's cooperative rule-making approach to the over-the-counter market by organizing a self-regulating group of professionals, the 1964 amendments imposed SEC disclosure requirements on a majority of the firms whose stocks traded in that market. Specifically, any company with more than 750 shareholders and $1 million in assets became subject to the agency's disclosure requirements (Cary 1967, 91–92).[5] Given their size and low capitalization, these firms had avoided SEC oversight by trading over the counter rather than through an exchange—where listing standards prevented their access. This extension of disclosure paralleled the legislature's 1940 approval of regulating investment companies and their advisors by means of disclosure. The SEC also recommended increasing standards for the participation of brokers and dealers in the markets, such as higher professional and financial qualifications (ibid., 91–92). In keeping with its reliance upon industry organizations to expand its regulatory reach, the SEC would oversee the enforcement of these new standards by the National Association of Securities Dealers, created under the Maloney Act, and by the stock exchanges.

Despite congressional support for a special study in 1961, the excitement generated by the American Stock Exchange scandal, and the sense of urgency created by the 1962 market decline, momentum for the legislation ebbed by 1964. Initial drafts of the amendments contained a controversial provision that would have included insurance companies in the new disclosure requirements. Insurance companies lobbied hard for an exemption, and the fight was tiresome for targeted members of Congress (ibid., 113–14). A compromise was eventually reached with the insurance industry, but it required the continued support of the SEC for the amendments as well as an endorsement by President Johnson before the bill was passed (ibid., 111–12).

Again, the concerns and priorities on both sides—the SEC and its legislative committees—were primary factors in expanding and further delineating the disclosure-enforcement framework in 1964. The SEC's concerns were developed in the *Special Study* and presented, in part, as amendments to the securities acts: an expansion of the disclosure-enforcement system to include over-the-counter firms and insurance companies. The AMEX scandal, the market crash, and Cary's lobbying efforts drew congressional attention, but committee preferences to exempt insurance companies from the disclosure-enforcement framework restricted the influence of SEC recommendations.

Amending the Investment Company Act

In the mid-1960s, the SEC began to examine the adequacy of investor protection under the Investment Company Act of 1940. Findings in the *Special Study* pointed out particular problems that the agency examined more closely in a subsequent report, *Public Policy Implications of Investment Company Growth* (Wexler 1975, 65–67). Using conclusions reached in both studies, the SEC recommended amending the 1940 act. Again, the legislation was an agency initiative based on its research of a technical area that had undergone fundamental change. However, where the agency first mobilized congressional support for the *Special Study* and the 1964 amendments in the wake of the AMEX scandal and the market crash, recommendations to amend the Investment Company Act had only the SEC's support. The fact that legislation was enacted testifies to the agency's influence as a source of expertise in Congress, as well as to the tenacious efforts of its chairman, Manuel Cohen.

The basic findings of the SEC's *Public Policy* study are best summed up by a former member of the SEC staff. In his unpublished history of the SEC, Bernard Wexler writes, "*Public Policy*'s general theme was that mutual funds were on the whole a desirable investment medium—but that they cost investors far too much" (ibid., 67).

The SEC argued that compensation for mutual fund managers was excessive, that the sales charges (including "front-end loads") levied against mutual fund investors were too high, and that arrangements between fund managers and certain broker-dealers were a breach of their fiduciary duty to investors. On this last point, the SEC focused primarily on a practice known as the "give-up." This typically involved a mutual fund manager who would pay one brokerage firm full commission for a particular service, such as executing the fund's trades on an exchange. The manager would then direct the broker to give up portions of the commission to other brokers for research they provided the fund, or for selling shares of the fund for the manager. Because the compensation of fund managers was often related to the number of shares sold, the SEC argued that the practice promoted a conflict of interest involving management compensation and shareholder concerns. The benefits of the give-up, the SEC argued, should have gone to the investors—the actual "givers" to the fund (Loomis 1967, 114).

When enacted in 1970, the Investment Company Act amendments were a much more modest reform of mutual fund practices than initially proposed by the SEC, yet the legislation was well within the bounds of disclosure-enforcement. Basically, the legislation gave the NASD and the SEC authority to prohibit "unconscionable or grossly excessive" fees charged to shareholders by investment companies. A fiduciary duty between investment advisors and shareholders was also established by the legislation, and the SEC was empowered to take actions against excessive fees or to sue for breach of fiduciary duty. However, the agency was not allowed to impose fair fees or set standards, and the burden of proving excessive or unfair fees lay with the SEC or the harmed shareholder (*Congressional Quarterly Almanac* 1970, 890–94).[6]

The watered-down legislation reflected congressional indifference as well as strong industry opposition to the SEC's initiative. As the *Public Policy* study concluded, the mutual fund industry was a prospering investment medium. But precisely because of the industry's prosperity, lawmakers failed to see the need for legislation. Neither the mutual fund industry nor the investors in mutual funds were clamoring for Congress to make any changes in the conduct of business. A former member of the House Interstate and Foreign Commerce Committee described his position on the legislation in the context of what appeared to be prosperity resulting from healthy competition: "I had a problem with intervention in the free enterprise system. . . . I guess I was described as a defender of the industry, but I just felt that whoever can sell at the best price to investors should be able to."

Similarly, a longtime SEC staffer argued that because there was no scandal or major crisis associated with the SEC's proposals, it was difficult to mobilize support for the legislation: "The problem was that nobody cared. It was too complex, and for the individual investors it was nickels and dimes. You couldn't get people excited about it."

As this former staff member pointed out, another obstacle faced by the SEC was the technical and complex nature of the agency's concerns. Issues raised by the SEC dealt with intricate transactions between various market professionals and involved the internal organization and operations of sophisticated investment mediums. The agency's concerns were obscure not only to members of Congress, but also to most of the investors in mutual funds. Consequently, the legislation was not easily debated in a congressional forum, nor easily presented as a means of protecting shareholders. For example, hearings on the SEC's proposals labored over points as fundamental as the definition of a mutual fund. Consider the comments of a former agency staffer who worked on the amendments:

> The big fight in the congressional hearings was over [excessive] management fees. The issue is controversial depending upon what your interpretation of a mutual fund is. If you think that a mutual fund is a separate entity with its own board of directors and a responsibility to shareholders, then the fund should bargain with managers for lower fees that are in the shareholders' best interests. But if you think that a mutual fund is just a vehicle for investments, then the fee is a bargain. Depending upon how you looked at it, [the fee] was either outrageously high or a bargain.

This individual went on to describe how these technical points clouded and confused the hearing process, as well as committee members' thinking on the issue: "These two arguments were debated in the congressional hearings just like two ships passing in the night. There was an air of unreality about the hearings, and [some members] were totally confused."

Yet the persistence of the SEC, primarily of Chairman Cohen, as well as the agency's reputation in Congress for expertise, were crucial to getting the bill passed in some form. When interviewed, former SEC staffers and former members of the legislative committees described Manuel Cohen's efforts as something of a crusade. One former agency staffer described Cohen's drive to pass the legislation over the stiff objections of the industry:

> The central provisions of the bill, the regulation of management fees and sales loads, [was] strenuously opposed by the investment company industry. It was the first time since the 1935 act that Congress passed regulation over strenuous opposition, although it was watered down; but still it passed. That was due to the indefatigable energy of career bureaucrat Manny Cohen. The legislation was not that important, but it became an obsession with him. He lobbied and lobbied and we got the legislation.

The SEC's reputation in Congress also went a long way toward convincing members of the legislative committees that the amendments were necessary. A former SEC staff member argued that "passage of the amendments was largely due to the SEC." He said that the SEC's proposals didn't receive much attention at first; however, "legislation that the SEC says is important eventually gets attention paid to it. That doesn't say it gets broad support, but it gets attention."

Another former staffer made the same observation. He pointed out that despite a lack of fanfare surrounding the legislation, the committees dealt with the recommendations—primarily because the agency had come to Congress well prepared. "The legislation was something the committees were interested in, and that was interesting because there had been no major scandal. No investment company had failed, no one went to jail. . . . But the SEC had done its job. It was very thorough."

These sentiments were echoed in interviews with former staffers and legislative committee members. In discussing the committees' willingness to take up the agency's proposals, several prefaced their comments with statements about the SEC's "integrity" and its "expertise." One former member of the House Commerce Committee noted the SEC's ability "to get things done" because it "just had a solid reputation" and "we could work together." Because the SEC was the designated expert for a technical area in which the outcomes of policies were uncertain, its recommendations apparently carried significant weight with its legislative committees. The fact that members of Congress saw the SEC as acting responsibly (SEC staffers were typically thorough in their research and came to Congress well prepared) further advanced its influence. Despite industry opposition and Congress's initial indifference, some of the SEC's concerns were incorporated into law—specifically, those in line with the disclosure-enforcement framework.

These roles were reversed at the turn of the 1970s when legislative committees were pushing for statutory reform. However, precedent (the disclosure-enforcement framework) and SEC expertise were again critical for adherence to the framework as a legislative solution to regulatory problems.

The 1975 Amendments to the Securities Acts

When Congress passed the Securities Exchange Act in 1934 to regulate stock market trading, existing regulations governing the stock exchanges were allowed to continue under SEC oversight, unless the agency determined that changes were "necessary or appropriate for the protection of investors or to insure fair dealing in securities traded in upon such exchange" (Schwartz 1973, 2699). In general, these rules set up guidelines for membership, listing a security with an exchange, and conducting business among exchange members. Many of these rules protected members from competition with other member firms and in other markets. For example, as members of the New York Stock Exchange, brokerage firms agreed to conduct business under a fixed-commission rate system for each round-lot order rather than compete for customers with lower commissions. Similarly, the exchange's rule 394 limited off-board competition for the "specialists" on the exchange—member firms that made a market in specific exchange-listed securities by matching buy-and-sell orders from brokers. In practice, rule 394 prevented member brokers from executing a trade (as buyer or seller) with exchange-listed stocks anywhere other than with a New York Stock Exchange specialist, even if the member could get a better price for the stock on another exchange or in the over-the-counter market.

At a time when most customers of the exchange were individuals placing small round-lot orders, the exchange argued that competitive restraints such as fixed rates and rule 394 helped to maintain a high-quality, primary-auction market for its customers: the fixed commission operated as an incentive for member firms to stay with the exchange (where their trading activities were carefully monitored and held to particular standards of quality), while the prohibition against off-board trading prevented the fragmentation of markets by concentrating trading activity in a single location. In both cases, it was argued that the benefit to the customer was greater depth and liquidity for buying and selling securities. However, throughout the 1960s these competitive restraints began to clash with fundamental changes in the securities markets.

Between 1960 and 1968, institutional investors grew to account for more than 42 percent of the trading volume on the New York Stock Exchange—up from a 26 percent average ten years earlier (Sobel 1975, 90–91). In contrast to an individual investor, institutions regularly traded "blocks" of stock—10,000 shares or more—in a single transaction. Under the fixed-rate system, the brokerage fees for block trades were exorbitant. The commission for a 10,000-share trade (100 round lots), for example, was 100 times more expensive than the commission on a single round-lot trade (SEC, *Annual Report* 1968, 2). Institutions typically responded to the cost in one of two ways. For those investors who continued to trade across the floor, byzantine schemes were developed to split up a single fixed commission among several brokerage firms for various services. Where one broker might receive a cut of the commission for executing the trade, others might take a cut for providing the institution with research or for selling shares in the institution (such as a mutual fund) to individual investors (Seligman 1982, 303; Loomis 1967). Other institutional investors dealt with the cost by patronizing the "third" market. Here, over-the-counter firms competed with NYSE specialists to make a market in exchange-listed stocks. Yet rule 394 limited participation in this market to brokerage firms that were not members of the exchange and forced investors who wanted to deal with exchange brokers to take the prices it offered.

Running parallel to the growth of institutional investment was a tremendous increase in trading volume on all of the nation's stock exchanges. Between 1964 and 1968, annual trading volume increased from 2 to 5.3 billion shares for all exchanges (SEC, *Annual Report* 1970, 1). The increase in volume, together with the competitive restraints, brought large profits to the brokerage industry in general and the New York Stock Exchange in particular. But the combination also brought the 1968 "back-office crisis" (Baruch 1971). Many brokerage firms "failed" owing to mismanagement of the increased income, as well as reliance on antiquated methods for clearing and closing stock sales—the delivery and receipt of buy-and-sell orders—in their back offices (Loomis 1968; Sobel 1975, 290–91). The fallout was indicative of a regulatory structure that had not kept pace with changing market conditions. In the wake of volume increases and a changing clientele, the initial logic behind protective rules (the need to maintain a primary auction market) promoted less than efficient management, encouraged circuitous trading techniques, and hampered the growth of a competing third market.

Both the SEC and its legislative committees addressed these regulatory problems, associated with the back-office crisis and fixed rates, in public hearings. SEC hearings began in 1968. Hearings held by the securities subcommittees of the House Interstate and Foreign Commerce Committee and the Senate Banking Committee were initiated three years later, in 1971. On the basis of extensive testimony and volumes of reports, the committees and the SEC came up with a legislative package for updating market regulation: the Securities Acts amendments of 1975.

The development and implementation of this legislation again illustrates the importance of both the SEC and the committees for perpetuating the disclosure-enforcement approach to regulation. This point is more obvious if we separate the legislation in two parts: that addressing the *regulatory* reform of the securities markets (the SEC's oversight and enforcement authority), and that addressing *structural* reform (the imposition of competitive conditions on the stock markets). With respect to regulatory reform, there was agreement between the committees and the SEC over how to address regulatory inadequacies to prevent another back-office crisis: the SEC proposed and the committees accepted a straightforward legislative expansion of the disclosure-enforcement approach.[7]

Regulatory Reform

First, the amendments supplemented the SEC's ability to oversee self-regulation. Although the Maloney Act authorized the agency to prevent rules from being implemented by the National Association of Securities Dealers, the SEC had been limited to merely protesting a stock exchange rule after its members voted to approve and implement the change. The 1975 amendments enabled the SEC to preempt exchange initiatives through approval or disapproval (*Securities Regulation and Law Report*, supplement to 5/21/75, 29). This new preemptive authority did not mean that the SEC would necessarily tell the exchanges what should be done; only what could or could not be done. It was therefore a means of enhancing the agency's oversight of the markets and market participants. The new authority did not place the agency in a position of initiating changes in market structure or behavior, but gave it a powerful veto over exchange rules that they opposed. The change was also sympathetic to the agency's traditional use of its rule-making authority: the SEC had its authority enhanced as a "shotgun behind the door," should the industry's internal governance system go awry.

Second, the amendments expanded the SEC's oversight to include more market participants. Clearing houses (firms handling the settlement and delivery of stock trades) and financial data suppliers (vendors providing current market prices and confirmations of transactions to brokerage firms) were also made subject to SEC regulation. This move paralleled the earlier inclusion of over-the-counter dealers and investment advisors within the agency's oversight authority (ibid., 30).

Third, the amendments enhanced the SEC's ability to enforce the Securities Exchange Act. They provided for additional means to censure or place limitations on the NASD or an exchange; expanded the grounds on which the SEC could sanction one of these industry organizations; gave it authority to remove officers and directors of an organization who did not enforce compliance with the act; and the commission was no longer required to give an exchange or the NASD prior notice when it planned to bring enforcement action against a member.[8] These changes also made the SEC better able to prompt industry cooperation in policing Wall Street activities.

However, the SEC and its legislative committees disagreed over how best to deal with structural reform in the industry. Where the SEC preferred an approach that was within the bounds of disclosure-enforcement, Democratic committee leaders favored requiring the SEC to initiate and enforce dramatic changes in the structure of the securities markets. Resolution of this conflict revealed how far Congress relied on the SEC to deal with technical aspects of securities law and the markets, as well as the agency's inability to stifle congressional initiatives framed in loose, nontechnical terms. The legislative result was that neither the SEC or Democratic committee leaders were able to entirely secure their foremost objectives.

Structural Reform

The SEC took a dual approach to market reform, as indicated by a series of rule-making initiatives and interviews with former agency representatives. First, after several years of hearings, the agency supported a move from the fixed-rate system to a system of competitive (or negotiated) rates. The SEC began to push for the removal of fixed rates as early as 1971, when it ruled that the commissions on all transactions over $500,000 were to be negotiated. In 1972, the agency increased the number of transactions subject to negotiated rates by lowering the minimum to $300,000 (SEC, *Annual Report* 1971, 5; ibid. 1972, xxiv). And in 1975 the SEC ruled that all commissions were to be negotiated as of May 1, 1975 (*SRLR* 5/21/75, 31)—or "May Day" as it was called in the industry. Under the Securities Exchange Act of 1934, the agency was charged with ruling on the "reasonableness" of fixed rates charged by brokers (Schwartz 1973, 2699), rather than on the continuation or cessation of a fixed-rate system. Consequently, in order to prevent a legal challenge from the NYSE to the agency's rule-making efforts, the SEC supported a legislative ban on fixed commissions to reinforce its actions. However, the agency also wanted an "escape clause" that would allow the SEC to reimpose fixed commissions if, as former staff members put it, "the world came unstuck" under competitive rates.

Second, the agency recognized the need to eliminate other anti-competitive features of the markets, as well. In its 1972 *Statement on the Future Structure of the Securities Markets* (pp. 7–9), the SEC expressed an interest in seeing the evolution of intermarket trading that would eventually remove barriers to market-maker competition, such as rule 394. However, the agency made it clear in other public documents that this transition to intermarket competition should come about naturally through industry cooperation and SEC guidance, not through edict or legislative mandate. This position was clearly articulated in the SEC's 1971 *Institutional Investor Study*. In the letter of transmittal to Congress (p. xxiii), the agency stated:

> We do not believe ... that it is either feasible or desirable for the
> Commission or any other agency of the government to predetermine
> and require a particular structure, and still less to specify now particu-
> lar procedures for the markets of the future. It is better to observe and,
> if necessary, to modify the structure which evolves through the ingenu-
> ity and response of the marketplace.

The Democratic leadership on the House Commerce and Senate
Banking Committees took a contrary approach to structural reform.
First, they supported the removal of fixed rates, like the SEC. However, the House committee was opposed to any type of escape
clause to reimpose fixed rates. According to congressional and SEC
staff members who worked on the drafting process, this was a serious point of contention. Committee members did not want the
securities industry (and the New York Stock Exchange in particular) to be able to fall back on fixed rates.

Second, the committees wanted to mandate structural changes
in the markets to promote competition. Rather than leave the development of competition up to the industry with SEC guidance, committee members supported the development of a national market
system as part of the legislative mandate. Further, both the House
and Senate committees supported the elimination of rule 394 as an
important first step. In its 1972 *Report on the Securities Industry
Study*, the Senate committee argued, "Barriers to competition
among markets, such as Rule 394 ... may cause an economically
inefficient allocation of business among markets. Such barriers
should be promptly eliminated" (p. 45). Similarly, in its 1972 *Report*, the House committee wrote, "In a central market system
whose objectives are that customers should receive the best possible execution of their orders in any market wherever situated and
that such orders be transacted at the lowest possible cost, rule 394
has no justification." Continuing, the House threatened that if the
New York Stock Exchange did not remove the rule "immediately,"
the committee would "introduce legislation which will have the
effect of abrogating the rule" (p. 127).

Finally, in contrast to the SEC's interpretation of future intermarket competition, committee members had a more rigid view
of what the national market system should look like. Whereas the
SEC promoted the concept of future competition between existing
markets, committee members advocated combining existing markets into a single, computerized market for the buying and selling of

securities. This congressional vision of a national market system was described by a former SEC staffer who was intricately involved in the drafting and passage of the amendments:

> For [Representative] Moss [chairman of the House Subcommittee] and particularly [Senator] Williams [chairman of the Senate Subcommittee], they wanted to abolish the floor of the New York Stock Exchange, and create this kind of... black box trading system, set up to [receive orders to trade stock and] disseminate information at the speed of light. There would be no coming together of people on the New York Stock Exchange floor.

This same staff member argued that the SEC's vision for market reform "was for a less structured approach, not one dictated and described by Congress." He argued, "The SEC clearly felt that the industry should be encouraged, nudged, and prodded to [implement intermarket competition] themselves, and that [the SEC] would implement SEC rule making when necessary." Expressing the SEC's opposition at the time to the congressional blueprint, this observer continued: "But don't drop this legislation in the lap of the SEC . . . to have full homogenization [of the markets] by date X, to take a specific direction and do it by a specific date. It would never happen. The SEC thought they couldn't do that and have it work."

With the exception of a mandated timetable for reviewing and removing anticompetitive rules, the SEC's priorities were paramount in the final legislative draft. In addition, the agency's preference for a gradual and cooperative approach to a national market system has been dominant in implementing the amendments. First, with respect to eliminating fixed rates, the legislation prohibited "fixed commission rates on and after the date of enactment of the Securities Acts Amendments of 1975." Yet, contrary to the initial congressional priorities, the conference draft allowed the SEC to "re-impose fixed rates prior to November 1, 1976, by rule, if the Commission finds that such fixed rates are in the public interest" (*SRLR* 5/17/75, 31).

Second, regarding a mandated change to a national market system, the legislation consisted of vague objectives that a future market system should achieve, rather than defining or describing what such a system would look like. *The Joint Explanatory Statement of the Committee of Conference* called for the SEC to "facilitate" the development of a national market system by promoting the following objectives:

> To provide fair and honest mechanisms for the pricing of securities, to assure that dealing in securities is fair and without undo preferences or advantages among investors, to ensure that securities can be purchased and sold at economically efficient transaction costs, and to provide, to the maximum degree practicable, markets that are open and orderly. (Cited in *SRLR*, supplement to 5/21/75, 26– 27)

As I have indicated, the House and Senate committees were explicit about the SEC's obligation to begin the transformation to a national market system. The agency was given ninety days from the enactment of the amendments to review the rules governing the various securities markets. If a rule with anticompetitive ramifications was found to block the objectives stated in the Exchange Act and to impede the development of a national market system, the agency was to remove or amend it within another ninety days (ibid., 27). However, the law gave the SEC tremendous latitude to interpret the stated guidelines for a national market system, as well as to determine whether a protective rule contradicted the Exchange Act. Nowhere did the legislation specify the criteria for "competitiveness," "fair and honest mechanisms," "economically efficient transaction costs," or "open and orderly" markets. Further, nowhere did the final legislation single out rule 394 for removal. Despite explicit language about the review and removal of anticompetitive rules, this vague approach to a national market system in effect left the SEC to resolve the debate between intermarket competition versus the consolidation of all markets into one system.

At this point, a possible counterargument might be that the initial congressional stance (1) in opposition to an escape clause, (2) in support of a mandated end to rule 394, and (3) in support of the consolidation of competing markets, was merely congressional posturing to push the industry and its regulators into some (albeit milder) reform efforts. With respect to market consolidation and the escape clause, this may very well have been the case. Obviously the implementation of intermarket competition would appear less onerous to the different markets than merging all markets into one computerized trading system, and persistent opposition to an escape clause could have merely signaled congressional resolve to see competitive conditions come about. However, mere posturing does not explain Congress's adamant efforts to push the SEC toward removal of rule 394 after the legislation was passed, particularly by the House.[9] One staff member involved in the oversight process summarized the position of committee Democrats on the rule, and what they believed was the SEC's "waffling" in its review of rule 394:

> One issue that was of particular interest to the oversight committee . . . was the breaking of the monopoly of specialists on the NYSE by getting rid of rule 394. The amendments didn't specify that rule 394 had to go. The legislators mandated the unfixing of [commission] rates, but the mandate was not as clear with respect to 394. Now, the members of the committee thought the mandate was clear. They thought the policy was clear, even though the law didn't say [that 394 had to go, but] after that kind of language and with all the evidence, the commission would have had to go through a convoluted process to say that rule 394 was O.K., that it was not an impediment to competition, but they did fudge in their report. . . . The commission waffled.

In its 1975 review, the commission did affirm the anticompetitive nature of rule 394, but "waffled"—as the congressional staffer argued—over the time and implications of its removal. Two rule-making proceedings followed, the first requiring the abolition of rule 394, and the second allowing for the abolition of off-board restrictions on all stocks listed with the exchange after April 1979.[10] However, the SEC did not act on either proposal, and the New York Stock Exchange's ban on off-board trades still stands. What is pertinent here is that the "shootout" over rule 394, as a former SEC staffer put it, reflected the agency's early stated preference to allow the stock exchanges to try to resolve the issue. Though in any legislative battle it is difficult to separate victories from compromises, the fact that the SEC preferred that a national market system "evolve" through industry cooperation rather than by an explicit mandate; that the legislation was truly vague on the dimensions of a national market system; that rule 394 was not explicitly singled out; and that the SEC was given broad discretion to implement the new system—all would seem to indicate that the SEC had the upper hand in the drafting process.

Further, the status of the national market system mandate today indicates that the agency has had tremendous leeway in implementing such a system. Fifteen years after the amendments were passed, it is evident that the *agency*'s long-term response to the mandate dominates development of the system. Even though rule 394 (now called rule 390) is still intact, the SEC's influence over the national market mandate can be found in the intermarket approach taken by the agency's Office of the National Market System—within the Division of Market Regulation. The office is charged with implementing the 1975 mandate. An agency staff member described their role as overseers of the process: "Our role is more supervisory. We encourage the exchanges [to move toward a national market system], and we make recommendations." The job of the SEC, as this staffer saw it, was to work with the different markets (the stock exchanges and the over-the-counter market) to develop, and slowly implement, trading linkages. After all, in the early 1970s the SEC's objective in addressing the future structure of the markets "was long-term. They thought about it for a while."

The Office of the National Market System points to linkages such as the Intermarket Trading System (ITS) as physical evidence of progress toward their mandate. The Intermarket Trading System was set up in 1978 as a communication system between competing markets: the New York, American, Boston, Philadelphia, Cincinnati, Midwest, and Pacific stock exchanges, and the National Association of Securities Dealers, representing the over-the-counter market. The system provides each market with current quotations—the prices that sellers of stock are "asking," and buyers are "bidding"— on a limited number of stocks. It also allows (but does not require) market makers to route an order to the market with the most competitive quote.[11]

Yet, despite this substantive project, staff in the office still recognize a national market system as an "ideal." When asked about the statutory objectives of the national market system, referred to earlier, one SEC lawyer called them "wide ... and subject to broad interpretation." The SEC has the opportunity to see national market system evolve under SEC guidance because "Congress doesn't understand the national market system."

The 1975 Amendments and the Independent Influence of the SEC

The SEC was able to fulfill its objectives in 1975 because of the regulatory environment and the professional and political incentives facing the SEC and the legislative committees at the time. Because of the technical and uncertain nature of a proposed national market system, the diversity of interests involved, and the SEC's ongoing enforcement program, members of the committees deferred to the priorities of the SEC in drafting and implementing the amendments, despite initially strong preferences to do otherwise.

First, consider the technical uncertainties surrounding a national market system. What would such a system look like? How would mandated changes affect the capital accumulation needs of the country and create incentives to invest? How would closing and clearing processes be affected by a new system? And what would happen to market liquidity and depth for small investors without rule 394? The committees wanted to address these complex issues, but, given the political and economic ramifications of market reform, they needed the SEC's imprimatur on the legislation.

Politically, if the committees had pushed ahead with an explicit definition of the national market system and a mandate for its implementation, final passage of the amendments might have been jeopardized without the SEC's endorsement. As I have indicated, members of Congress typically rely upon the SEC's opinion as a voting cue with respect to securities issues. Yet even if the committees had succeeded in winning the reforms they preferred, as opposed to the SEC's, committee members faced the possibility of an economic backlash—a downturn in the stock markets. Just as members of the Congress look for the SEC's approval as a measure of confidence in securities legislation, the agency's approval of legislation represents a measured, objective analysis of a particular problem that diverse industry interests can also more readily accept. In the case of the amendments, the SEC's imprimatur no doubt gave the industry and investors some much-needed confidence in the reform effort.

Consequently, the potential for blame resulting from political or economic fallout prevented the committees from getting what they wanted most: the immediate elimination of rule 394 and a single national market for securities. Instead, they secured a mandate for the review of all anticompetitive rules within a ninety-day period and their elimination within another ninety days if such 'rules were found to be unnecessary under the Exchange Act. Again, given the uncertain implications of enforced competition between market makers, the committees had to rely upon the SEC (the accepted expert) to review and remove rule 394. And in their vision for a future national market system, the committees deferred to the agency's initial approach to market reform: changes in market structure should not be mandated or imposed, but evolve through cooperation between the regulators and the market. Where the legislation was explicit about structural reform—the mandated end to fixed rates—legislators were protected by the fact that the SEC had already acquiesced in the policy through its rule-making initiatives.

Without a specific SEC blueprint, Congress was in no position to define a national market system legislatively. Instead, the lawmakers depended on the agency's expertise, and hence the influence of its own preferred approach, to implement structural reform. One SEC staff member who worked on the legislation commented on this congressional "reliance" on the SEC: "Congress recognized that the SEC would have to have latitude in implementation. . . . The end product contained a lot of trust and reliance on the commission."

Consider also the role of diverse interests involved in structural reform that reinforced Congress's deference to the SEC. Contrary to the position taken by other analysts of these events, there was not a clean division between the interests of the New York Stock Exchange who opposed reform and the institutional investors supporting it (Weingast 1984; Phillips and Zecher 1981; MacKay and Reid 1979; and Jarrell 1984). Within the New York Stock Exchange, for example, several prominent voices *favored* changes to enhance competition. The president of the exchange, Robert Haack, mentioned a need for fixed rates as early as 1970. Though he did not speak for the majority, he represented the position of several large brokerage firms, including Merrill Lynch, the largest broker on Wall Street (Loomis 1970). Merrill Lynch and other large public brokers were financially sound, despite the back-office crisis that struck the profit margins of most other firms, and they were prepared to compete for customers.

Institutional investors also differed in their ideas about reform. For institutions that wanted to control costs by trading exchange-listed stocks in the third market, or by executing their own transactions, reform was a top priority. Negotiated commissions and removal of rule 394 would have significantly cut the cost of trading and boosted the quality of the third market. However, for institutional funds that hired investment managers to trade for them, the issue was somewhat murky. Under fixed commissions, the practice of splitting up one commission among several different brokers often involved reimbursing a broker for selling shares in the fund to customers. The arrangement was particularly lucrative for fund managers who were reimbursed according to the size (outstanding shares) of the fund, as well as for the participating broker. Further, many institutional funds were—and still are—willing to pay an exchange commission to ensure that, in the event of a market crash, the New York Stock Exchange specialists would give their orders first priority. The removal of rule 394, in particular, could have jeopardized these and similar arrangements.

Despite a strong interest in reform, the committees were unable to demand a national market that would clearly benefit a particular constituent group without harming a variety of other powerful interests. Hence, members of the committees concerned about reelection and the support or opposition of these industry interests had a strong incentive to defer to the SEC's approach and let the agency work out the details between conflicting groups.

Finally, consider the impact of SEC enforcement actions on congressional deference to the SEC's position. The debate over structural reform ran parallel to a massive enforcement effort by the SEC to clean up the brokerage industry after the back-office crisis. In fact, a significant number of the amendments were aimed at strengthening the SEC's enforcement of the Securities Exchange Act. Recall that the amendments gave the SEC additional means to censure or place limitations on the NASD or an exchange; they expanded the grounds on which the SEC could sanction one of these industry organizations; they gave the SEC authority to remove officers and directors of an organization who did not enforce compliance with the act; and the commission was no longer required to give an exchange or the NASD prior notice when it planned to bring enforcement action against a member.[12] These changes also helped the SEC to secure industry cooperation in policing Wall Street activities.

Much of the new enforcement authority represented the joint priorities of the SEC and the committees. For Congress, in particular, the boost in authority was a popular policy approach to the problems of the industry at the time, and the SEC's traditionally thorough investigation of fraud could be relied on to produce solid prosecutions. What is important here is the role of the SEC's enforcement activities in promoting congressional deference to the agency's priorities for market reform. Its traditionally rigorous enforcement efforts, as well as the professional ambitions of its personnel (who typically do not go to work for the securities industry) assured members of Congress that the SEC did not necessarily act as a mouthpiece for any particular segment of the industry. Rather, it was seen as a competent expert that could be relied on and trusted.

For agency personnel, a boost in the SEC's enforcement authority was a good alternative to an explicit definition for market reform that it would have to implement. To regulate the industry primarily as a rule maker would have been to jeopardize the agency's standing as independent from the securities industry, as well as its role as a securities expert in congressional decision making.

First, to engage in routine decisions that allocated wealth among regulated interests—such as where stocks listed with the New York Stock Exchange can trade, or whether commissions should be negotiated—would drag the agency into constant frays with the industry. (This topic is discussed in chapter 4.) Such battles are draining and would eventually reduce the agency's clout in resolving industry disputes. Thus the SEC has traditionally preferred to encourage industry solutions and to use its rule-making authority only in times of stalemate or as a lingering threat to prompt an acceptable industry solution. Nevertheless, its strong enforcement policy places the SEC in an adversarial position vis-à-vis the industry and consequently bolsters the agency's position as a rule maker when it does choose to invoke its authority. A strong policy also allows agency attorneys to demonstrate their legal skills (their application of the law) to future employers—law firms that hire the best securities lawyers. This explains, in part, the SEC's opposition to specifying rules to be removed as well as explicitly defining future market competition in the amendments. With greater leeway, the agency can work with the industry to promote change and invoke its own rule-making authority only as a last resort.

Second, by maintaining its independence from the industry, the SEC has maintained a reputation in Congress as a detached expert in complex and technical policy debates. This reputation is critical for members of the agency interested in having a voice in legislative policy making, as they had during the drafting of the 1975 amendments.

Summary Remarks

Both the SEC and its legislative committees emerged from the amendment process having achieved some of their goals, but having made concessions on others. The result of this tug and pull between legislative authority and regulatory expertise was to reinforce the agency's disclosure-enforcement approach as a way of dealing with changes in the securities industry. Recall that in 1940 the SEC requested the authority to go beyond its activities under disclosure-enforcement: the agency wanted to rule on the "fairness" of investment companies' organization and activities to shareholders. In denying the request, Congress reinforced the agency's mission as the enforcer of disclosure, rather than the initiator of structural reform.[13] In 1975, the tables were turned. The SEC originally advocated a national market system that evolved from within the industry with the agency's guidance; Congress pushed the agency to take a more activist role in restructuring the markets. In this case, it was the relaxed implementation by the SEC, and the agency's recommendations to expand its existing enforcement authority, that kept the disclosure-enforcement approach intact—that is, retained the SEC's reactive (or prosecutorial) regulatory posture. Specifically, in addition to a mandate for structural reform, the legislation increased the SEC's power to oversee self-regulation, enhanced the SEC's preemptive rule-making authority, and increased the agency's enforcement capabilities.

4 Maintaining Disclosure-Enforcement

Disclosure-enforcement, which took shape under Chairman James Landis (1936–1938), was institutionalized through legislative expansions of the SEC's mandate and is the premise of the agency's regulatory activities today. For example, still central to investor protection is the SEC's emphasis on disclosure. This tendency is reflected in the agency's recommendations for greater and more timely disclosure of information to protect the interests of shareholders in takeovers and leveraged buyouts.

In addition, the agency continues to make frugal use of its rule-making authority to initiate change in the securities industry—a practice set early in the New Deal. Rather, its broad authority is used more as a "shotgun behind the door" to prod the industry toward acceptable solutions. Thus, after the 1987 stock market crash, the SEC encouraged and approved a New York Stock Exchange initiative for "circuit breakers" to halt trading in times of dramatic market declines, as well as a NASD proposal to ban use of its automated order system for large ("program" type) traders. However, when an industry stalemate threatens investor interests, the SEC will make a ruling. For example, to preempt takeover attempts, many companies began to alter the voting rights on existing shares of stock so as to place more votes in "friendly" hands. When the different markets failed to agree on restrictions on the practice, the agency set a one-share, one-vote standard.

Finally, the agency's ability to deter fraud and market manipulation still depends greatly on its high-profile enforcement activities. The recent prosecution of inside traders has generated enough concern within the industry to demand an explicit definition of the crime, and the popularity of the SEC's cases in Congress has meant that the agency's domestic and even international enforcement capabilities has expanded in recent years.

This chapter examines the incentives facing both the SEC and members of its congressional committees for maintaining the disclosure-enforcement framework. That framework is maintained today, I will argue, because it is a workable aggregation of preferences between the SEC, members of the House Interstate and Foreign Commerce Committee (now the Energy and Commerce Committee) and the Senate Banking Committee, and their constituents in the securities industry for regulating the capital markets. The role of the administration as a potential destabilizing force will be addressed in chapter 6.

Disclosure-Enforcement and the SEC

The staff and commissioners of the Securities and Exchange Commission have maintained the disclosure-enforcement framework for two fundamental reasons. First, all seek to protect the agency's reputation as an successful enforcer of the law. Regulation through disclosure-enforcement is universally seen as a success. Second, staff and commissioners, for the most part, desire to maintain the framework because of their connections to the securities bar. Making regulatory policy within the framework has created an economic niche for securities lawyers, elevated their prestige, and increased the private-sector demand for their services.

The Risks of Rule Making

It is difficult for any agency to take the initiative when the enabling statutes provide little guidance for action. Consider the SEC's mandate to regulate the markets for the "protection of investors" (Schwartz 1973, 2556, 2685, 2690–91, 2693–96). The SEC must first decide what investors should be protected: the small investor who buys a hundred shares of AT&T through a New York Stock Exchange broker; the small investor who purchases shares in a mutual fund; the institutional investor, perhaps the manager of a mutual fund, who trades tens of thousands of shares in one transaction; or the professional-risk arbitrageur who executes a flurry of trades throughout the day speculating in takeover stocks.

The agency's mandate to "maintain fair and orderly markets" (ibid., 2691) provides no more guidance. Fair and orderly for the institutional investor might mean the markets' capacity to absorb, for example, a pension fund's trading volume and quickly reflect the new information in the price of stocks—regardless of price volatility. Yet fair and orderly for the small independent investor might mean protection from market swings that can occur when a large investor enters the market. Finally, far removed from the concerns of both large and small investors, the risk arbitrageur, as well as other specialist traders, capitalizes on the perversities of fair and orderly markets—that is, they profit from the difference between the value of a stock reflected in its market price and the price an aggressor company is willing to pay in a takeover bid. Yet their buying and selling might very well be in the small investor's best interests by stabilizing the market—trading against the trends—at times.

Market diversity only further clouds the "public interest" objective for rule making. What is good for members of the New York Stock Exchange and investors trading in that market may not be good for members of the smaller regional exchanges, or participants in the over-the-counter market and the private placements market—where nonpublic issues of stocks and bonds are sold without being registered with the SEC.

As these few examples illustrate, there is nothing intrinsically obvious about the public interest in regulatory matters. In recent years protecting the public has increasingly been defined as maintaining competitive markets and efficient pricing that benefit some broad-based interest such as consumers (Kohlmeier 1969; Noll and Owen 1983; Viscusi 1984). Applied to securities regulation, this definition of the public interest means lower brokerage fees for large and small investors achieved by competition (Phillips and Zecher 1981). It has also been the impetus for preventing, or removing, restrictions on corporate takeovers in order to expose top-heavy, poorly managed companies to the rigors of the market (Grundfest 1989). However, the public interest could as readily be defined in terms of protecting investors, broadly defined, and companies from the rigors of a volatile market by checking and limiting competitive conditions. Agencies must deal with many different interests, each of whom claims to represent the public. In reality, they simply represent another interest broadly or narrowly defined.

When the SEC does make rules, it is placed in the difficult position of ruling in the public interest, yet unavoidably ruling on behalf of some special interest over others. For example, in 1982 the SEC issued the controversial rule 415—"shelf registration." The rule was welcomed by large corporations that could now register a large issue of securities but then had the flexibility to bring the issue to market in pieces without reregistration through the SEC. Investment bankers, on the other hand, opposed the rule because it jeopardized their syndicate activities that were facilitated by the twenty-day registration period (to be discussed later). To routinely impose its rule-making authority would no doubt draw tremendous resistance from these various interests and perhaps induce recalcitrance. Further, if the agency's rule-making authority were to be questioned or routinely challenged in court, its legitimacy as an enforcer and overseer of the markets might also be questioned.

In addition, the risks incurred by making rules that concerned the first commissioners still exist: judicial censure, industry opposition that might result in economic downturns, and consequently the instability of the agency. Rather than routinely test the limits of its authority to intervene, the SEC has reasons to remain aloof.[1] Part of this caution is demonstrated by the agency's role as mediator in its oversight of the governing bodies within the industry—in particular, the National Association of Securities Dealers (NASD) and the stock exchanges. These are called self-regulatory organizations (SROs) because they monitor the behavior and qualifications of their members. Yet they are still subject to the SEC, which can veto or approve proposed rules. An SEC staff member with responsibility for overseeing these organizations' activities described the role of the SEC: "We are in the middle. We try to resolve differences, encourage them to discuss things. We sit there and listen to the issues ... we conduct oversight."

In its role as mediator, the SEC protects the public interest by encouraging solutions from within the industry that it will eventually approve or disapprove. This approach is less of a risk to the agency's reputation: if the industry is more likely to accept a mediated solution than an imposed one, the agency will more likely succeed in enforcing the policy. Further, rules developed out of mediation are less likely to be challenged in court. This last point is important, because the bulk of SEC policy is developed through adjudication. The fewer the legal challenges, the more stable and successful the agency's policy stance will be.

According to SEC officials, a rule initiated by the agency is rare compared to the number of rule proposals generated through the self-regulatory organizations. As described by a senior staff member, the SEC issues rules only in a case of stalemate: "We don't issue a lot of rules. Most come through the SROs [subject to SEC approval]. When the commission does issue rules it usually reflects deep divisions, like intermarket issues."

Throughout the commission, staff members see this restrained use of the agency's rule-making authority as key to successful regulation. Members equate the approach, first, with their perceptions of the appropriate role for the government in relation to the regulated interests. One staff member's comments were typical: "I personally think the role of government is to be reactive, unless you can demonstrate some need to act." This perception contributes to the enforcement focus of the agency[2]—interpreting the securities statutes through the enforcement of the securities laws and regulations, rather than through rule-making initiatives.

Second, staff members draw parallels between the restrained approach and the SEC's primary responsibility as a disclosure agency. One senior staffer described the connection as follows: "[The SEC has] pretty much restricted itself. Its main thrust is disclosure [and] it's described as a disclosure agency.... When the SEC acts to limit choice [by issuing rules], it does badly. If disclosure is an alternative to limiting investor options, it's better. We have leaned in favor of permissiveness, but we demand disclosure."

If risks are defined by the possibility of negative judicial reviews, or by the recalcitrance of the industry—thus invoking a threat to the agency (difficulties could lead to congressional hearings, staff turnover, or internal apprehension and possible division about policy and the role of the agency)—the cautious use of the SEC's rule-making authority helps to minimize such risks. However, just as the SEC's reluctance to make rules is intrinsic to its vague public-interest mandate, so the soundness and wide acceptance of the disclosure laws provides the foundation for strong SEC enforcement actions. When the agency acts to enforce disclosure, it does so from an explicit statutory base.[3] Further, the fact that investors and market professionals have come to accept, and even rely upon, the enforcement of disclosure gives the SEC strong backing for this type of regulatory action. As characterized by one member of the SEC staff:

> Disclosure and the rules of disclosure are important because contracts are important; the rules are well known and well defined.... [Disclosure] imposes costs, to be sure, but it seems that the lack of hue and cry from the markets is a good test. By and large, the benefits of disclosure helps with writing contracts and raising capital, [but] the ultimate test is the market place.... When Boesky [an arbitrageur convicted of trading on nondisclosed information] was caught, the markets seemed to appreciate the fact.

A former member of the SEC staff saw similar support for the agency's disclosure efforts. This staff member characterized the enforcement of disclosure as an easily implemented policy. In addition, the former staffer argued that because disclosure was central to the agency's activities, it placed the agency out of the reach of congressional criticisms that other agencies typically incur:

> The fundamental policy behind all securities regulation is: as long as you tell the investor what you are doing, you're O.K. It's the essence of disclosure. It's not like the clean air act. Government is not telling you what to do, just to make sure you give investors enough information.... If the agency can make an argument [for Congress] that the disclosure they require is enough, they are O.K.... It would be hard to be [a bad agency]. Enough disclosure, enough market efficiency, they are all right.

These sentiments were reiterated throughout my interviews with former and current members of the SEC staff. Time and again staffers noted that a major strength of the SEC was the centrality of disclosure to its regulatory efforts. As one former staffer put it, "The concept of disclosure, placing information in the glaring light of the public as a guidelight, rather than the use of regulatory intervention in the corporate area . . . is a healthy one." As long as the disclosure-enforcement approach maintains the agency's reputation as a successful regulator, and the staff of the agency continue to perceive the connection, there is no strong incentive to deviate from the established disclosure-enforcement framework.

Lawyers and the Common-Law Approach

Securities lawyers make up 62 percent of the SEC's professional staff (SEC, *Self-Funding Study* 1988, II-1). Further, nearly 70 percent of the agency's commissioners have been securities lawyers or lawyers with experience in securities law.[4] Some observers have argued that the agency's regulatory approach parallels the common-law training of the SEC staff (Chatov 1975; Kripke 1979; Karmel 1981). Lawyers, it is argued, react to violations and build regulatory policy through adjudication. This approach to regulation has been reinforced over the years by the relationship between the agency and the private securities bar.

In a tradition established by Landis, the agency has been the beneficiary of excellent legal talent. Unlike many regulatory agencies, a relatively low government salary has not kept good lawyers from coming to the agency because it offers legal experience that is in high demand in the private sector. Young attorneys are willing to take on the government job for the potential of making, as one SEC official put it, "enormous big bucks when you leave." A senior staffer described the phenomenon: "The revolving door works well here. . . . [The] government doesn't pay well, but the commission can offer highly marketable skills. . . . We get good people coming in the front door. People get the experience and move on. That way, we don't get ossification." A colleague concurred: "People who come here can get jobs when they leave. The SEC is not a place to retire like other regulatory agencies, it's a beginning. It's like a finishing school. You can spend a few years here and it's not wasted, but instead it enhances your credentials. Then you can go back to a law firm."

A prominent member of the securities industry (and sometime adversary of the SEC) gave a similar response when asked to elaborate about the quality of the agency's work. He noted the incentives for young attorneys to join the agency and their willingness to work very hard for a future in the securities bar:

> I guess because they are a bunch of hard-grinding young lawyers who aspire to have a career in the securities industry, and they are willing to spend two or three years in the SEC to prove that they are Jack the Giant Killer, and that they can do good work for the commission.

To prove that they can do good work, these attorneys must demonstrate their legal expertise. This has enormous implications for the agency's regulatory approach—its adherence to disclosure-enforcement—as well as for its relative independence from the interests that it regulates.[5] Law firms will evaluate these staff members, as aspiring members of the securities bar, by their legal skills rather than by the impact of rules or decisions on particular interests. Consequently, rule making is approached as a legal exercise, and there is no incentive to favor a particular economic interest in agency decision making. The comments of two former members of the SEC staff note the value of legal expertise for future employment:

> When you go to the SEC you don't work for much, but when you go back [to the private sector] you can make a lot. At the SEC, it doesn't do you any good to curry favor with the defense contractors, for example, because when you go to work for law firms after the SEC they rate you not on what you decided, but how you did it, in legal terms. . . .
>
> People don't go to work for the industry, they go to work for law firms, not brokerage firms. They can't be captured by the New York Stock Exchange [for example] when 99 percent of them don't have an intent to work for these entities.

In addition to the training and experience the SEC can offer young attorneys, the kind of work done by the agency can be a powerful attraction. Consider, for example, the SEC's recent enforcement actions against inside trading (the trading of securities based on nonpublic information that can affect the price of the stock, such as an impending takeover). As I have noted, several of these cases have resulted in the disgorgement of hundreds of millions of dollars and civil and criminal convictions of individual traders and investment banking firms. In a *Washington Post* story (7/25/87, D10:c) on the work of the SEC, an attorney from the Division of Enforcement reflected on her two years of work related to these cases: "Sometimes I get lost in day-to-day work and forget how exciting this is. Then I'll talk to a friend who is sitting in a [law] library researching water rights."

The enforcement work of the division can be exciting, and it is obviously an important draw for the agency. As a senior member of the securities bar and former member of the SEC staff argued, "The

SEC has been a little lucky. . . . It does exciting work. At a time when most lawyers want hot and heavy cases, the SEC has had big cases, exciting cases. . . . It's a lawyers' agency."

The demand for securities lawyers in the private sector clearly explains the agency's ability to attract good legal talent. Public corporations, institutional investors, the various securities markets, brokerage houses, investment bankers, and accounting firms need securities lawyers (or law firms with securities lawyers) precisely because of the need to comply with the federal securities laws and SEC policies. The agency's policy making has therefore created an economic niche for lawyers specializing in securities. This mutual relationship gives the agency a strong constituency and the securities bar professional security. It is also a strong incentive to maintain the agency's emphasis on disclosure and enforcement. As long as all corporate issues, mergers, acquisitions, and other means of finance must be disclosed to the SEC, securities lawyers will be needed to file myriad SEC forms; further, as long as the SEC's enforcement team polices the Wall Street beat, bringing civil and administrative actions against violators of the statutes and rules, the lawyers' litigation skills will be in demand.

When President-elect Reagan's transition team recommended massive budget and personnel cuts for the SEC (see chapter 6), securities lawyers were quick to come to the agency's defense. In a letter to White House counsel Edwin Meese, former SEC commissioner A. A. Sommer (1973–1976) expressed the views of a securities law conference by arguing that the proposals "might well destroy" the agency. He pointed out the need to increase, not decrease, the SEC staff; to retain senior staff officials for policy continuity; and to maintain the agency's enforcement efforts so as not to violate the intent of Congress in the securities statutes (*Washington Post* 2/5/81, B1).

Several current members of the securities bar, many of whom have been affiliated with the SEC, point out another important reason for the bar's support of the SEC. If the agency cannot function efficiently, these attorneys' clients might suffer. Crimes that go unprosecuted can erode investor confidence (thus affecting both responsible and irresponsible firms), and long delays in registering a securities issue can mean the possible failure of an initial distribution as a result of changed market conditions. Therefore, the more capable and efficient the SEC is in handling its regulatory responsibilities, the better a securities lawyer's clients will be served. These sentiments were summarized by a current member of the bar and former SEC staffer:

> Before some current [SEC] procedures were institutionalized, a lawyer could tell a client that it would take three to six months for a registration statement to be processed. For a company in business, that is a long time to wait to get your money. If you could know that young lawyers were doing this work and that they were over worked, and if you knew that if things were changed, your clients will do better, then you would support those improvements in the SEC. . . . To the extent that the commission is not getting [the quality staff] that they would like, the people who suffer are those who have to deal with the commission, the clients. As an attorney, you want the best possible treatment for your clients.

The connection between the SEC and the securities bar takes on greater significance within the agency's own decision making. In the Landis tradition, the legal profession clearly takes precedence in the agency's responses to both external and internal pressures on SEC decisions. For example, one SEC commissioner stated, referring to possible outside influences on his decision making, "If we look anywhere beyond these four walls, it is to the D.C. Court of Appeals and the Supreme Court to see if we are acting within the law, and if the courts will uphold our actions."

The point may be obvious, but highly relevant. When the SEC makes a decision—approving a rule proposal submitted from an industry organization, imposing its own rule, taking an enforcement action, or participating as *amicus curiae*—considerations of judicial review are fundamentally important. It is questions of law (statutory interpretations) that dominate internal decision making. One member of the SEC staff put the point succinctly: "We start with the statute! That's our form of government decision making." In other words, how the SEC applies the securities statutes is the essence of its work.

The relationship between the securities bar and the SEC is also crucial to the agency's reputation. As I have noted, many agency officials attribute the success of the SEC to its regulatory approach. Further, they see the agency's connections with the securities bar as protecting that reputation. When asked about the strengths of the

SEC, one official made this connection between the quality of the agency and its personnel, and the support of lawyers specializing in securities:

> We are sometimes rather haughty and arrogant, but maybe that is one of our strengths. It is a very proud agency, and there is a strong alumni group that is constantly elevating or promoting the agency, because I guess it elevates them at the same time.

However, that prominence and reputation of the agency is not necessarily accepted by everyone in the agency. Indeed, some officials blame the lawyers who serve the agency briefly before moving on to the private sector for perpetuating the SEC's inflated image. In contrast to the previous remark, consider the comments of another agency official:

> This would be heresy here, [but] notions of high regard are repeated more in this building than anywhere else.... It's too esoteric.... This place produces people who go on to become prestigious people of the securities bar. You get a lot of lawyers saying it [is a great agency]. That's how they got into the business.... The SEC is the graduate school in securities law. You get the nuts and bolts of how this place works, the details of the securities laws. Most in the securities bar have spent time at the SEC. They are the ones who talk a lot about how they worked hard and had an esprit de corps.

The point here is not to question the success of the SEC or the dedication of its staff. Rather, it is to emphasize the mutual reinforcement of what agency personnel see as the source of the agency's success—that it is a disclosure-based, rather than a merit-based, agency—and the predominance of securities lawyers. Upholding the agency's success record and its ability to attract high-quality lawyers are strong reasons for maintaining the disclosure-enforcement approach. If, as suggested above, the two are interrelated, those reasons are intensified.

The foregoing comment also provides a glimpse of a growing challenge to the agency's decision making and its dominance by the legal profession. The challenge comes most directly from economists who are the mavericks in the SEC and whose impact on the disclosure-enforcement approach will be addressed later. Here I simply note that throughout the 1980s economists became increasingly prominent in SEC decision making, and by questioning the processes and logic that have produced SEC regulations for more than fifty years, they have become a source of instability.

Constituent Support and Reelection

Members of the House Energy and Commerce Committee and the Senate Banking Committee have maintained the disclosure-enforcement framework chiefly by expanding the SEC's mandate. A primary reason for supporting disclosure-enforcement is that their constituents in the securities industry endorse it and appreciate the professionalism that securities lawyers bring to the SEC. If special interests in the securities industry favor a professional SEC and the agency's regulatory approach, members of Congress will support those features of the agency as well.

It would be easy to assume that members of Congress adopt the preferences of these special interests because they can materially affect their chances of reelection (Mayhew 1974). Interviews with Senate and House legislative committee staffers made it clear that many actions taken by committee members affecting the SEC (hearings with the agency, the introduction of securities legislation, or commenting on a rule proposal) are indeed motivated by the concerns of special interests. For example, one Senate staff member connected senators' preeminent concern with fund-raising and the money that the special interests can provide with members' periodic public derision of the SEC:

> Fund-raising is so important. These guys don't want to eat up [former SEC chairman] David Ruder, but their survival depends on it. . . . Politicians are like an issuing corporation; investments are made in them. . . . Investment bankers can raise capital. They are important to the process. . . . When the SEC tries to stop [an investment banker, bankers] hold a fund raiser; [then] the Senate comes down on David Ruder.

Yet to assume that all of Congress's interest in the SEC's work and the agency's professionalism is driven by special interests and the pressures of reelection could oversimplify the policy process. Members might also be motivated by a genuine interest in developing good securities policy (Fenno 1973). A House staff member gave an example of this concern:

> [Representative Matthew] Rinaldo [R-N.J.] is a big fan of pushing a new special study [of the securities markets].... Rinaldo wrote a letter to Ruder and the OMB to include five million dollars for the study in the budget proposal.... I don't believe this is constituent-driven. He is interested in a long-term plan for the securities markets. Most Republicans have supported the study in deference to Rinaldo, and some share his view that it is important.

There was no doubt a mixture of both electoral and policy concerns in 1934 when members of Congress were faced with balancing (1) the opposing special interests of the securities industry and the New Deal reformers, against (2) the nation's economic recovery and the need for capital accumulation. For our purposes, we can assume that even a member concerned solely with making good public policy will have an interest in the security industry's acceptance of the SEC and its regulatory approach: Specifically, the nation's capital accumulation needs might suffer from industry protests against poor or unworkable regulation.

Industry Support for a "Professional" SEC

Bolstering the support of securities lawyers, particularly when the SEC's budget and staff are threatened, is the backing of the securities industry itself. According to both SEC officials and industry leaders, there is generalized support for a "professional" agency. That means an agency independent of the industry whose personnel are guided by professional standards—the principles of securities law. The explanation is twofold. First, a commission obedient to professional standards can provide a regulatory balance among the industry's multiple economic interests. Second, a strong agency capable of policing the markets maintains public confidence in the markets; people are not willing to invest in securities when fraud is prevalent.

On the first point, one SEC official illustrated the diversity of interests by citing the variety of industry positions on the SEC's rule 415—also known as the "shelf rule."

> There was strong support from issuers, opposition from underwriters, and the brokerage industry was mixed. . . . The underwriters were concerned about "due diligence," and the brokers were concerned about timely information, or dealing with out-of-date information.

A description of the shelf rule illustrates the industry's heterogeneity and the need for a professional agency. Rule 415 was an effort by the SEC to give large corporations more flexibility in timing an initial distribution of securities. Any new issue of securities to be traded in the public markets must be registered with the SEC. The agency has twenty days to review the registration documents, after which time the securities can be sold to the public if the SEC finds nothing wrong with the prospectus. Throughout the late 1970s and early 1980s, the twenty-day waiting period became a snag in capital accumulation because of volatile interest rates and rising inflation. A large swing in interest rates during the twenty-day period could prevent the successful distribution of even a "blue chip" stock—those issued by a well-known company with a reputation for profits and dividends.

Large corporations such as Du Pont and Exxon expressed concern over the cumbersome SEC procedures. To liberalize the capital accumulation process, the SEC proposed "shelf" registration. The rule was possible under the SEC's mandate because of the parallel disclosure requirements in the 1933 and 1934 Securities Acts. The rule allowed a company to register an issue one time with the SEC by stating its long-term plans for the issue. The company could then bring the issue to market in pieces—"off the shelf"—whenever market conditions were most favorable (*Wall Street Journal* 2/25/82, 7:1). Throughout this period, investors could still secure material information about the issuing company from the company's periodic reports to the SEC required under the 1934 Securities Exchange Act.

As we have seen, investment bankers and brokers were opposed to liberalizing the twenty-day waiting period for bringing issues to market. First, the rule was a direct threat to traditional investment banking through syndicates. Second, it increased the risk that a banker might be held liable for fraudulent information in an issue's prospectus.

In 1982, investment banking was dominated by seven large firms: Morgan Stanley, Merrill Lynch, Goldman Sachs, Salomon Brothers, First Boston, Lehman Brothers, and Kidder Peabody (*Wall*

Street Journal 11/2/82, 4, 2). These were known as the "bulge bracket" firms because they sat on top of the syndicated brackets used to distribute and sell securities issues. One of these firms typically served as a company's banker, providing advice and assistance in determining the types of securities to be issued and the terms and timing of the distribution. The firm then financed and distributed an issue by bringing in brackets of progressively smaller (regional) firms to form a syndicate. The twenty-day registration period gave bankers time to finalize the bracket—for example, time to determine the number of shares to be sold by each firm in the syndicate. The time also allowed bankers to give "due diligence" to the issue: the liability provisions of the securities acts require bankers to consider carefully the information in the prospectus and the quality of the issue (Schwartz 1973, 2559–62).

Under cumbersome SEC registration requirements, companies had depended on their traditional investment banker for the successful distribution of an issue. Under shelf registration, that dependency was eased by competition. First, investment bankers had to bid competitively for issues that companies could bring to market at will. There was no time to set up a syndicate to distribute an issue; rather, those bankers who could take the entire issue alone (financing and distribution) soon dominated the market for initial distributions (*Wall Street Journal* 11/2/82, 4). Second, because investment bankers now had to bid for shelf distributions, their fees were cut by competition. Investment banking money went toward advertising their capability to finance and distribute an issue immediately; and, for those "bulge bracket" firms that controlled the syndicates but had no extensive sales offices, there were expansion costs. In addition, investment bankers themselves had to find ways to generate capital in order to snatch up an issue when it was brought to market (Brooks 1987, 9–10).

Small investment bankers and brokers stood to lose most in the breakup of syndicate banking. If the large firms could handle the entire issue, there was no need to bring in the smaller-bracket firms for financing and distribution. A controversial SEC study of regional firms bore this out. In February 1987 (one year after the study was conducted), the SEC reported that regional firms each lost an average of $432,000 annually in underwriting fees (*Investment Dealers' Digest* 2/2/87, 16).

The shelf rule illustrates how the SEC can mediate a difficult transition period when diverse economic interests are at stake. With issuers clamoring for a better way to raise capital, and investment bankers rooted in a traditional system, the SEC stepped in to issue a modified version of 415 on a trial basis. For nine months, only companies with widely held stock that had regularly filed with the SEC were eligible for shelf registration. When a company used the shelf rule, it could issue only 10 percent of the securities at a time (*Wall Street Journal* 2/25/82, 7, 1). The nine-month period allowed large and small syndicate bankers to prepare for what appeared to be an inevitable shift in the way they did business. Further, the restrictions on use of shelf registration kept the power of issuing companies (vis-à-vis the capital markets) in check.

Throughout the trial period (February–November 1982), the SEC studied the impact of the rule on the markets. The agency voted in late 1982 to make the rule permanent, but—as just mentioned—they continued to monitor its impact. With such diverse interests, an imposed solution is possible only if it is promulgated by an authority that is accepted as the technical expert: industry participants will know that the rule was based on careful consideration of the securities statutes, empirical evidence, and the public record. "If the commission were to become political or weak," as one SEC official stated in an interview, "it would throw off the delicate balance."

However, industry divisions are more fundamental than differences among brokers, investment bankers, and issuers, so the need for an agency that can mediate among industry interests is more conspicuous. As I discussed in chapter 1, the structure of the industry pits strong producer interests against strong consumer interests. The diversity of customers—institutional versus individual—pits one brokerage house against another. The over-the-counter market competes with the exchanges. And, finally, industry interests are divided by size—the interests of large brokerage firms differ from those of small (regional) firms; those of large investment banking concerns differ from those of smaller underwriters; and those of small regional stock exchanges differ from those of the New York Stock Exchange and the American Stock Exchange. In an industry where technological change and competition have blurred the lines between underwriting, securities trading, and banking, and where innovation in investment vehicles and trading techniques constantly threatens a firm's economic niche, large and small participants have an interest in a regulatory process that is not biased in favor of one group and that will give careful and knowledgeable consideration to regulatory change. An SEC staffed by professionals and guided by expert standards gives some assurances to the industry that decisions are not arbitrary or politically motivated.

A *Strong Agency and Well-Policed Markets*

In addition to a need for a mediator among industry interests, there is support in the industry for a strong (well-staffed and well-funded) SEC that can control fraud. If the public loses confidence in securities as investments, brokers lose commissions; investment funds lose business; issuers have a tough time selling an initial distribution; and investment bankers take on a greater risk in underwriting issues.

Though the public may decide to pull out of the stock market for a number of reasons—for example, a recession, inflation, higher interest rates in the money markets—fear of fraud is often cited as a cause. If brokers can "churn" an account—excessive trading of a customer's account in order to generate commissions—without being caught; if mutual funds can charge a customer hidden fees and place prohibitive restrictions on an account; if someone can claim to be an investment advisor without credentials; if inside traders can profit at the expense of shareholders; and if fraudulent issues of stock can easily be peddled to the public, people will consider securities a risky investment and pull out. Therefore, a strong agency to police these activities is important to maintain investor confidence.

The comments of a Securities Industry Association official illustrate the point. When asked whether the industry supported strong SEC enforcement, he replied:

> Absolutely! Our entire business is entirely intangible. It is dependent on conditions being honest and above board. Every day, trillions of dollars change hands on word of mouth. Securities... is a business where belief in the system is critical. You will find that our association has supported greater funding for the SEC than it is receiving. . . . There needs to be a timely review of disclosure, *and there needs to be strong enforcement.*

Similarly, an attorney with a New York Stock Exchange broker-age firm noted the industry's strong support for SEC enforcement efforts: "The one thing that would hurt the most is if the public lost faith in the industry. Protecting the public is something that can only be done by a regulator. . . . A majority of the industry desires to have a strong SEC. It keeps the industry cleaner." When asked to define a strong SEC, he mentioned the agency's budget and its ability to hire sufficient personnel—the SEC needs "enough funding so they could do [brokerage firm] audits and follow ups. Enough so they could investigate alleged wrongdoings, fraud, anything that could actually hurt the purchaser of securities."

The industry's concern to maintain public confidence was also pointed out by a former SEC staffer who worked extensively with Capitol Hill. He described industry support for SEC enforcement as essential. To come out against tough enforcement, he argued, would hurt investment confidence in general and a firm's business reputation in particular:

> If the SEC is perceived to be a tough cop, it is good. Even if you think the SEC was too tough on Boesky and Drexel, (a) it is never in your interest to stand up and say so, and (b) [good enforcement] creates public confidence in your business.

The industry's support for tough enforcement sends an important signal to members of the legislative committees and may explain Congress's interest in supporting the agency's enforcement efforts. (See, for example, Senate Banking Committee, *SEC Reauthorization Hearing* 1983, 113, 120–121.) Indeed, many industry representatives come forward at authorization and appropriation time to request more funding for the SEC. One explained why the mutual fund industry has supported greater resources for the SEC before Congress: "If anything, we often feel that the SEC doesn't regulate and enforce enough." That was a problem, he continued, because of the "tremendous growth in mutual fund–like entities at the periphery of the industry." Under its current level of resources, the SEC was unable or unwilling to expand its regulatory activities to include firms at the periphery as well as to reach a greater number of less-than-honest entities. Thus he supported increased funding by calling and writing to members of the SEC's legislative and appropriations committees.

Industry Participation Through Disclosure-Enforcement

The securities industry has also learned to work with the SEC's regulatory process. In some cases, groups such as the securities bar have developed professional stability from the disclosure-enforcement system. If diverse interests can operate within the framework, and groups with economic interests are concerned to maintain it, then members of the legislative committees are more apt to support the framework.

The SEC's efforts at joint rule making with the industry's governing organizations may minimize some of the conflicts between interests seen by members of Congress as important constituent groups. Chubb (1983) and Culhane (1981) argue that one way to respond to clashing constituent interests is to expand an agency's decision-making process. For example, when environmentalists became as important a constituent group as ranchers, the Bureau of Land Management allowed more information to be brought into the public record—more public hearings, consideration of environmental impact statements, and informal meetings between opposing groups mediated by the bureau (Culhane 1981).

Although rule making in the securities industry does not necessarily result directly from congressional efforts to expand those involved in making decisions, the existing process holds similar benefits for members of Congress. Whether a rule is initiated by NASD, an exchange, or a regulatory division within the SEC, the agency's final verdict is based on a public record—an accumulation of research and comments generated from within the SEC, as well as from the industry and the public.

Consider a NASD rule initiative limiting the use of its Small Order Execution System (designed for the automatic execution of orders for 1,000 shares of stock or less) by market professionals, particularly during volatile periods. Such a regulation was recently approved by the SEC (*Securities Regulation and Law Report* 12/16/88, 1931). A rule dealing with operations in the securities markets is first submitted to the Division of Market Regulation (one of the agency's four regulatory divisions) for consideration and approval. Market Regulation then studies it, accepts public comments for a specified time, holds hearings (if necessary), and, on the basis of the amassed public record, recommends that the commission approve or disapprove the rule.

One of the three specialist offices (the General Counsel, the Office of the Chief Accountant, and the Office of Economic Analysis) or another of the four divisions may also review proposals and make recommendations to the commission. When there is disagreement within a division, stated one official, the division "goes through a quasi-legislative process to come to a decision." According to SEC staff officials, such disputes are usually resolved before the commission goes public with a rule. However, interdivision (or interoffice) disagreements are not uncommon, and any controversial proposal usually goes through extensive internal and public debate prior to a final decision.

For members of Congress concerned not to exclude an important constituent group, SEC decision making offers two ways of contributing to the public record. First, because NASD or an exchange can propose a rule as readily as a regulatory division, members of these organizations, or the SRO itself, can initiate the decision procedure. Without joint rule making, the industry would have to rely on its power of prevention (its power to oppose proposals) to affect the policy process. Second, regardless of the source of a proposal, SEC decision making gives all interested groups ample opportunity to contribute to the public record—particularly when an issue is controversial.

Directly interested groups can participate in public hearings, submit written comments to the agency, or alert members of Congress to their position on an issue. Consider, for example, the SEC's one-share, one-vote rule of July 1987. The issue involved economic differences between the stock exchanges and over-the-counter market (each with its own listing requirements for companies), for corporations that wanted to alter the voting rights on stock to stop a takeover threat, and for shareholders interested in the profits gleaned from a takeover (*Investment Dealers' Digest* 3/30/87, 22). Because the issue was so controversial, there was extensive direct participation in the rule-making process. The agency received a thousand public comments favoring the rule and ninety-one oppos-

ing it (*SRLR* 7/15/88, 1126–28). One senior SEC official commented, "One-share, one-vote was controversial. All you have to do
is count the comment letters we received. It was a tough issue."

When decisions are made, the preferences of interested groups
are indirectly represented by their elected officials and members of
the SEC. Describing the agency's ruling on the one-share, one-vote
question, one official observed: "We base our decisions on the public record. In this case, the record was voluminous. We had comments from the industry, Congress, and the White House. We based
our decision in light of the record."

On Capitol Hill, this method of decision making is seen to produce good results. A Senate staff member who deals directly with
the agency believes that "final rulings for the commission have had
filtering. . . . Different points of view create a product that is fairly
washed . . . a good product."

Not surprisingly, elected officials who participate in rule making
often reflect their constituents' concerns. When asked how often
members of the House Energy and Commerce Committee are in
contact with the securities industry, one congressional staffer replied, "All the time . . . mostly they come to see us about legislation,
but *that is not to say they don't come and see us about rulings*. . . .
It can be anything and everything."

Further, the more contested the issue, the more likely elected
officials are to write letters to the commission for the public record.
Several SEC officials admitted that congressional participation in
rule making was infrequent, but that debatable issues—such as the
one-share, one-vote rule—provoked letters from Congress. However, in SEC decision making, whether an issue is controversial or
not, such participation is considered another aspect of the total
public record. One senior staffer put it this way: "Congressional
[opinions] are considered part of the mix of information that goes
into the decision."

Like debates between politicians, disputes between varying
groups of specialists within the SEC can parallel special-interest
positions. As professionals, SEC staff members assert their autonomy
in their decision making at all levels. The comments of a senior staff
attorney are typical: "We are an independent agency, and we remain
so as long as we stay independent. . . . [You] just keep doing what
you think is right [even though] people are going to get mad."

However, despite professional impartiality, fundamental differences between the decisions of economists and lawyers in the SEC enable opposing groups and politicians to substantiate whatever policy they prefer with expert opinions. The Division of Market Regulation supported the one-share, one-vote rule, while the Office of the Chief Economist opposed it. Staff dissension over the rule, however, reflected a deeper division that has been developing between lawyers and economists for some time: specifically, the appropriate role for economic analysis in an agency traditionally dominated by legal considerations. For the lawyers in Market Regulation, the rule was justified by the agency's statutory authority to protect the rights of shareholders (*SRLR*, "Text of the SEC Final Voting Rights Rule," 7/15/88, 1130). The agency's chief economist, on the other hand, opposed it, arguing that it would "enmesh" the SEC in "corporate capitalization" (*Wall Street Journal* 7/8/88, 3)—an issue of corporation governance traditionally left to state regulators.

The specialist offices (such as Office of the Chief Economist) cannot initiate policy. Only the regulatory divisions (in this case, Market Regulation) have that authority. But the information the offices bring to bear on policy positions can figure into the commissioners' decision calculus.

Before 1980, the role of an SEC economist was ad hoc: nearly every commission chairman in the previous twenty years had reshaped the economic staff for his particular purposes, while always keeping it tangential to the agency's decision making. However, as the demand for economic analysis has grown outside the agency, its economic staff has gained significance. According to several SEC staff members, the stock market crash of 1987 was particularly important in bringing about this shift. Consider the comments of a senior staffer about a presidential commission's report on the 1987 crash:

> When asked who should be the final arbiter between the SEC and the CFTC [Commodity Futures Trading Commission], the Brady Commission said the Federal Reserve Board. That is the only depository of economic wisdom with quality economists. That, I think, presented [the SEC chairman] with the stark realization he wasn't going to bury economics at the SEC, that he needed economics. Outside forces . . . were at work. The crash was an economic event and legal scholars cannot be relied on to solve the problem.

This apparent shift in priorities—the recognized need for analytical, research-oriented economists—is reflected in the most recent restructuring of the economic staff. In February 1988, the Office of the Chief Economist was merged with the Directorate of Economic Policy and Analysis (a unit created by a previous chairman but not considered a key player in SEC decision making) to form the Office of Economic Analysis. The new office has since hired about a dozen additional economists with Ph.D.s, to replace approximately twice as many economists who had been engaged in gathering statistics rather than research and analysis. Despite the impact of the crash, the status of economic analysis has been gradually changing over the last decade. However, the transition has met, and continues to meet, strong opposition from the lawyers on the staff. In particular, many lawyers take offense at the implication that economic analysis can be broadly applied in the work of the commission. As one lawyer put it:

> I always say, there's only one person who's a bigger fool than someone who thinks economic analysis can be used for any question, and that is the one who thinks it's good for every question! We deal a lot with fraud. I don't think I've ever thought of fraud in economic terms.

Similarly, when asked if he saw a role for economic analysis at the SEC today, a former staff attorney first acknowledged that economists could play a supportive role, but criticized their efforts to initiate or guide policy. He also argued that economists should be secondary to the legal staff: "Economists are important, but they shouldn't dictate policy. The SEC has been accused of being a lawyer's agency, but that has always been its best strength. . . . Economists shouldn't drive the policy wagon."

The internal debate among professionals over what information is relevant for agency decision making is a relatively recent phenomenon. The impact of this debate on SEC decisions, and the role of Congress and the administration in the controversy, will be discussed in later chapters. But the debate has paralleled changes in how securities are traded and marketed as well as in the interests involved in those processes. What is significant here is that the agency's decision making—allowing for public comment and internal debate before a rule is issued—can accommodate increasingly eclectic interests. For members of Congress, the conflicting positions of economists and lawyers often reflect the diverse positions in the industry.

On the one-share, one-vote question, the positions of Chairman William Proxmire (D-Wis.) of the Senate Banking Committee and groups supporting antitakeover legislation (particularly the Business Roundtable) matched those of SEC economists (*Investment Dealers' Digest* 6/6/88, 11). Similarly, the positions of Chairman John Dingell (D-Mich.) of the House Energy and Commerce Committee and advocates of shareholder rights corresponded with those of the legal staff (*Congressional Quarterly Weekly* 7/4/88, 1507). However, the consistency of professional judgment rarely provides political ammunition for the same interests in different disputes.

It should be noted that the final rule did not fully satisfy either side. Whereas Dingell felt the exemptions diluted the strength of the rule, Proxmire felt any SEC interference with corporate governance was wrong (ibid. 7/9/88, 1921–22). In this case, the decision making produced a compromise: shareholder rights were protected to the degree that corporations would be limited in their ability to alter voting rights on specified categories of stock; however, exemptions on several kinds of securities issues left corporations some flexibility in structuring voting rights.

When controversial issues are at stake, the SEC's balanced approach to decision making is perhaps safest. For opposing economic interests and their representatives in Congress, a definitive win today may be eliminated by an opponent's victory tomorrow. Such ups and downs are not only unpredictable, but also costly. A decision-making process that encourages broad participation in amassing the public record, with decision makers who are accepted as technical experts, reduces uncertainty and minimizes controversy. The system produces rules that a divided industry can live with. In the words of one SEC official:

There is wide divergence in the industry. The commission [uses] restraint. There [is] an awareness of institutional boundaries. . . . There is a difference between taking the initiative and ramming a rule down people's throats. When the [SEC] does take the initiative, it takes comments, questions. . . . There is an exchange of ideas . . . a willingness to give and take.

Professional and Economic Enhancement Through Participation

Various industry groups can take part in SEC rule making by actually initiating the rule—in the case of the self-regulatory organizations—or by placing comments in the public record. For some groups more than others, however, participation in rule making is critically connected to their professional and economic positions in the securities industry. Specifically, they have gained professional stature precisely because the SEC has relied on their respective industry organizations to initiate rules governing their members' behavior and to oversee their members' practices as an extension of SEC authority. Interests with a stake in maintaining the agency's regulatory framework can have a substantial influence on members of the legislative committees.

Consider the role of SEC regulation in the development of the accounting profession. Under the 1933 Securities Act, the SEC (initially the FTC) was given authority to set up general criteria for the report of financial data. This grant of power was first overlooked by accountants, investment bankers, and corporate financial directors, who focused instead on the act's liability provisions. After these provisions were amended in 1934, the accounting profession lobbied specifically to contain SEC initiatives to set standards for financial reporting.

To assume that the SEC *could* delineate immediate standards was unrealistic. Before any general guidelines could be established, research was necessary. But at the time of the New Deal the SEC faced an obstinate profession in which the balance of power opposed any restrictions on the reporting of financial data. Accountants were divided into two groups with different agendas. The practitioners—a group dominated by certified public accountants (CPAs)—advocated flexibility in the reporting of financial data. On the other hand, the academic accountants—usually college professors—often proposed research initiatives as a way of establishing generally accepted principles. But in both the state and national professional organizations, in which the academics were relegated to second-class citizenship, CPAs and other practitioners held the leadership positions. The academics' own organization had only a weak and insignificant voice in the profession. The domination of practitioners was also reflected in professional journals, where academic initiatives received a cool reception (Chatov

1975, 38–54). Thus, given the status of the academics in the profession, the SEC would have to rely on its own internal research if it were to promulgate standards. With its resources stretched to the limit simply to enforce the basic aspects of the 1933 and 1934 acts, such an effort was out of the question (ibid., 97–98, 277–78).

In some respects, flexibility, the byword of practitioners, could be interpreted as client domination of financial reporting. Without a core of accepted principles, the accountant could select a technique preferred by a client so as to present a client's financial position most favorably. Instead of fighting the practitioners over the imposition of general standards, the SEC offered accountants a chance to gain some independence from their corporate clients. The SEC delegated its own standard-setting authority to the profession's most nationally recognized organization: the American Institute of Accountants. General standards remained the goal, but the profession controlled the pace of their promulgation (Chatov 1975).

By bringing the profession into the rule-making process, the SEC gained a somewhat cooperative ally in its enforcement efforts. More important for the profession, the SEC's authority to impose guidelines forced accountants to organize around the development of standards—at least as a long-term goal of the profession (McCraw 1984, 188–92).[6]

Today the Financial Accounting Standards Board (FASB) works with the SEC in formulating standards. As with the other self-regulating entities, the SEC oversees the process. The agency's chief accountant—a position created under Chairman Landis when intra-agency disputes over different means of reporting required a final arbiter—issues Accounting Series Releases to guide self-regulation and imposes standards when the process itself does not produce a resolution (Chatov 1975, 102–03).

Over-the-counter dealers, too, have benefited from the SEC sharing its rule-making authority. As discussed in chapter 2, the 1938 Maloney Act established a self-regulatory system for traders in the over-the-counter market. The formation of the National Association of Securities Dealers lent status to the profession: it controlled the quality of its practitioners by setting standards for membership; it controlled trading practices that harmed the investing public by restricting particular actions and monitoring member behavior; and it gave over-the-counter dealers (as well as exchange brokers who would become members to realize the many pecuniary benefits) an organized voice in regulating the securities industry. Further, internal regulation—with SEC oversight—boosted public confidence in the profession and the markets that they made (Jennings 1964).

To this point I have argued that the securities industry has an incentive to support a strong, professional SEC and the agency's disclosure-enforcement framework. A professional SEC can mediate between heterogeneous economic interests and offer acceptable solutions to disputes, and a strong SEC can practice vigorous enforcement and keep the markets free of fraud. This helps to maintain investor confidence, which is considered key to the industry's economic health. In addition, the agency's regulatory framework gives diverse interests ample opportunity to debate controversial issues. These interests are also indirectly represented by members of Congress and in the SEC's internal debates. In the Landis tradition, the agency is thorough in its approach to rule making. Its extensive internal decision making process and use of the public record produces rules that, as one Senate staffer observed, are "fairly washed . . . a good product." In other words, the industry does not view SEC rules as biased toward one or more special interest. Finally, the SEC's regulatory framework has enhanced the professional status of several groups. The agency's disclosure and enforcement activities have created an economic niche for securities lawyers; accountants became organized as a profession in reaction to the liability provisions in the 1933 Securities Act and in response to corporations' need to comply with disclosure; and over-the-counter dealers have become professionally established, given their organized participation in self-regulation.

Congressional Support for Policy That Is Both Good and Popular

The centrality of disclosure to the SEC's approach assures members of Congress that the agency's regulations will be generally accepted as good public policy. First, investors receive a benefit that the market would have never provided on its own. Before the 1933 and 1934 acts, companies that issued publicly traded stock used a mixture of disclosure practices. Where some offered scant information about company finances in a stock prospectus, most treated that information as privileged. Even when information was given, underwriters of the issue, accountants, and the company's officers were not liable for losses caused by false information. Therefore, rather than revealing a firm's financial status, information could even be used to inflate or misrepresent a company's potential. In other words, the industry operated on the watchword, "Let the buyer beware" (McCraw 1984, 166).

Without mandatory disclosure, no member of the securities industry had to fully disclose the financial status of an issue: accountants could not independently certify the information as accurate; investment bankers would not stake their reputation on the stated soundness or riskiness of an issue; and corporate directors (often the inheritors of family operations) did not have to reveal finances that might be considered confidential or damaging to sales. In an atmosphere of secrecy, unsound issues were sold as readily as sound ones. Even when an honest company might have benefited from the disclosure of information relating to its less stable competitors, there was no incentive to incur the costs of disclosure simply to demonstrate financial stability—it was not required to sell an issue. The 1933 and 1934 acts solved the disclosure problem through enforcement. Full disclosure meant better information, and better information meant more efficient markets, or stock prices that reflected a more accurate market assessment of a company's worth (Cohen 1966).[7]

Enforcement of disclosure by the SEC, therefore, reduces the risk and cost of participating in the markets. Investors do not have to rely on the reputation of an underwriter or broker-dealer as assurance of the soundness of a new issue; in demonstrating their financial stability, stable companies and unstable ones alike incur the same costs; finally, broker-dealers can back up sales of securities with prospectus information.

The SEC's enforcement of full disclosure assures a level playing field and produces a valuable good—material information—for market professionals, the investing public, and the economy in general. If we were to rely on voluntary full disclosure, this collective good would not be realized.[8]

Second, disclosure might also be deemed good policy because the practice and the costs of compliance are an accepted part of doing business. As noted earlier, the lack of hue and cry from the markets over compliance seems to indicate that the enforcement of full disclosure is actually appreciated by members of the industry. When I asked the director of compliance for a large brokerage firm whether the industry would favor voluntary disclosure, he responded, "The industry would be afraid of that. No one would comply with voluntary disclosure because disclosure is too costly." In other words, compliance with mandatory disclosure may be cumbersome to the industry, but the need to maintain fairness—everyone in compliance—is seen as important and therefore an accepted cost.

Third, disclosure is good policy in that it protects the investing public. It leaves the nation's capital-raising mechanisms intact without limiting or intervening in the options of investors. Rather than impose structural limitations on the industry's growth and development, the policy simply requires that all relevant financial information be made public. Further, protection through disclosure does not limit investors' choice: it does not require the government to rule on the viability of a company or the value of its stock. That is the investor's decision, based on available information. As I discussed in chapter 2, an initial draft of the Securities Act was rejected precisely because of a requirement that the regulating agency should pass judgment on issues in the public interest. And a 1940 SEC proposal for ruling on the fairness of investment company organization and practices was similarly rejected.

Members of Congress are ready to promote the agency's enforcement efforts because attacks on fraud and abuse—hardly a controversial policy—gives a lawmaker's agenda momentum. Consider, for example, the 1988 legislation dealing with insider trading. In an immediate response to the largest fraud and insider trading case ever brought by the SEC—against the investment banking firm of Drexel Burnham Lambert—the House of Representatives passed legislation that bolstered the agency's ability to restrict insider trading by a vote of 410 to zero (*Congressional Quarterly Weekly* 9/17/88, 2580). The unanimous vote reflected the political capital to be gleaned from the SEC's civil complaint.

Scandals on Wall Street have traditionally provoked hearings, investigations, and new legislation in Congress. As described in chapter 2, the 1933 and 1934 Pecora investigations into the financial community were a source of political momentum for congressional Democrats. Similarly, the chaos that accompanied institutional trading in the late 1960s and the countless brokerage firms that failed during the same period (Loomis 1969) spawned three years of congressional hearings that eventually produced the 1975 amendments.

Members of the legislative committees can hardly lose when they go after the rogues on Wall Street who violate ethical and fiduciary principles. The SEC's emphasis on enforcement provides continuing evidence of financial wrongdoing that lawmakers can draw upon from time to time. Throughout the 1970s and the 1980s, Congress pressured constantly for better and more SEC enforcement efforts—particularly for the type of activity that produces high-profile cases. For example, in an SEC authorization hearing before the Senate Banking Committee in 1985, committee members were concerned that the agency's recent cost-cutting efforts would jeopardize its enforcement capacity: Senator Proxmire questioned Chairman John Shad (1981–1986) about how many times the Enforcement Division recommended enforcement actions that the commission voted down. And Senator Jim Sasser (D-Tenn.) was interested in the SEC's commitment to prosecuting hostile takeover violations and insider trading in general (Senate Banking Committee, *Hearing for Reauthorizations for the SEC 1986–88* 1985, 57; ibid., 49–53).

Insider trading and hostile takeovers still attract national attention. These illicit transactions (when insider trading is involved or violations of the takeover laws occur), involving millions and sometimes billions of dollars, can affect the stability of entire companies and therefore threaten their employees' welfare. Further, they can dramatically redistribute the wealth between the parties involved. Therefore, it is profitable for members of Congress to push the SEC to take more enforcement actions, or to push legislation aimed at curbing and punishing securities violations. As a former SEC official argued, "It's motherhood and apple pie. No one argues with the SEC when it is trying to help widows and orphans or when it's going after fraud in the market." Another congressional staffer described legislators' support for SEC enforcement activities as follows:

> The Enforcement Division of the SEC is the darling of the U.S. Congress. Whenever they come up to the Hill, [members of Congress] ask, 'How many people do you need? How much money do you need?' . . . With

the Boesky and Levine cases, [the] Enforcement [Division] got a tremendous increase in their budget—a lot of new [staff] slots.[9]

Enforcement is popular because it promotes investor trust and market stability. A former member of the House committee contended that enforcement is "critical to public confidence in institutions where investors must place dollars at risk; . . . public confidence is a fragile thing, and it can easily be shattered."

Congressional support for more enforcement is a reasonable alternative to Congress's intervention in the more complicated SEC rule-making activities or initiating controversial legislation. SEC activities affect the nation's capital-raising capacity and can have strong repercussions in the economy as a whole. The markets are sensitive not only to official proposals, but also to hints of policy changes made by public officials. For example, in 1987 a brief comment by SEC Chairman David Ruder about closing the stock markets under highly volatile conditions was cited for precipitating a 508-point drop in the Dow Jones industrial average that same day (*Wall Street Journal* 10/21/87, 36; ibid. 11/3/87, 1). Similarly, as I mentioned in chapter 1, comments by Chairman Rostenkowski (D-Ill.) of the House Ways and Means Committee on the elimination of tax deductions for corporate debt were credited for fueling a selloff in takeover stocks involving leveraged transactions (ibid. 12/11/87, 10; ibid. 10/30/87, 20).

To take a stand or move in a new direction in sensitive policy areas can be costly for members of Congress. One SEC official described the willingness of Congress to abstain from direct or explicit policy making as follows:

> It's too risky. They know the expertise lies here [in the SEC] and not with them. If they override the SEC course, they will have egg on their face if they fail. They would rather engage in puffery and [point out] foolish actions. They would much more do that than take the risk of trying to implement policy.

Instead, the visible support of enforcement bolsters a popular policy and satisfies industry concerns for investor confidence. Further, the only direct way in which members of the legislative committees can influence the SEC's enforcement agenda is by providing money and personnel. They have no direct influence over the kinds of cases pursued by the commission, the speed of prosecution, or outcomes. Again, intervening directly runs the risk of being implicated in the fraudulent activities under investigation. As a result, Congress depends on the SEC to implement a policy that is popular among the public and the industry, leaving support for enforcement as the only means by which Congress can influence it—a demand, in a sense, for more of the same.

The Securities Law "Expert" and Support of Disclosure-Enforcement

Key to maintaining the disclosure-enforcement framework is the nomination of qualified individuals to serve the agency—or commissioners who will work within the framework. Given the interest of the Senate Banking Committee (as well as the House committee, even though it has no formal role in making appointments), their constituents, and the SEC career staff in sustaining the disclosure-enforcement framework, there is mutual agreement about the ideal qualifications of the securities law "expert."

First, a nominee that best fits the profile is a lawyer who has specialized in securities law. The typical candidate will also have served on American Bar Association committees that focus on securities issues. Having chaired the ABA's Corporation Law Committee or Securities Committee brings recognition within the more specialized securities bar. When asked to describe a qualified nominee, a former commissioner focused on this type of special background: "[The candidate should be] a securities lawyer, not just a lawyer but a securities lawyer. . . . I think being a lawyer is not enough. This is a statutory position, and I think you need to have been steeped in the statute."

A senior member of a New York Stock Exchange investment firm declared that training in securities law was the necessary "technical competence" for serving on the commission. When asked what the securities industry would consider a "qualified" nominee to the SEC, he replied: "Someone with a background in securities law. An in-depth knowledge of securities law and how the industry works. Competence is the issue. . . . [We] are looking for technical competence."

Second, a securities expert will ideally have had some previous experience in dealing with the SEC, or will have been an agency staff member. Some of the most heralded appointees in the 1970s, for example, were commissioners who rose through the ranks. (See chapter 5.)

Finally, an expert is free of political ties to the White House and (particularly) the securities industry. A former commissioner and member of the bar talked about the proclivity among agency professionals to distrust Wall Street connections. The agency and those who are regulated have antithetical interests, he argued; for the most part, SEC staffers have never been on Wall Street before coming to the agency.

The SEC staff, members of the Banking Committee, and representatives of the securities industry distinguish between nominees who fit the profile—qualified professionals—and those who do not—those recognized as "political," whatever their qualifications. The latter type of nominee typically comes from a Wall Street investment house, a corporation, or—during the 1980s—from the economics profession. Staff and commissioners who are members of the securities bar view the nomination of such a candidate as an effort by the president to inject politics into the work of the agency. In other words, those who do not fit the profile threaten the disclosure-enforcement framework.

Interestingly, the relation of "experts" to the bar is not seen as political. Rather, it is viewed as preserving the agency's apolitical tradition and pursuit of its mandate. As an SEC staff member commented: "Political pressure does not do well at this agency. [We're] not a political agency. Perhaps it's the nature of securities law and securities experts—above politics, maybe. What [commissioners] deal with are not political matters. Perhaps it's the legacy of the SEC." Another staffer agreed, asserting that since the beginning of the New Deal, those nominated to serve on the commission have been "the best and the brightest" securities lawyers—again defending the belief that a nominee's strong ties to the bar preserved the agency's apolitical tradition.

Summary Remarks

Both the SEC and its legislative committees have good reasons to maintain the disclosure-enforcement framework—incentives strengthened by their interaction when policy is made. Consider how the committees reinforce the agency's reliance on coopera- tion to exercise its rule-making authority. If the legislative commit- tees restrict the SEC's resources by limiting the agency's reauthori- zation,[10] the agency must find other means to do its job. A key reason for the commission's initial cooperative approach to indus- try regulation was that it lacked the resources to oversee all of the industry's activities. Self-regulatory organizations accountable to the SEC enabled the agency to spread its regulatory reach without adding more staff.

The agency's relationship to the securities bar reflects a similar need. Without larger staffs to police the disclosure activities of corporations, for example, the agency requires the vigilance of law- yers to alert it to discrepancies.[11] This may appear to entail a conflict of interest between a securities lawyer and his or her corporate client, but members of the bar want to cooperate with the SEC: violation of the SEC rules could lead to censure and disbarment from practicing before the commission. Such disbarment includes every aspect of SEC regulations from filing a disclosure document, to representing a client in litigation before the agency (SEC, *Rules of Practice* 1964, 1). Given the desire to support the SEC in the first place (employment in a valuable training ground in preparation for the private sector and maintaining a private-sector demand for one's services), it is unlikely that a securities lawyer would risk being excluded from agency-related activities.

To the extent that the legislative committees have been responsi- ble for limiting the agency's resources, therefore assuring the agency's incorporation of the private sector, they have helped to uphold the disclosure-enforcement framework. If the SEC had re- ceived larger budgets or more staff positions, it might not have enlisted the cooperation of the industry to such an extent. As it stands now, the securities bar extends the SEC's regulatory arm, and the SEC gives the bar a professional niche—relationships that re- inforce SEC's approach to regulation.

Members of the legislative committees have two reasons for supporting the SEC: strong enforcement is supported by the indus- try (important constituents), and it is a popular way of dealing with industry problems and shoring up investor confidence. Conse- quently, the committees have typically used their power to reau- thorize SEC funds as a means to push for greater enforcement. At oversight hearings, legislators have exhorted the agency to spend more on enforcement and have pledged to authorize more money for this purpose.[12]

Whether or not as a direct consequence, the SEC continues to give high priority to enforcing the law. In 1983, the agency reported that, on average, a third of its annual budget goes toward enforcement (House Energy and Commerce Committee, *Hearing for SEC Authorization Request* 1983, 22). With more funding for enforcement than, say, research, the agency inevitably makes policy through adjudication rather than rule-making initiatives. Further, with its resources concentrated on enforcement, the agency's ability to oversee the markets is limited; this reinforces the cooperative approach to industry regulation.

Dependency, however, runs both ways. The committees' reliance on the SEC for its policy expertise also strengthens the legislators' determination to uphold disclosure-enforcement. Consider Congress's incentive to support a regulatory approach that is acceptable to constituents. The economic interests of the securities industry are divided according to the size of firms, type of clientele, trading activities, and between industry producers and consumers. If the industry wants a professional SEC that can negotiate acceptable solutions to controversial issues, and if it has come to accept the agency's regulatory framework as necessary and even beneficial, members of Congress will support the framework, as well.

The SEC's regulatory approach meets the needs of a heterogeneous industry. How it has dealt with problems in the past, therefore, is important for members of Congress trying to deal with new securities legislation. If solutions offered by the SEC to current problems include greater disclosure and intensified enforcement, the committees are driven to accept those solutions. Given the SEC's expertise, the agency's support could make new legislation more acceptable to important congressional constituents, as well as to other members of Congress (see chapter 7).

Because both the SEC and its legislative committees influence the formation of policy, a unilateral move by the SEC or by Congress to alter the regulatory strategy can be checked by the other. The history of securities legislation demonstrates this point: any attempt by the SEC to vary the framework, such as the SEC's 1940 proposal to rule on the fairness of investment company plans, must contend with congressional authority over its mandate and resources. Similarly, any attempt by Congress to change the approach, as in the 1975 mandate for greater SEC activism in restructuring the markets, has had to rely upon the SEC's interpretation and implementation of the statute. (Recall that in this case, members of the SEC staff pointed to the gap between the national market concept and its implementation, and it has since fallen from the agenda.)

Precisely because of this mutual ability to check initiatives, both sides have settled on disclosure-enforcement as the framework for making federal securities policy. The time and resources spent by either side to try to change the system would no doubt end in a compromise. Yet disclosure-enforcement meets key professional objectives of SEC personnel, it satisfies the needs of diverse interests in the securities industry that are important to Congress, and it gives members of Congress noncontroversial solutions that are seen as good policy.

5   A Decade of Activism

For nearly a century, government reformers have equated professional expertise with political neutrality. Yet there is nothing politically neutral about institutionalized expertise in an agency's structure and decision making. Decisions made by experts or professionals have political consequences, because how a decision is made affects the distribution of costs and benefits associated with public policy. Further, like any other special interest group, the lawyers, scientists, economists, and engineers who staff many government agencies have demands and priorities regarding how policy is made, and they seek to influence the political process to achieve their demands in various ways (Kaufman 1956; Mosher 1982; Knott and Miller 1987).

Nevertheless, the legacy of neutrality is strong, and the term *political* is typically reserved for efforts to tamper with or abolish decision making processes so as to advance a particular interest or limit the reach of bureaucratic expertise (Goodsell 1985; Seidman and Gilmour 1986). Indeed, protecting the disclosure-enforcement system has become synonymous with keeping politics out of SEC decision making. As I discussed in chapter 4, the professional career officials in the SEC and members of the agency's legislative committees have the greatest incentive to maintain the framework and have the most at stake should it be threatened—that is, should "politics" get a foot in the door.

This chapter addresses, first, efforts by the SEC staff and legislative committee Democrats to fortify the disclosure-enforcement framework throughout the 1970s in order to keep politics out of agency decision making. Second, I address the impact of the disclosure-enforcement framework on the SEC's regulatory activism during the same period. Despite harsh criticism from the business community and attempts by presidents Nixon, Ford, and Carter to appoint chairmen who supported regulatory restraint, the SEC pursued its disclosure and enforcement activities with unabated intensity until the end of the decade. Efforts by the Reagan administration to alter the behavior of the SEC by undermining the rules that maintained disclosure-enforcement will be discussed in chapter 6.

Economic and Political Disarray

During the early 1970s, the SEC embarked upon an enormous enforcement effort because of a plague of brokerage failures on Wall Street, complicated by a declining market. At the same time, public confidence in the SEC was at a low ebb. The agency was the focus of political scandals that ruffled its independent status, as well as the professional standing of career staff. The situation on Wall Street and in the SEC largely conditioned the regulatory agendas of the agency and of Congress throughout the 1970s.

The "Back-Office" Crisis

Chapter 3 described the tremendous increase in the volume of stocks traded across the floors of the various exchange markets in the 1960s. (Volume reflects securities listed with an exchange and the turnover of those shares each day.) Between 1965 and 1967, the daily volume on the New York Stock Exchange alone increased from 6 million shares a day to 10 million (NYSE, *Fact Book* 1966, 44; ibid. 1968, 64). The increased volume meant an increase in brokerage income for members of the exchange, as well as for brokers in other stock markets that shared in the boom.[1] However, the antiquated operations of many firms for the settlement of trades eventually led to their demise.

Trades are "settled" when brokers on both sides of a trade receive and pay for the securities involved. For example, a customer may place an order with a broker, Merrill Lynch, to buy 500 shares in Corporation X; another customer may place an order with another broker, Payne Webber, to sell 500 shares of the same stock.

Once these two orders are matched and executed, the first investor will typically receive securities, and the second, cash, from the account of each broker. However, the settlement between the Merrill Lynch and Payne Webber brokers will not take place for five more working days, during which time the trade is cleared. The Merrill Lynch broker will receive the securities purchased, while the Payne Webber broker receives payment for the securities delivered (Teweles and Bradley 1987, 273).

With an average trading volume of 6 million shares a day on the New York Stock Exchange (usually consisting of small orders), these "back-office" activities were adequately handled through a combination of computerized confirmations, hand delivery of securities, and hand processing by clerks (Loomis 1968). But when volume nearly doubled by the late 1960s, back-office operations were overloaded (NYSE, *Fact Book* 1969, 3).

The immediate impact was an increase in the number of "fails" to deliver and receive in the settlement process. To accommodate the increased trading volume, brokerage firms tried to expand their back-office operations, many by simply hiring more clerks to process the work. The difficulty was that clerks were often inadequately trained, and commitments to buy and sell were lost in massive paper shuffles. A failed settlement went against a brokerage firm's capital base.

Not merely a lack of long-term planning took a toll on brokerage firm capital. Indeed, many firms attempted to adapt to the increased trading volume by implementing large computerized systems to handle settlements (*Securities Regulation and Law Reports* 6/18/68, A 12). Such efforts, however, lacked the trained personnel necessary to ensure smooth operation. Further, the operations often included unanticipated cost overruns (SEC, *Annual Report* 1969, 1).

When a firm's capital dropped below a mandated level, the firm itself often failed.[2] Given the considerable number of settlement fails by the late 1960s, the liquidation of whole firms became commonplace. By December 1968, fails-to-deliver reached a record $4.1 billion (SEC, *Annual Report* 1969; 2). The drain on brokerage capital forced nearly a hundred firms on the New York Stock Exchange alone to close their doors, sell out, or merge with other firms (NYSE, *Fact Book* 1971, 4).

Following the 1963 failure of a New York Stock Exchange member firm, Ira Haupt and Company, the exchange created a special trust fund to cover the losses of Haupt customers. The fund was also intended to insure against other customer losses in the future. The American Stock Exchange took similar actions to protect the customers of its member firms. However, by the late 1960s the New York Stock Exchange's $10 million fund had to be increased three-fold to cover impending customer losses. A $30 million capital commitment was difficult to maintain, even for the New York Stock Exchange (Loomis 1970; *SRLR* 1/20/71, B 1–9).

The situation was complicated in 1970 by the end of the "bull" market—a market in which orders to buy stock consistently exceed orders to sell (NYSE, *Fact Book* 1970, 3; ibid. 1971, 3). Between 1968 and 1970, trading volume on the nation's exchanges declined by 18 percent (SEC, *Annual Report* 1970, 1). The consequent decline in the prices of securities and in trading volume took an additional toll on the capital bases of brokerage firms. First, the value of securities owned by the brokerage firms themselves were calculated as part of a firm's capital base. A decline in securities prices was a decline in assets and, therefore, in the capital base. Second, while the risks of brokerage firm failures no doubt drove some investors from the market, investors pulled out of the declining securities markets for other investment options. Fewer customers meant lower trading volume and lower brokerage incomes for Wall Street firms (SEC, *Annual Report* 1970, 2).

The fallout from the back-office crisis required an enormous regulatory effort by the SEC to deal with the structural problems of the industry, as well as violations of the securities acts that took place throughout the crisis. The fallout also alerted members of the legislative committees eager to bring market professionals under greater scrutiny, as well as to intensify the prosecution of market fraud and manipulation (*SRLR* 11/3/71, A 5; ibid. 2/16/72, A 11).

Political Scandal in the SEC

Amid Wall Street's problems, the SEC was trying to deal with two successive blows to its reputation as an impartial regulator. Between 1971 and 1973, the Nixon White House used its connections with Chairmen William Casey and Bradford Cook to interfere with ongoing SEC investigations. In both cases, the investigations turned up incriminating evidence that would have harmed the administration. The chairmen's interference, and the political repercussions, were viewed by observers as a blemish on the agency's tradition of independence from outside political influences (Fowlkes 1971a; *Wall Street Journal* 7/5/73, 2).

President Nixon appointed William Casey chairman of the SEC in 1971. As with several previous chairmen, Casey had financial connections to the Nixon presidential campaign in particular and to Republican causes in general (*New York Times* 2/3/71, 1). Yet regardless of their ties to the White House, the majority of SEC chairmen had accepted the position in the twilight of their legal and business careers, or as a prelude to a more lucrative career in the private sector. Observers of the Casey nomination, on the other hand, viewed it as a political stepping-stone en route to a position in military intelligence (ibid. 3/26/71, 53).

Casey's political connections to the White House became a concern for the agency when the new chairman interrupted an SEC investigation into the activities of the International Telephone and Telegraph Corporation (IT&T). The SEC investigation revealed communications between officials of IT&T and the Nixon administration during negotiations to settle charges of antitrust violations. It was alleged that IT&T promised to help fund the Republican National Convention in 1971 in return for favorable treatment by the Department of Justice (*SRLR* 12/20/72, A 13–17).

Simultaneously, the Senate Judiciary Committee was investigating IT&T. When the committee tried to secure the incriminating documents from the SEC, the agency voted in a session not attended by the staff to send the case to the Department of Justice for review. The termination of the SEC inquiry and the transfer of some thirty-four cartons of documents to Justice kept the incriminating evidence away from Congress in an election year (*Wall Street Journal* 6/9/73, 1; *Pollack's Confirmation Hearing* 1974, 10–16).

In 1972, Casey left the SEC to become undersecretary of state for economic affairs (*SRLR* 12/6/72, A 7). Nixon appointed the agency's director of the Division of Market Regulation, Bradford Cook, to fill the position. Like Casey, Cook had financial connections to the Nixon presidential campaigns. His father was the president of Bankers Life Nebraska in Lincoln and was the state chairman of the president's election campaigns in 1968 and 1972 (*Washington Post* 2/4/73, A 18). Cook first came to the agency as general counsel. He reportedly accepted the position at the urging of then Chairman Casey, with the administration's promise that a commissionership was not out of reach (*New York Times* 2/19/73, 33). When Casey split the responsibilities of the Division of Trading and Markets into two divisions, he named Cook to head the new Division of Market Regulations. After a brief stint as division director, Cook was named chairman.

Ten weeks into his term, however, a grand jury's scrutiny of Cook's role in yet another SEC investigation forced the new chairman to resign. During Casey's tenure, the SEC began an investigation of a New Jersey financier Robert Vesco. The inquiry led to charges that Vesco defrauded investors in a mutual fund by channeling the revenue from fund sales to shell corporations (*SRLR* 11/29/72, A 11–12). Further, it revealed that Vesco had contributed $200,000 to the president's reelection campaign. To protect the administration from the taint of an impending indictment against Vesco, Attorney General John Mitchell and Maurice Stans, head of the campaign finance committee, approached Cook about deleting any reference to the contribution from the SEC complaint. A grand jury found that Cook, as director of market regulation, had complied with the request (*New York Times* 7/8/73, 30; *Wall Street Journal* 7/5/73, 2).

It was not unusual for a chairman to have connections to the White House. Contrary to expectations that a securities expert would be appointed to fill SEC vacancies and that they would be independent of the White House (see chapter 4), the choices of chairmen were often exceptions to the rule. President Roosevelt set the precedent in 1934 when he named Joseph Kennedy, a personal friend and a large contributor to the Democratic national party, to be the agency's first chairman (de Bedts 1964, 88). What was unique about the Casey and Cook appointments, however, was that their White House connections were alleged to have disrupted the work of the agency.

For the SEC staff, conditions on Wall Street and in the agency provided two motives for regulatory activism. First, as regulator of the brokerage industry and protector of the investing public, the agency had to deal with the back-office crisis. Second, the Casey and Cook scandals threatened the agency's reputation as an independent (neutral) regulator and the professional credentials of the agency's career staff. Tougher enforcement and oversight activities could restore that status, and the disclosure-enforcement framework provided the means.

Members of the House and Senate legislative committees also had two reasons for supporting SEC activism. First, the back-office crisis was harming their constituents in the securities industry; strong enforcement could renew public confidence in the safety of securities as an investment; as a strong overseer, the agency could use its expertise to resolve differences among conflicting economic interests. Second, the scandals at the SEC gave legislative committee Democrats some political capital to use against a Republican administration. Support for the SEC staff's activism would place these members above executive branch meddling.

The SEC's Motivations for Rigorous Regulation

During an interview, a longtime Capitol Hill staffer referred several times to the "tremendous reputation" of the SEC as an independent regulatory agency. He argued that because of the agency's efforts in controlling stock fraud, "No one [in Congress] thinks the SEC isn't *very* vigilant." Yet he made a distinction between the SEC of the 1970s and the commission in the mid-1980s. He saw the difference as a loss of charisma: "I don't feel like the SEC is as known as when [Stanley] Sporkin [director of enforcement] was there—a real personality. They used to have longstanding commissioners, too. You could pick up the paper and recognize their names. It isn't like that now."

Throughout the 1970s it was not uncommon to read about agency personalities, particularly career staff, in the print media. For example, in 1973, the *Wall Street Journal* (6/9/73, 1) featured the director and associate director of enforcement in a front-page article, "SEC's Top Cops; Enforcement Chieftains Push Cases Vigorously." Similarly, in 1977, the *New York Times* (1/23/77, III 1) featured the agency's five division directors, its chief accountant, and its general counsel in an article, "Where the Power Lies at the S.E.C."

The rigor of the agency's enforcement efforts, as well as the reach of its rules regulating disclosure, were controversial in the 1970s. However, as indicated in the above title, "Where the Power Lies at the S.E.C.," supporters and critics alike placed responsibility for agency policy with the SEC senior staff. Commission approval was (and is) required for agency investigations, enforcement actions, rule proposals, and rules. But it was the staff of the agency's regulatory divisions that initiated the controversial policies. Therefore, supporters praised the staff for the agency's vigilant efforts to pursue market fraud and manipulation. Critics, on the other hand, argued that in its zeal the staff had overstepped the agency's mandate.

The attention focused on the agency's career staff was a direct reflection of staff efforts to reestablish the agency as a sagacious, independent regulator. The Casey and Cook episodes tarnished its reputation. In turn, the career staff bolstered the SEC's professional status by pursuing more vigorous enforcement and disclosure programs and by supporting legislation that enhanced its regulatory authority and fortified the disclosure-enforcement framework. Their careers were built upon service with the agency; they had professional reasons for insulating their work from the "political" overtones of recent chairmen.

The Reputation of a "Professional" Staff

In February 1977 the Senate Governmental Affairs Committee released a *Study on Federal Regulation*, an assessment of nine regulatory agencies based on a survey of members from the Administrative Conference of the U.S. (an advisory board made up of agency heads, other federal officials, attorneys, university professors, and other administrative experts), administrative law judges, and members of the private bar who practiced before the agencies. Among these agencies, the SEC was ranked highest for "technical knowledge, impartiality, legal ability, integrity, and hard work."[3] When I interviewed past and present members of the SEC and staff members in Congress about this laudatory assessment of the SEC, most attributed its reputation to the agency's senior staff, which they viewed as highly professional and committed. This meant that the staff had talent and took an *apolitical* approach to the job. One Senate staff member said: "For the most part, it's been a repository of very talented people. It feeds on itself. Good people go there because it has a good reputation." A House staffer who had formerly been with the SEC made a similar observation: "They have terrific lawyers. I'm not saying that because I used to be one. There are people there that I would feel dumb as a doorknob next to.... It's the quality of people."

Finally, a former member of the House committee referred to

the traditional high quality of the agency's staff and Congress's and the industry's reliance on their judgment when dealing with complex issues:

> From the beginning, it was a blue-ribbon selection for staff and commissioners, and there was great dependence placed on the agency and reliance to help steer the country to better economic footing. . . . And I think that there are many people in the industry who feel more secure knowing that regulation is even-handed and fair.

The staff's freedom from political bias—having no personal or financial ties to elected officials, particularly the White House—was often noted as a professional attribute. A staff member from Senate Banking felt that the SEC staff was "somewhat above the political fray. It's not viewed in that light; . . . [because of the] continuity of the senior staff, [the SEC] avoids the politics of other agencies." In other words, long tenure with the agency was seen as reinforcing the professional ties of agency employees, whereas high turnover among senior staff was seen as opening the door to patronage-type personnel policies.

A senior staff member from the House told a story that revealed a similar appraisal of the agency as apolitical. During the chairmanship of Hamer Budge (1969–1971), a Nixon appointee, a particular senator tried to make the SEC his "private fiefdom." In a blatant display of patronage, this staff member recalled, the senator sent "all these cronies" to the SEC. However, Stanley Sporkin (then a senior staff member in the Division of Trading and Markets) frustrated the effort. This House staffer, relieved that the SEC was not a reservoir of employees receiving political payoffs, described what happened: "Sporkin, bless his heart, told all these people they were going to be on a special enforcement group, policing the streets! They all quit within a few days, and it preserved the SEC staff. . . . Historically [it has been] a good staff."

As this observer saw it, Sporkin upheld the agency's professional integrity by minimizing the number of political, or patronage, positions in the agency. By political posts, he meant those filled by unqualified candidates who get jobs because they know someone in Congress. One SEC official confirmed that the agency is still wary of newcomers with connections to elected officials; even though she was well qualified for her staff position, because she was brought in

from outside to fill a principal position and had previously worked
on the Hill, her appointment was received with apprehension: "I
was a political appointment and had to go through a period of
scrutiny. . . . 'Who are you? Where do you come from?' [The staff] is
very suspicious of outside influence, in general, but political influence, in particular," she noted.

The term *apolitical* also applies to the staff's lack of partisan
connections. A former deputy director of one of the SEC's regulatory divisions described his appointment by an SEC chairman to
become division director.

> What was most striking was the lack of concern over political party
> affiliation: When [the new chairman] came in, he appointed me head of
> the division, and he didn't ask what party I was with. You don't find that
> in other agencies, particularly in the executive branch. . . . I suppose
> you could find other nonpolitical [nonpartisan] agencies that don't
> have the clout of the SEC, but I think that that is one important reason
> for the agency's standing.

In several interviews, the terms *outside* and *political* were
loosely distinguished, representing a general apprehension toward
any source of influence beyond the realm of securities law that
might threaten the stability of the disclosure-enforcement framework. Agency staffers recognize that to have decisions influenced
by any other criteria than the standards of the legal profession is
possibly to damage the agency's professional reputation (a point
discussed at length in chapter 8). Of course, the agency's protection
of its legal expertise through disclosure-enforcement is just as political as the influence of cronies or elected officials. Yet maintaining
the disclosure-enforcement system was portrayed by the SEC staff
as the politically neutral means to regulate the markets.

Another commonly cited reason for the agency's success was
the long-term commitment of the senior staff, already alluded to.
The turnover of SEC staff, in general, is high—an average stay being
two or three years.[4] But it was different for the senior, or career,
members of the staff. In nearly every interview with former and
current staffers on the Hill, in the SEC, and industry representatives,
this group was credited with being both proficient and committed.
An official in the SEC described the agency's regulatory success as a
direct reflection of their diligence:

[They] work like hell. I've been quite a few places in private industry and we are like a law firm. We have dedicated staff trying to do a good job. We try to work in the public interest, not succumbing to pressure from the White House. . . . We have a hell of a staff. It's infectious, it's everywhere. We get a lot of turnover, but we have a core group that is a stable staff. They've stuck around, giving continuity. . . . It's a people thing.

It is widely agreed that the career staff are not only committed to the agency, but also above politics—in this case, independent of White House pressure. As the above comment also conveys, the praise given the senior staff also explains the success of the agency as a whole. This is important: for career officials, their professional success is closely connected to the success of the agency. Moreover, the agency's reputation as a legal (and therefore apolitical) decision maker is directly connected to the clout the SEC carries on the Hill. A former SEC staffer noted the correlation between the apolitical nature of the staff and the agency's ability to serve the public interest:

In dealing with people on the Hill, the SEC was never political. Politics was absent, and it was an inherent policy of the agency. People on the Hill had confidence [that] when we would tell them X, it was X. When there were queries, we could tell them it involved things of a factual, legal nature. . . . [Committee members] had the view they could trust the agency. It was fair, aggressive, and it put the public interest on top of anything we did. It was rare confidence on the Hill.

A Senate staff member agreed: "There is a deference for the SEC bills that are sent up [to Congress] because of the agency's abilities, capabilities, and forthrightness." Similarly, when asked about the agency's reputation and influence with the Senate Banking Committee, a former congressional staffer argued that, particularly in the 1970s,

the SEC certainly had a big influence. A lot of members of Congress looked to the Enforcement Division for information and guidance on SEC matters. . . . [Particularly if it was a] technical issue that was not hotly contested in the industry, there was great deference given to the SEC. It was always seen as having a competent, professional staff. . . . The professional competence of the SEC stands out, and there is a reluctance [on the Hill] to tamper with it.

This forthrightness and competence was in question immediately following the Cook and Casey incidents. Further, the career staff had the most at stake in restoring that reputation. The young attorneys who worked with the SEC for two or three years, as well as the commissioners, typically moved on to private practice or business. Restoring the agency's independent status was less critical to their future success. The professional reputation of the SEC career staffers, however, was intricately linked to the reputation of the agency, and they did all they could to reinforce its status as a vigorous regulator independent of executive branch influence.

Career Staff Autonomy

Because the career staff was held responsible for the SEC's regulatory efforts, they sought to keep a distance between themselves and the commissioners. A former division director during the 1970s assessed the agency's strengths:

> The biggest thing is that it has always had an outstanding staff. Unlike other agencies, it's staff-driven. In a commission where tenure is not long, that can be a disaster. But at the SEC [senior staff stay on, and] there are a lot of staff-driven projects. They are creative people at the peak, pushing, pushing, always pushing. . . . Second, by and large, the chairmen were always supportive of the commission's work. . . . Those who came in to support the agency, support the staff, went out on a white horse.

What is most interesting about these remarks, echoing a widely held opinion, is its reference to the work of the *staff* as the work of the agency or the commission itself, and the chairman as a supporter of the staff, rather than a leader or an agenda-setter. Critics of the agency's regulatory activities during this period argued that it was inappropirate for the SEC chairmen to play a secondary, or support, role, and that stronger leadership might have checked the staff's regulatory zeal.[5] For example, in 1975 President Ford selected Roderick Hills to be SEC chairman. Hills had served as a White House counsel and chaired the president's deregulatory task force. Hills had been a corporate lawyer before his government service, but his experience in dealing with the SEC, or with securities law in general, was limited. Representatives of the securities industry criticized the nomination. A member of a Wall Street con-sulting firm was quoted as saying, "As far as I can determine, this guy knows zilch about the brokerage business. . . . *That means the staff at S.E.C. will walk all over him* (*New York Times* 10/3/75, 44, emphasis added).

However, the staff's autonomy was also a problem even for commissioners who did have a background in securities law and who questioned the agency's regulatory policies. Commissioner Roberta Karmel, appointed by Carter in 1977, had served as a branch chief of the SEC's New York office. In 1969 she joined a prominent New York law firm where she represented several large Wall Street enterprises, a career which gave members of the staff reason to believe she had a "proindustry bias" (*New York Times* 11/27/77, III 1). Throughout her term (1977–1980), the SEC's senior staff and Commissioner Karmel frequently disagreed over staff initiatives concerning disclosure and corporate governance. Karmel argued that many of the proposals were excessive and be-yond the scope of the agency's mandate. A comment in the *New York Times* made by a senior staff member indicated the staff's view of its autonomous role in the commission: "New members [commis-sioners] always tend to have a sense of paranoia about the head-strong staff. . . . But after a while she'll discover that the staff is somewhat like a large, nonthreatening St. Bernard, seeking direc-tion and trying to keep peace in the family" (*New York Times* 11/27/77, III 1).

By stating that the staff seeks direction, rather than following the lead of the commissioners, this observer suggested a leadership role for the "headstrong" staff. During the early 1970s, when several commissioners were representative of, or closely allied with, the staff, consensus between the staff and commission was generally the norm. However, when policy positions taken by staffers were chal-lenged by a few commissioners with conflicting views, the auton-omy of the SEC staff became more prominent. Its leadership role in making regulatory initiatives was something that a commissioner would perhaps come to accept (making "peace in the family") or tire of fighting.

Indeed, before leaving the commission, Karmel told the press that clashes with the staff had "made life very difficult." Reflecting a growing debate over the efficacy of the staff's ambitious disclosure and enforcement agenda, Karmel added that the staff positions on regulatory issues weren't "automatically the best expression of what is in the public interest" (*New York Times* 2/20/79, IV 1). After leaving the SEC, Karmel argued that when the agency should have been a leader in addressing problems such as capital formation in an inflationary market, the priorities of the Enforcement Division continued to dominate the agency's agenda (Karmel 1981, 73–74).

The division between staff and Commissioner Karmel indicated not only staff autonomy but also the staff's efforts to reaffirm the agency's political independence. Part of that drive was the staff's promotion of their views and concerns as representing the public interest.[6] As Karmel argued, what would benefit the public may very well have gone beyond staff concerns. Yet the connection between staff initiatives and the public interest was powerful, and it fueled a historical high point for SEC disclosure and enforcement efforts in the second half of the 1970s (to be discussed later).

What makes this noteworthy is that the increase in regulation occurred during two administrations that were pushing deregulatory agendas as well as attempting to change the character of appointees to the agency. Commissioners sympathetic to the staff remained with the commission throughout the decade, but several vacancies were filled by commissioners who represented the deregulatory efforts of the Ford and Carter administrations. These nominees, such as Hills and Karmel, apparently found the staff to be an impediment. They were unable to override the staff's determination to increase regulatory activity throughout the decade.

The staff's commitment to regulation was bolstered by the stability of the disclosure-enforcement framework. Standard operating procedures and institutional inertia go a long way toward frustrating leadership efforts (Kaufman 1981), especially when upholding those institutional arrangements is portrayed as keeping politics out and serving the public interest. But disclosure-enforcement was also a barrier because of the imperatives driving career staff, as well as Democrats on the legislative committees, to fortify the framework.

Questions of Reelection, Oversight, and Policy

Members of the congressional committees overseeing the SEC had invested time and effort in the development and maintenance of the disclosure-enforcement framework. Their strategies for reelection, constituent relations, and legislative initiatives were built upon the framework. To alter it, or to allow outside "political" intervention in how the SEC did its job, would threaten those strategies and consequently pose significant legislative costs. The problems of the securities industry in the early 1970s gave Congress members an opportunity to reinforce the disclosure-enforcement framework through legislation.

Chapter 3 describes how subcommittees of the House Interstate and Foreign Commerce Committee and the Senate Banking Committee initiated comprehensive hearings in 1971 to address structural reform—the organization of trading within and between the securities markets—and regulatory reform—the SEC's ability to oversee the markets and bring enforcement actions. The result was the 1975 Securities Acts amendments and the regulatory reform aspects of the legislation, which former members of the SEC staff referred to as the "nuts and bolts" of the legislation, fortified disclosure-enforcement.

Regulatory "Reform" and Reelection Finance

Members of the committees used the 1971 hearings to build financial support for their reelection efforts, to shore up their position as SEC overseers, and to try to improve securities policy. Several former SEC staffers analyzed the legislators' motives for backing initiatives such as the 1975 amendments. One implied that when committee members held hearings on legislative initiatives, special interest groups responded with campaign contributions:

> Around 1971, [the committee members] knew a good thing when they saw it—that's my own cynical view. Senator Williams was chairman of the Securities Subcommittee and securities was his territory, legislatively. That meant Wall Street and lots of campaign dollars. The SEC had found all this stuff [the trading abuses and problems related to fixed rates and capital requirements] with all this money lying around, and Congress thought it should be involved.

Whether or not this view is cynical,[7] others offered a similar interpretation of congressional interest in hearings and legislation. One Senate staff member explicitly connected calling for hearings

and passing legislation to members' fund-raising needs by discussing the Glass-Steagall Act. The legislation, which prevents commercial banks from underwriting securities issues, consequently pro-
tectd the securities industry from commercial banking competition.
This staffer argued that members of the Banking Committee used
this mandated split between the two banking industries to raise
money:

> It's the annual Glass-Steagall Derby, the goose that laid the golden egg.
> Every year members drag it out to repeal [it], and everyone comes out
> of the woodwork to hold fund-raisers to prevent it from happening.
> Then [members] don't do anything. If they ever did repeal it, they
> would be out of a fund-raising source.

He continued by elaborating on congressional interest in legislation
in general: "These guys will announce a controversial bill, and then
go up and do fund-raisers. They threaten to do things, and then go
exact resources. If they get enough, they don't do anything."

But in 1975 members did do something. They passed the comprehensive Securities Acts amendments. Apart from campaign financing, legislators no doubt had other interests. For example, they
might also have wanted to sustain the disclosure-enforcement
framework for their own long-term ability to oversee the SEC, and
thus claim credit for successful policies or readily intervene in the
event of policy failures.

Reform and Congressional Control

For members of the legislative committees, a "political" SEC was
an SEC that was influenced by (or accountable to) other elected
officials. Consequently, congressional activism favoring regulatory
reform was also a battle for influence over the SEC. The Nixon
administration's efforts to influence the agency through various appointees directly challenged the legislative committees that assured
the agency's accountability. The House Interstate and Foreign Commerce Committee and the Senate Banking Committee were interested in firming up the disclosure-enforcement framework so as to
exclude presidential influence and reassert their own position as
overseers.

One former SEC staff member illustrated this battle by arguing that in the hearings held by the House Subcommittee on Commerce and Finance, congressional interest in the 1975 omnibus legislation was prompted by a concern for the autonomy of the SEC. More specifically, he argued that Representative John Moss (D-Calif.) was worried about the "responsiveness of the SEC to Congress" and the agency's independence from the executive branch. These concerns are highlighted in the subcommittee's 1972 *Report* (pp. 114–15), and in the Independent Regulatory Agencies Act, introduced by Chairman Moss during the hearings.

First, the bill required the Office of Management and Budget (OMB) to submit a budget recommendation for the SEC to Congress, as well as the original agency request. The intent was to help the legislative committees make a better assessment of the SEC's needs, rather than accepting the OMB's request as the agency's. Second, the bill released the SEC from the need to clear with the OMB all communication with Congress over legislation or changes in disclosure rules (*SRLR* 6/28/72, A 18). The purpose was to nullify (or at least reduce) White House influence over the agency's regulatory activities. Portions of the bill were passed as part of the omnibus legislation of 1975.

The amendments also established an important oversight link between the legislative committees and the SEC. In particular, the legislation amended the Securities Exchange Act to require SEC authorization for appropriations; the agency had previously had permanent authorization. In conference, members settled on a two-year authorization for 1976 and 1977. If the SEC required appropriations over the authorized level, it would have to come before the legislative committees to make the request (supplement to *SRLR* 5/21/75, 32).

On the one hand, the action was viewed as a substantial boost to the oversight authority of the House and Senate committees (*SRLR* 5/21/75, A-5). On the other hand, adding another authorization gave the committees a visible means to support the regulatory activities of the agency. The inadequacy of SEC resources was a constant theme throughout the hearings. Members of the legislative committees pledged to increase the agency's staff and funding, with the three-year authorization a way to achieve that goal. In 1975 the final appropriation for the SEC was just over $43 million (*Congressional Quarterly Almanac* 1974). The conference version of the 1975 amendments authorized $51 and $55 million for fiscal years

1976 and 1977, respectively (supplement to *SRLR* 5/21/75, 32).
Though the authorization did not necessarily diminish the role of
the OMB and the appropriations committees in determining the
agency's resources, it did enable the legislative committees to endorse a stronger, more capable regulator.

Reform and "Good" Policy Considerations

Some who had worked on the amendments denoted their interest in securities legislation as a "policy" concern. When asked why
they initiated the legislation, a former House member said, "We felt
we had to meet the regulatory challenges of an ever growing market." Others pointed to what they saw as abuses in the industry and
the need to correct for those practices in the interest of investors.
For example, a former House member described his battle with the
specialists on the New York Stock Exchange during the legislative
process. (His allusion to the "mutual fund question" refers to legislation passed in 1970, and an "open book" means the New York Stock
Exchange practice of placing market orders with a specialist who
records the orders in a book—to which the specialist has primary
access.) "Now the specialists, they hated me," he said. "If they could
burn anyone in effigy it would probably be me. They were running
around talking about an open book and there is no such thing!
Never mind the mutual fund question; look, here's your biggest
crooks of all!"

Though a distinction was made in these interviews between
reelection concerns (fund-raising), questions of oversight and control, and to a lesser degree, policy concerns, there was no doubt
overlap among them. As I argued in chapter 4, segments of the
securities industry prefer an impartial regulator among competing
interests rather than an agency that might favor one set of interests
over the other. The ability of the White House to intervene in
agency policy could have been viewed by these interests as a
source of bias (or outside influence) in SEC decision making. Therefore, congressional concerns for the agency's independence may
have represented these economic interests. If so, the oversight concerns of Representative Moss and others were as relevant to reelection as Congress's interest in the campaign contributions generated
by threatening to tamper with the industry's regulatory structure.

Regardless of the motivation, conditions on Wall Street in the early 1970s were sufficiently troublesome to get the attention of lawmakers. However, in order to hold the hearings and pass legislation, members of the legislative committees needed the SEC's expertise to draft workable legislative proposals. They also depended on a capable SEC to implement new mandates in the face of stiff opposition from segments of the securities industry. Consider, for example, the controversy surrounding the fixed-rate system for brokerage fees. Lawmakers, regulators, and members of the New York Stock Exchange acknowledged that fixed rates would eventually give way, but there was a recognized need for a period of adjustment (Glass 1973). A strong, objective enforcer able to assess the impact of competitive pricing was needed for the transition (*SRLR* 2/16/72, A 11).

Congress's Reliance on the SEC

During the early 1970s, cooperation between the SEC and its legislative committees was not necessarily a given. According to a former SEC staffer, members of the House and Senate legislative committees felt that during Casey's tenure "SEC decision making was too political." In other words, it was too easily swayed by partisan considerations and White House concerns. This former staffer said that when the legislative process began in 1971, "it started with a lot of mistrust."

To address the industry's problems (for whatever electoral, oversight, or policy reasons), members of the legislative committees needed to overcome that mistrust. They did so by cultivating a working relationship with the agency's career staff, who were considered above the fray of recent political events. After all, it was the investigations by the SEC Enforcement Division that turned up the evidence on IT&T, as well as the Vesco campaign contribution. The Vesco investigation, in particular, demonstrated to members of Congress that the agency's career staff was independent of the political connections that commissioners may have had. In 1972, Stanley Sporkin (then the associate director of enforcement) convinced Chairman Casey to continue the early investigation of Vesco, despite White House pressure to back off (*Washington Post* 4/22/81, E 1).

The strong ties that developed between the SEC staff and Congress during the decade were very important for the direction of securities policy, according to former staffers and SEC members. Of particular significance were those between committee Democrats and senior staff in the Division of Enforcement. A former SEC official stated:

> There were some very close relations between . . . the SEC and the Hill at the staff level, up. Stanley Sporkin, the director of enforcement, had tremendous influence over what the SEC did, and he was very close to people on the Hill. . . . You didn't have to talk about what would be the Hill's reaction [to SEC actions] because people in the SEC knew what their reaction would be.

In fact, according to several persons who were integral to these agency-Hill connections, the SEC staff began to define congressional oversight, not as a check on the agency's behavior, but as a means to support the staff's agenda—particularly if the commission was recalcitrant. When asked to describe the relationship with committee Democrats, a former SEC official replied:

> At times, it was extremely terrific, at other times it was bad. . . . I would like to say that I think the oversight we received from Congress was great. When I say it was terrific, it was when we were working together. . . . Close oversight of the SEC, I think, was good. . . . As director of [a division], I wanted tough oversight, support that what we were doing was right, or done the right way.

The staff typically had the committees' support, he continued, even when the commission didn't support the staff. However, he limited his praise of congressional oversight to Congress's support for the staff. "Oversight is good," he argued, "if it doesn't impede the work of the commission." Here again the term *commission* is used to represent the staff's work.

For committee members, the agency's enforcement activities demonstrated the independence of the SEC staff. In addition, those activities had turned up incriminating evidence against the Republican administration. An alliance with the career staff proved therefore to be an important resource for Democratic members of the legislative committees. First, support for the SEC's regulatory activities was a political counter-punch to an administration that was caught meddling in an independent agency. Given the agency's reputation protecting the small investor from securities fraud, support for the enforcement staff also placed the Democratic Congress on a symbolic high ground. For example, the SEC's case against Vesco revealed a mutual fund scheme that defrauded hundreds of investors. Following the attempt at interference in the Vesco indictment, members of the legislative committees expressed outrage over the White House's willingness to tamper with an independent agency's investigations. Members made commitments to "beef up" the agency's enforcement staff and funding, as well as its power to sanction violators of the securities laws (House Subcommittee on Commerce and Finance, *Securities Industry Study* 1972, iv, xii–xiii; *Wall Street Journal* 6/9/73, 1).

Second, members of the legislative committees enjoyed their working relationship with the securities experts on the SEC career staff. They needed the SEC's assistance in drafting new bills, and they needed the agency's cooperation to ensure that their proposals were workable. This relationship produced legislation that fortified disclosure-based enforcement, an activist regulatory agenda within that framework, and mutual support for nominees to the commission with a career staff background. On this last point—support for internal appointees—the logic on both sides was straightforward: commissioners with a career staff background would support the staff's efforts and work within the disclosure-enforcement framework. In fact, as I discussed in chapter 4, support for the "right" nominee became one of the rules or norms essential to upholding the system.

Career Staff Nominees and Maintaining Disclosure-Enforcement

Between 1971 and 1975, four nominations were made to fill commission vacancies that reflected the working relationship between Congress and the SEC staff. Each nominee resembled the ideal securities law expert profiled in chapter 4. Each had a background in securities law, three were previous SEC staff members, and each was said to be independent of the White House and Wall Street. Congress's endorsements of these candidates showed support for strong market regulators at a time of low investor confidence and support for nominees who were "above the politics" of previous chairmen. These nominations further enhanced the professional status of the senior staff: first, they became a represented group on the commission; second, because the nominees were independent of the White House, the autonomy of the agency was enhanced.

Consider the nomination of Philip Loomis in August 1971. Loomis was named to the commission before the Casey and Cook scandals, but after the back-office crisis and the market downturn. He initially joined the SEC in 1954 as a staff consultant. In 1955 he was named associate director of the Division of Trading and Markets, and shortly thereafter, division director. Eight years later, he was appointed to be SEC general counsel, where he served until his nomination to the commission (SEC, *Annual Report* 1972, xi).

The respect and admiration of the SEC staff for Loomis was obvious. As general counsel, he was described by staff members as the agency's "resident genius." One staff member stated, "Almost nothing of importance goes on that Loomis isn't consulted on" (Fowlkes 1971a, 380). Loomis also symbolized the agency's reputation as a regulator who was independent of the industry and the White House, and as a policeman of the stock markets. For example, Loomis was the agency's chief drafter of the 1964 amendments to the Securities Exchange Act—an expansion of the agency's authority over disclosure. He led an agency investigation of the American Stock Exchange in 1961 that resulted in sweeping reforms, and in 1966 he participated in an agency study of the mutual fund industry that charged the industry with using pressure tactics to sell fund shares to low-income investors (*New York Times* 8/8/71: 58).

It was perhaps his reputation as a strong regulator that induced President Nixon to pass over Loomis for earlier openings (Fowlkes 1971a, 380). However, in the wake of the back-office crisis, as well as other emerging problems, he was chosen as a competent securities expert. Loomis was well known to members of the Senate Banking Committee. As general counsel and agency draftsman, Loomis had worked closely with the Securities Subcommittee. More important, as revealed in his confirmation hearing, he was welcomed by Banking Committee members as one who could address the problems of the securities industry. The SEC's own hearings on commission rates, initiated in 1968, and the congressional hearings, begun in 1971, had uncovered a wide range of difficulties. Committee members used Loomis's confirmation hearing to get an assessment of the testimony to date. Questions addressed efforts to secure the safety of the small investor in the stock markets, back-office tangles, and computerized closing and settlement (*Loomis's Confirmation Hearing* 1971, 1–6; ibid. 1974, 2–6).

The nominations of Ray Garrett as SEC chairman and A. A. Sommer as commissioner came in the wake of the Cook and Casey episodes. The press explicitly referred to these selections as efforts to shore up the commission's reputation and to rebuild investor confidence (*Wall Street Journal* 7/5/73, 2; *New York Times* 7/6/73, 29). Others argued that it was also an attempt to salvage the administration's faltering image by showing it could still attract talented and qualified people (Seligman 1982, 448).

Ray Garrett was a professor of law before joining the SEC in 1954. He served as the director of the Division of Corporation Finance for three years and as the agency's associate executive director in 1958 (SEC, *Annual Report* 1973, ix). He left the SEC for private practice shortly thereafter. Sommer, on the other hand, had no experience as an SEC staff member, but had presided over the Board of Governors of the National Association of Securities Dealers (ibid., xi). He was therefore well known in the industry and by the SEC—which oversees NASD activities. Both were described as "widely known in securities circles" (*Wall Street Journal* 7/5/73, 2). Further, given the competence of both men as securities experts, both nominations were welcomed "with relief" by the financially beset securities industry (*New York Times* 7/9/73, 51).

The nominations were some of the best in the agency's history, said former SEC staffers. One current member of the securities bar stated, "Now, Ray Garrett—he was selected as being the best qualified they could find." Another former staffer, a lawyer, respectfully referred to Garrett as a "brilliant" chairman and to Sommer as a "self-taught scholar." He said that with Garrett and Sommer, the SEC had a "very knowledgeable set of commissioners."

Although observers expected members of the Senate Banking Committee to grill the nominees on their independence from White House influence (*Wall Street Journal* 6/9/73, 1), no one questioned the qualifications or expertise of the nominees in the least. As in the Loomis hearing, senators used the opportunity to address issues raised in the Securities Subcommittee hearings on the industry—the role of the small investor and the impact of competition on brokerage firms (*Garrett-Sommers Confirmation Hearing* 1973, 21–25).

The joint confirmation hearing was also used to address the adequacy of SEC disclosure efforts. Banking Committee Chairman William Proxmire (D-Wis.) questioned the nominees about the SEC's disclosure efforts pertaining to defense contractors. His interest in the topic was evidence of the SEC staff's credibility in the eyes of the examiners—in contrast to their distrust of past commissioners. Consider, for example, Proxmire's question to Garrett:

> Are you aware also that less than a year ago the SEC staff recommended to the Commission that formal, specific guidelines be issued directing defense contractors to make full disclosure of cost overruns and other matters . . . and that the Commission killed the guidelines and instead put out a practically meaningless press release stating, in effect, that defense contractors should try to do a better job of making full disclosure? (ibid., 19)

Proxmire continued to discuss a proposal that the SEC should audit defense contractors and expressed his willingness, as chairman of the appropriations subcommittee with SEC jurisdiction, to provide funding to hire the necessary staff. These questions were some of the first indications that committee members were looking to the SEC staff for reliable advice about regulating the securities markets— in this case, disclosure by defense contractors. Also this attempt to focus congressional concern on the newly appointed commissioners foreshadowed future congressional support for the agency staff's sweeping proposals on disclosure, to be discussed later.

Nominated in 1974, Irving Pollack typified the independent regulator as well as the characteristic securities expert. Pollack joined the SEC in 1946 as a staff member for the agency's general counsel and in 1956 was named assistant general counsel. Five years later he moved to become associate director of the Division of Trading and Markets and was named full director in 1965. Finally, in 1972, he was named director of the Division of Enforcement after the functions of Trading and Markets were split (SEC, *Annual Report* 1975, x–xi).

Pollack had an illustrious record as a professional public servant. He received the SEC Distinguished Service Award for Outstanding Career Service in 1967, and the Rockefeller Public Service Award in Law, Regulation, and Legislation in 1968 (*New York Times* 6/28/75, 37). More important to members of Congress, however, was his record as Wall Street's "top cop." It was Pollack's investigation of Vesco that revealed the $200,000 connection to the Nixon administration (*Wall Street Journal* 12/17/73, 2). Further, his reputation as a protector of investor rights on Wall Street was welcomed as a means to shore up investor confidence in the markets (*Time*, 2/11/74, 72). Members of the Senate Banking Committee agreed on the "demonstrated honesty, integrity and candor" of the nominee (*New York Times* 1/31/74, 45).

There was some strong opposition on Wall Street to Pollack's nomination because of his former position in the Enforcement Division (*Wall Street Journal* 12/17/73, 2). However, the fact that the Nixon administration went through with the nomination reveals the impact of combined SEC and Senate Banking Committee support. According to a former member of the SEC staff who was closely involved in the debate over Pollack, elements of the financial community were opposed to the nomination because "he was a cop, and also because Stanley Sporkin would become director of enforcement." But a meeting between SEC Chairman Garrett (who recommended Pollack), the Senate liaison at the White House (who represented Senate Democrats), several senior SEC staffers, and White House Chief of Staff Alexander Haig resulted in Pollack's nomination. Apparently, the need to rebuild confidence in the administration was more important than giving in to protests from the industry. One SEC staffer was quoted to say, "Because of Watergate, the administration had to come up with a completely honest guy" (*Time*, 2/11/74, 72). Further, as a member of the SEC staff, Pollack was well known to members of the legislative committees: as division director, he had testified before the committees on several occasions (*Pollack's Confirmation Hearing* 1974, 7–8). Not only was he a trusted member of the SEC staff, but also he represented the agency's independent enforcement efforts that contributed to the Nixon administration's decline.

The Pollack nomination revealed Congress's priorities at the time. First, Congress sought to rebuild investor confidence in the faltering markets partly by supporting commissioners who favored strong enforcement of the securities laws. Second, congressional support for the Pollack nomination was politically fashionable in the wake of revelations of attempts by the Republican administration to meddle with the agency; Pollack was considered to be independent of both the industry and the administration. Third, his knowledge of the markets and market structure (*Wall Street Journal* 12/17/73, 2) gave members another source of expertise for dealing with the problems of the industry.

In sharp contrast to the Pollack nomination was President Ford's selection of Patrick Delaney to serve on the commission in 1976. Delaney was a White House aide at the time of his nomination, and his father was the second-ranking Democrat on the House Rules Committee. However, any loyalty to a Democratic colleague was overcome by the Senate Banking Committee's concern over Delaney. Members reportedly thought Delaney was too closely connected with the White House and not qualified to serve. In other words, he did not fit the profile of a securities law expert. The committee refused to call a hearing to confirm Delaney and let the nomination die (*New York Times* 1/7/77, IV 3; ibid. 5/15/77, III 18).

To address the problems of the securities markets, Congress needed the SEC's drafting expertise and cooperation. Further, the legislative committees supported a strong and independent SEC that would carry out the new mandate. They therefore supported the agency's increasingly vigorous enforcement and disclosure efforts. Their support of Loomis, Garrett, Sommer, and Pollack, and their rejection of Delaney contributed to those efforts.

The Product of Mutual Agendas

The regulatory policies of the SEC during the second half of the 1970s focused on the behavior and governance of corporate America. It was a campaign aimed at making corporations more accountable to their shareholders. It was also a drive to elevate the status of the SEC as a regulator that served the public shareholder and the public in general. The agency's senior staff, which focused on expanding the number of investigations and enforcement actions taken by the SEC to uncover corporate abuses and on broadening the agency's authority through disclosure, had the support of committee Democrats.

SEC Enforcement Initiatives

The SEC has the authority to bring administrative and civil actions against violators of the securities laws and regulations. If an investigation reveals criminal (as opposed to civil) violations, the SEC can recommend a case to the Department of Justice for prosecution. These actions are statistically recorded in the number of administrative proceedings instituted by the SEC, the number of injunctive actions taken (actions filed with the district courts to order a halt in activities), and the number of criminal cases referred to Justice annually. As shown in table 1, all of these enforcement activities significantly increased during the seventies.

Three features of table 1 stand out. First, administrative actions jumped from a low of 42 in 1968 to 133 the following year. Actions increased through 1971 to a decade high of 217, then settled to a level equal to case loads of the early 1960s. The immediate increase in administrative proceedings is most likely attributed to the number of broker-dealer abuses related to the back-office crisis. Further, the number of registered brokers, dealers, and investment advisors (most commonly the subject of an administrative proceeding) significantly increased during the period (SEC, *Annual Report* 1970, 82–83).

Second, the number of injunctions instituted by the SEC, and the number of criminal cases referred to the Department of Justice, had increased substantially by the mid-1970s. The increase in injunctive actions reflected the fallout of the back-office crisis in 1970. However, unlike administrative actions, the number of injunctions instituted continued to rise through the mid-1970s. Further, though there was a decline from a high of 178 in 1973, injunctive actions initiated in the late seventies were significantly higher than the equivalent years in the previous decade.

Whereas the number of injunctive and administrative actions reflected a more immediate agency response to the back-office crisis, the number of criminal referrals did not show a significant increase until 1974. In that year the agency referred 67 cases, up from 49 in 1973. However, like injunctive actions, by 1976 referrals were more than double the average number of cases referred throughout the 1960s (47): the agency referred 116, 100, and 109 cases in 1976, 1977, and 1978, respectively.

Finally, all three categories of enforcement declined noticeably in 1979. Administrative actions instituted in 1979 dropped to 81, down from 122 in 1978. The number of injunctive actions instituted fell from 135 in 1978 to 108 in 1979, and the number of cases referred to the Department of Justice for criminal prosecution were cut by more than half, from 109 to 45.

TABLE 1. SEC Enforcement Actions, 1960–1979

	Injunctive Actions	Referrals to the Department of Justice	Administrative Actions[a]
1960	99	55	190
1961	84	42	137
1962	99	60	159
1963	109	49	175
1964	76	50	163
1965	71	52	131
1966	67	44	64
1967	68	44	52
1968	93	40	42
1969	94	37	133
Mean (1960s)	86	47.11	24.6
1970	111	35	138
1971	140	22	217
1972	119	38	165
1973	178	49	198
1974	148	67	175
1975	174	88	142
1976	158	116	129
1977	166	100	142
1978	135	109	122
1979	108	45	81
Mean (1970s)	143.7	66.9	150.9

Source: SEC, *Annual Report*, 1960–1979.
   a. Includes all broker-dealer proceedings instituted during the year, investment-advisor proceedings, stop-order proceedings, and suspensions of Regulation A exemptions under the 1933 Securities Exchange Act.

The immediate increase in administrative actions instituted has been attributed, as already noted, to brokerage abuses during the back-office crisis. What is less readily explained is the increase in injunctive actions and criminal referrals several years after the back-office crisis, as well as the precipitous decline in all three categories of enforcement in 1979. To explain that increase, we must consider the parallel increase in the realm of disclosure—what the agency demarcated as information "materially" relevant to the investing public. Further, to understand the swift decline in all three categories of enforcement, we must understand the controversial policy that these efforts produced. Each category fell to pre-1970 levels at the close of the decade, perhaps indicating that an atypical period of SEC regulation was coming to a close.

SEC Disclosure Initiatives

Running parallel to an increase in SEC enforcement activity was an increase in the agency's mandatory disclosure program. Disclosure is the cornerstone of the federal securities statutes. Both the 1933 Securities Act and the 1934 Securities Exchange Act require corporations that sell their stock to the public to disclose all material information to the SEC. An informed investor, according to advocates of disclosure, is an investor protected from fraud (Cohen 1966, 1985). However, the SEC has discretion to determine what information is relevant, or *material*, to the investor. The SEC staff campaign to expand the domain of material information became controversial because—as critics saw it—the agency was requiring the disclosure of information that was not relevant to an investment decision (see, for example, Freeman 1976; Kripke 1979). Instead, critics argued that the SEC was attempting to use its authority over disclosure to regulate corporate behavior—an illegal extension of its mandate.

Perhaps the best example of this expansion in disclosure requirements was the agency's voluntary disclosure program for "questionable" payments. The SEC described its efforts as an attempt to "restore the efficiency of the system of corporate accountability and to encourage the boards of directors to exercise their authority" (SEC, *Annual Report*, 1976, 26). Specifically, the agency urged companies to voluntarily disclose questionable payments (or bribes) made overseas to secure a share in foreign markets, or favorable legislative or regulatory treatment. Through its own investigations, the SEC found what it alleged to be the misuse of corporate funds by publicly owned companies. If corporate managers and directors were willing to initiate their own investigations of possible misuse and to report the findings to the SEC, the implication was that their firms would avoid prosecution by the agency (see Karmel 1981, 149). However, such cases could be referred to the Department of Justice for criminal prosecution under the securities laws.

In 1977, the SEC reported that nearly 400 companies came

forward to disclose information voluntarily (SEC, *Annual Report* 1978, 27). But by 1977, the director of enforcement and other senior staff members indicated that the agency would begin phasing out the voluntary program and, instead, would begin to expand its own investigations of questionable payments (*SRLR* 11/9/77, AA 3–4; ibid. 3/9/77, A 10–11). Further, Congress gave the agency's program statutory backing in 1977. The Foreign Corrupt Practices Act of 1977 incorporated the SEC's questionable payments program (in words basically identical to those of an SEC legislative proposal), which made failure to disclose illegal payments a criminal violation (*SRLR* 7/14/76, A 16; ibid. 12/14/77, A 3).

In defense of the agency's expanded program for corporate disclosure, Stanley Sporkin, then director of the Division of Enforcement, argued that the information was material to making an informed investment decision:

> The shareholders are entitled to know about the quality of a company's earnings and the risks associated with the business. If there is anything that is material, it is information that pertains to the quality of a company's earnings and the high- risk methods of a company's doing business. (*New York Times* 10/5/75, III 1)

In 1977, the agency also required the disclosure of executive perquisites in SEC registration documents. This included the disclosure of "salary, fees, bonuses and certain personal benefits" received by corporate officers and directors (SEC, *Annual Report* 1977, 37–38). The required disclosure was viewed as proof of the agency's determination to uncover management fraud and to increase corporate accountability to shareholders. As in the case of questionable payments, the commission ruled that executive "perks" were material to the investing public.

The Consent Decree

What made these SEC initiatives so controversial was the SEC's "creative" use of its enforcement authority to back them up. Consider the agency's use of a consent decree. In a consent decree, an alleged violator neither admits nor denies charges brought by the SEC. Instead, the individual agrees to settlement conditions specified by the agency. Use of the decree expedites the judicial process because the case does not go to court.

During the 1970s, the SEC used consent decrees to induce corporations to implement structural reforms in the interest of the public investor. Specifically, part of the settlement included SEC-prescribed changes in corporate governance. Among some of the most publicized uses of the consent decree were SEC investigations that revealed questionable overseas payments (that is, bribes) made by Exxon, Lockheed Aerospace, and Gulf Oil. As part of a settlement with the SEC, all three corporations instituted reforms in their corporate governance (*SRLR* 10/5/77, A 20; ibid. 4/21/76, A 3; ibid. 3/19/75, A 23–24).

Opponents of the SEC's campaign for corporate responsibility claimed, first, that the SEC exceeded its statutory authority in its definition of material information. In a speech addressed to the community of business lawyers, a member of the New York securities bar and former staffer for the SEC argued that the SEC's disclosure program went beyond the legal meaning of material information. He stated that as an SEC staff member he had determined the materiality of information by using a "simple rule":

> It was the kind of thing that affected an investor's judgment as to whether to buy or not. It was the kind of information that could be expected to affect the market value of the stock in a substantial way. . . .
> In those simpler days, which I say have not passed, investors were interested only in what was happening to the bottom line in their companies. (Freeman 1976, 1295)

Rather than identifying information that was truly relevant to the investing public, he argued, the SEC was using its authority to impose its own moral standards on corporate behavior (ibid., 1295–1303).

Second, critics charged the agency with violating the due-process rights of subjects of a consent decree (*New York Times* 10/5/75, III 1). The SEC could use the threat of full prosecution as leverage over a company. In turn, a company was forced to waive its due-process rights and submit to SEC demands for structural and operational changes. During her tenure, Commissioner Karmel was one of the strongest critics of the staff's use of consent decrees, and this was a source of conflict between Karmel and the staff. Though she recognized that more cases could be "disposed of" and fewer resources spent, she argued that heavy reliance on consent decrees "cheapened" the federal securities laws (ibid. 2/20/79, IV 1; see also Karmel 1981, 148, 151, 155).

To the charge that the SEC was trying to impose a code of behavior on corporate America, the agency replied that its efforts were aimed strictly at improving the information available to investors. Responding to critics of the SEC's extensive program, Commissioner Sommer argued (1976, 1292):[8]

> The commission ... is not concerned with remaking the world in its own image and likeness. We're not trying to extrapolate out from our offices our notions of morality as it should govern the conduct of American businesses, or the way in which business is done overseas. If, as a collateral consequence of the policies that we are pursuing with regard to the requirements of disclosure, there are changes in the practices of American business, I would suggest that while that is not our objective, it may be one of the happier results.

The agency defended its use of the consent decree by arguing that the technique allowed the commission to regulate more effectively despite scarce resources. First, although the size of the enforcement staff had not increased in ten years, the number of cases brought by the agency had more than doubled. This was because, rather than going to court, the agency had begun to settle more than 90 percent of its cases by using the consent decree (*SRLR* 7/19/78, A 12). Second, the agency's senior staff argued that the decree allowed the agency to supplement its disclosure efforts in preventing fraud. A company that implemented management reforms as part of a consent decree might be less likely to violate the securities laws in the future (Levine 1978). Reacting to criticism, the agency argued that the consent decree

> is a vehicle by which the Commission accomplishes the statutory objective authorized by Congress and a vehicle by which the Commission has obtained significant other equitable relief, all of which has worked to the benefit of investors in the U.S. and ultimately to the public interest in general. (Cited in *SRLR* 7/19/78, A 13)

Summary Remarks

Both the SEC and its legislative committees had a stake in preventing politics from creeping into the disclosure-enforcement framework. To prevent executive influence from tainting the agency, both sides worked to reinforce the system. Publicly, the protection of investors and the prevention of future violations were used to justify the agency's regulatory actions. However, the increase in enforcement and disclosure activities represented an effort by the career staff to bolster the SEC's autonomy—particularly from the executive branch. Strong enforcement actions and tough rules for disclosure rebuilt the agency's reputation for integrity that was tarnished by the Cook and Casey episodes.

That agenda also reinforced the SEC's prestige with Congress as the definitive securities expert. By demonstrating its autonomy from the industry and the White House, the agency staff was able to work closely with the legislative committees to develop the 1975 Securities Acts amendments. The legislation significantly enhanced the agency's authority over the markets and market participants.

The staff received strong support from its congressional legislative committees who also had a stake in maintaining disclosure-enforcement. First, senators and representatives looked to the SEC to handle the growing pains of the securities industry. In the fallout from the back-office crisis, both the industry and Congress were looking for a technical mediator to address developing regulatory issues. Second, Congress wanted to pass legislation to deal with the industry's troubles, and to do so it needed the assistance of the SEC staff. Finally, the committees used the meddling of the Nixon administration as a pretext for supporting the SEC's independence from the executive branch.

The compatibility of congressional and SEC objectives contributed to a statutory increase in the agency's authority; an increase in the agency's oversight of the disclosure process and of the operations of the securities markets; and an enforcement effort that statistically more than doubled the efforts of previous years. The legality of this agenda was questioned by critics of the agency, yet throughout the 1970s the career staff prevailed.

6 Breaking the Rules

*T*he American governmental process, with its elaborate system of checks and balances, contains ample barriers to changing the formal rules that guide regulatory policy. Any presidential effort to alter regulatory policy legislatively requires extensive coalition building and bargaining between the White House and Congress, which is most difficult and rarely succeeds (Peterson 1990, 179–80). This is not to say that presidents cannot bring about—or at least lead a supporting coalition in favor of—significant regulatory change through legislation. Laws to deregulate depository institutions and the trucking, airline, and natural gas industries were passed with the support of President Carter and through earlier efforts by President Ford (Eads and Fix 1984). Yet, as attested by the many failed attempts to pass substantive regulatory reform, legislative changes face an obstacle course of veto points in Congress, where committees have strong means to maintain the status quo (Hammond and Knott 1988), and members of those committees care a great deal about policy outcomes that affect their constituents (Jones 1961; Fenno 1973; Shepsle 1978). Consequently, advocates of change are likely to focus on the rules of regulatory policy that can be amended without new legislation—perhaps through executive order or administrative procedure.

This was the strategy used by the Reagan administration to bring about across-the-board regulatory "relief." Political appointees and staff positions were filled with nontraditional and controversial personnel (Moe 1988), agency rule-making initiatives were pushed to the OMB for review by executive order (Weidenbaum 1984;

Viscusi 1983), and agency leaders used their discretion to set and pursue priorities that deviated from the norm (Miller 1989).

This politicization of regulatory policy was also used in an attempt to change the SEC's behavior. The formal aspects of the disclosure-enforcement framework were formidable barriers; any attempt to alter the securities statutes would have no doubt met swift and stinging opposition in Congress. However, the informal aspects of disclosure-enforcement—interpretation of the statutes and the rules or norms observed in maintaining the approach—were seen as a bit more pliable.

One important rule or norm sustaining the framework was the expectation that appointees to the commission should fit the profile of a securities law expert—they should have a securities law background, and (particularly for a chairman) should have no political connections to the White House during their tenure. Another was that attorneys should play a central role in SEC decision making, while economic analysis was relegated to a minor advisory capacity. Each of these rules was attacked by the Reagan administration in an attempt to alter the content and procedure for decision making in the SEC.

The Reagan administration succeeded somewhat in destabilizing, or at least shaking up, the disclosure-enforcement system—its effort facilitated by budget-deficit politics and intensified partisan disputes between congressional Democrats and the White House. Both factors weakened the ties between the SEC and its legislative committees that had fortified the framework in the previous decade. For example, federal deficit politics reduced the legislative committees' power to determine the SEC budget. Recall that the link between the committees and agency resources had been strengthened in the previous decade by a 1975 provision for a budget reauthorization. However, because there was less money to spend, the authorization had less influence at appropriations time. Further, Democratic members of the legislative committees used the SEC to play partisan politics with a Republican administration. In contrast to the high degree of cooperation between the agency and its committees over the previous decade, this aspect of change perhaps soured the relationship most.

As a result, the direction of federal securities policy was open to debate throughout the much of the 1980s. Chapter 7 will focus on the struggle between the SEC and its legislative committees to shape securities policy in this altered political context. Here my point is to establish the challenge to some of the informal rules of the game that were fundamental to disclosure-enforcement.

The Reagan Agenda and the Transition Team Report

In 1980, segments of the securities industry and business community were looking for less financial regulation. A decade of spiraling inflation and fluctuating interest rates hampered the capacity of issuers and investment bankers to raise needed investment capital (Brooks 1987, 9; *New York Times* 5/6/80, IV 9). In addition, by the late 1970s and early 1980s, the trend toward buying and selling securities on international markets began to have a competitive impact on the U.S. securities industry. Whereas American markets grew at an annual rate of 14 percent between 1978 and 1986, those in Japan and the United Kingdom grew at annual rates of 23 and 18 percent, respectively, during the same period (SEC, *Internationalization of the Securities Markets* 1987, I-3). The SEC's disclosure regulations and enforcement activities throughout the 1970s were seen as additional impediments to America's competitive edge (*New York Times* 10/31/79, IV 1). Discontent within the business community was addressed by the new Reagan administration, which made changing securities regulation a primary goal in its transition team's report.

The Final Report of the SEC Transition Team recommended three significant breaks with the policies of the 1970s. First, it suggested deep cuts in the agency's budget and personnel, contradicting previous congressional recommendations and SEC requests for increases in the agency's budget and staff. Specifically, the report suggested that the agency's budget be reduced in FY 1981 from an authorized and approved $85.5 million to $71 million; in FY 1982 from $98 million to $60 million; and in FY 1983 from $108 million to $53 million (cited in *Securities Regulation and Law Report,* 1/21/81, K-2). The report also recommended a 30 percent reduction in staff over the same three-year period, including the replacement of existing senior staff officials (ibid., K-2, K-17–18). The recommendation was said to promote efficiency and ideological compatibility. In the words of the report:

> At the present time, the leadership of the staff of the Securities and Exchange Commission has . . . remained from previous Democratic administrations. In virtually every area the leadership of the various divisions is unsatisfactory either because of philosophic incompatibilities or competence. . . . Therefore, the new chairman should make sweeping changes in senior staff promptly. (Ibid., K-2)

Second, the report recommended that the activities of the Enforcement Division be scaled back. It suggested a reduction in staff at the Washington headquarters from 200 to 50 over a three-year period; decentralizing the enforcement effort by shifting resources to the regional SEC offices; a more rapid termination of SEC investigations if charges of securities law violations were not imminent; and a shift from the large enforcement efforts (such as prosecution of Wall Street firms or corporations) to individual violations of the securities laws (ibid., K-7–9).

Recommendations to reduce the agency's resources and enforcement activities were a prelude to a third controversial suggestion. Instead of emphasizing the SEC's role as enforcer of the securities laws—the "police" of the markets—the Reagan team suggested that the SEC should instead actively encourage capital investment and accumulation (ibid., K-22–25). The suggestion challenged what was seen as the fundamental role of the SEC and threatened the source of the agency's independent status vis-à-vis the securities industry and corporate issuers of securities. Transforming the agency into a facilitator of capital accumulation would place it among "industry-driven" agencies (as members of the SEC staff call them), making it an advocate of industry interests rather than an independent regulator. For example, in describing the strengths of the agency, a member of the senior staff contrasted the SEC to its counterpart in the futures industry—the Commodity Futures Trading Commission (CFTC): "The SEC is not controlled by any segment of [the securities] industry. The CFTC [on the other hand] is the regulator as well as the chamber of commerce and promoter for the futures industry."

The extent to which the CFTC actually promotes the futures

industry is no doubt open to dispute. What is important here is that SEC personnel have traditionally perceived themselves to be independent of the securities industry, and members of the industry corroborate those sentiments. That perception of autonomy is meaningful largely because of the leverage it has given the agency in the legislative process. Another member of the SEC staff commented on the commission's influence on Capitol Hill, as opposed to the influence of the Federal Energy Regulatory Commission (FERC):

> We are taken seriously because we have no axe to grind. Our work is more respected than, say, FERC. They are industry-driven. When we send a bill [to Congress], from a technical standpoint, no one would suggest anything [about the SEC's motives]. We are a cleaner agency. I say cleaner; I mean less industry-dominated.

In 1981, agency personnel saw the SEC's status as an independent regulator—and, possibly, their own standing with Congress—openly challenged by the transition team's proposals to curtail the agency's enforcement activities and to redefine the agency's role as a promoter of capital accumulation. In other words, the proposals might have made the SEC the "chamber of commerce and promoter" of the securities industry.

These proposals cut to the core of the disclosure-enforcement framework and congressional-SEC relations throughout the 1970s—when there had been support for more enforcement, higher budgets, and greater disclosure. The Reagan administration sought to implement its goals, in large part, by appointing John Shad to be the agency's twenty-second chairman.

The Nomination of John Shad

John Shad's chairmanship (1981–1986) represented a break with the disclosure-enforcement system in three ways. First, throughout his tenure, Shad had ongoing contact with the White House and openly endorsed the administration's plans for deregulation. This overt connection with the executive branch was a source of congressional criticism of particular SEC nominees during the 1970s and was generally discouraged by the legislative committees.

Second, Shad objected to the agency's enforcement-driven regulation of corporate America that had received the support of committee Democrats. Instead, he favored assisting U.S. corporations and Wall Street in capital accumulation.

Third, Shad created his own economics office within the SEC. Whereas attempts to bring economic information to bear on commission decisions had often failed in the past, Shad was somewhat more successful. The use of economic data was controversial within the commission because the economic staff usually disagreed with the agency's legal staff. The economists also brought information to agency decision making that was considered outside the realm of securities law. The use of economic analysis was also disputed by congressional Democrats because economists promoted deregulation in areas where regulation hurt the economic status of powerful constituents.

White House and Wall Street Connections

John Shad was financially connected to the 1980 Reagan election campaign. He served as the chairman of Reagan's finance committee in New York and was the link between candidate Reagan and large financial backers on Wall Street. In 1980, he arranged a meeting between Reagan and members of the New York Stock Exchange (*Washington Post* 2/5/89, A 1). The new chairman was also a long-time contributor to Republican Senate campaigns in New York State. Included on his list of contribution recipients in early 1981 was Republican Senator Alfonse D'Amato (R-N.Y.), then chairman of the Senate Banking Subcommittee on Securities (*New York Times* 2/20/82, 26).

Shad's professional background was in brokerage and investment banking. For twenty years, he had served as vice-chairman of E. F. Hutton and Company (ibid. 4/7/81, IV 6). He held a law degree from New York University (SEC, *Annual Report* 1982, xiii), but, as indicated by his plans for the agency, Shad did not share the perspective of the agency's legal staff and other commissioners. As chairman, he openly supported the Reagan administration's deregulatory agenda, urging that the SEC should become a participant in capital accumulation instead. Further, Shad saw a prominent role for economists in a decision-making process hitherto dominated by lawyers.

Shad's executive branch and Wall Street connections were

points of contention for Democratic committee members. During the 1970s, congressional Democrats sought legislation to protect the SEC's independence from the White House. Recall, for example, that Chairman Moss of the House Subcommittee on Commerce and Finance had introduced legislation to bring the agency's budgetary needs under closer congressional scrutiny and to reduce the influence of the executive branch (*Congressional Quarterly Almanac* 1974, 196). But doubtless Shad's open White House connections also concerned senior members of the SEC staff who had spent the previous decade trying to reinforce the agency's political independence.

Disclosure and Enforcement Under Shad

As SEC chairman, John Shad supported administration proposals to scale back the agency's intervention in the markets. Consider, for example, efforts to implement the 1975 congressional mandate for a national market system. In that legislation, Congress required the SEC to facilitate changes in the structure of the stock markets with the goal of developing a single market for securities. (Chapter 3 examined the SEC's evolutionary approach to this mandate, which was to let the private sector lead the way.) According to SEC staff members, John Shad reinforced this approach. The comments of a senior staffer who served under Shad are indicative: "When Shad became chair, it put the nail in the coffin [of the national market system]. Shad was a deregulator, a child of Wall Street. He would see the national market system come about in an evolutionary sense, and it wouldn't be done by edict!"

What Shad did support was a new role for the SEC. Rather than enforce what he saw as barriers to capital formation, he envisioned the SEC as a participant in the process, a position articulated in the *Report of the SEC Transition Team*. Shortly after taking office, Shad told the *Washington Post* (7/26/81, F 1), "What I'd like to communicate is the things the commission is doing to facilitate capital formation."

According to Shad, the SEC could best support capital formation by cutting back on the amount and kind of information publicly traded companies were required to disclose to the SEC and by refocusing the case load of the Enforcement Division. Both points of this agenda were opposed by legislative committee Democrats, who particularly resisted any shift in the agency's enforcement policies that threatened a valued congressional staple—high-profile cases that often took powerful corporations and Wall Street firms to task.

With respect to the first point, Shad advocated peeling back and integrating agency disclosure requirements that had grown throughout the 1970s. During that time, the agency's staff justified the expansion of mandatory disclosure as a way of providing additional protections to the investing public (*New York Times* 10/5/75, III 1). In contrast, Shad argued that more disclosure—such as information about executive perquisites and a corporation's governing structure—did not necessarily mean better or more useful intelligence for the investing public (*Washington Post* 7/26/81, F 1).

As evidence that disclosure did not help the investor, Chairman Shad pointed to the SEC's "questionable payments" program. The program required companies to come forward voluntarily to report overseas and domestic payments thought to be suspicious—that is, illegal payments to foreign governments for access to the market. By 1977 the SEC reported that more than 400 companies had reported illegal foreign payments (SEC, *Annual Report* 1978, 27). In that same year, however, the director of enforcement and other senior staff members announced that the agency would begin phasing out the voluntary program, implementing its own investigations of questionable payments (*SRLR* 11/9/77, AA 3–4, A 10–11). Committee Democrats were so impressed with the program's results that they introduced legislation to make illegal foreign payments a criminal offense, and the full Congress passed the Foreign Corrupt Practices Act in 1977 (ibid. 7/14/76, A 16; ibid. 12/14/77, A 3).

Chairman Shad argued that the program impeded capital accumulation and was therefore a "competitive problem" for American enterprises (*New York Times* 4/7/81, IV 6). First, he said, the program imposed excessive disclosure requirements on corporations. Second, he argued that the program forced "overkill compliance with disclosure requirements" by private members of the securities bar in an attempt to prevent an SEC investigation (*Washington Post* 7/26/81, F 1). The overly detailed disclosure forms took too much time for the SEC staff to review and contained such an abundance of information that they were more confusing to investors than helpful (*New York Times* 8/3/81, IV 1). Finally, the program promoted the negative aspects of corporations through disclosure. Shad, on the other hand, advocated a role for the SEC in establishing a "positive" image for corporations (ibid. 8/3/81, IV 1).

In advocating a change in the SEC's enforcement procedures, Shad was confronted by members of Congress who opposed any diminution of the agency's efforts. To blunt congressional critics, Shad stressed the continuity between the SEC's past enforcement efforts and those planned for the future. He attempted to do this in two ways.

First, in laying out his priorities for the agency over the next several years, Shad emphasized to the press that the agency's enforcement efforts would be changed only in kind, not in intensity. For example, he wanted to shift resources from a emphasis on large cases that often ended indeterminately—a common situation in the 1970s—to explicit violations of the securities laws by individuals (*Washington Post* 2/14/89, A 1; see also Eads and Fix 1984, 198– 200). Rather than pursue the questionable payment practices of a corporation, for example, the agency would go after individuals who participated in insider trading, market fraud, and market manipulation. Strong enforcement in these areas, he argued, would help to maintain fair and open markets in a deregulated environment (*Washington Post* 7/26/81, F-1).

Second, Shad tried to offset criticism by pointing to the number of cases brought during his first years in office against the number of cases brought in the past. The statistics were strategically released just before a critical appearance by the SEC before the legislative committees (ibid. 10/20/82, D 8; *New York Times* 10/25/82, IV 2) and before a hearing with the House Appropriations Subcommittee (*Washington Post* 2/8/83).[1] The agency's increased case load made it more difficult for critics to argue that the SEC was not continuing the rigorous enforcement policies of previous commissions.

The Office of the Chief Economist

Perhaps more suspect in the eyes of SEC personnel than the introduction of outside influence by elected officials and political parties was the growing prominence of economists among agency decision makers. It is not surprising, therefore, that John Shad's efforts to counterbalance decision making by attorneys with economic analysis was met with resistance and skepticism. In 1982 Shad created the Office of the Chief Economist (OCE) within the chairman's office. Eventually, the OCE's work contributed to the agency's adoption of controversial policy positions that were opposed by members of the legislative committees; consequently, the incorporation of economic analysis became a significant factor in fomenting hostility between some members of the SEC and Congress.

There has been a semblance of an economic staff throughout the agency's history. But in an agency dominated by lawyers, economists have traditionally played an insignificant role. Shad's efforts to alter the status quo were not unique. As I noted in chapter 4, Chairman Roderick Hills created the Directorate of Economic and Policy Research in 1975 (later changed to the Directorate of Economic and Policy Analysis, or DEPA). In a 1976 speech, Hills addressed the need for economists in the SEC: "We must instill in our regulators an appreciation of the therapeutic value of competition and a willingness to temper the lawyers' urge to regulate relentlessly with economic data that tests the need for regulation" (cited in Kripke 1979, 69).

In an interview, Hills reflected on his role in bringing economics into commission decision making:

> I think that anybody who believes that they can or could change the course of events is somewhat arrogant. The timing was good in 1975. A lot of things weren't working in the markets.... A lot of people got excited about the use of economic analysis to deal with these questions, but I think it was a good idea that we began. We got them thinking about it.... When Shad came in, he boosted the role of the economist back up . . . but we made it O.K. to bring economic analysis to bear.

Chairman Hills did inaugurate a role for economic analysis in the agency that was different and new. But his statement that the commission *began* to use economic analysis during his tenure indicates the lack of an institutional history that would reveal the intermittent (and sometimes ad hoc) role played by economists in the agency. Several years before Hills's appointment, the Office of Economic Research and its chief economist actively supported the commission in the policy debates and hearings over fixed commission rates and in the early debates over rule 394.[2] However, according to staff members serving in the agency at the time, that participatory role began to fizzle when a new chairman—Casey—was appointed in 1971.

What has prevented economics from becoming institutionalized in SEC decision making, from playing more than a supportive role, is the pervasive feeling among agency attorneys that the economic staff is somewhat "political"—that their standards depart from those of the legal profession. As one former official and current member of the bar put it, "For lawyers, there are notions that economists can be found on both sides of the fence." In other words, when economic analysis substantiates and supports policy preferred by the staff's attorneys, as in the case of the Office of Economic Research and the commission rate debates, the agency has a use for it; when the two do not mesh, it is viewed as being "on the other side of the fence." The comments of another former SEC official, currently a member of the bar, also reflect the skepticism toward economic analysis that prevails in the agency:

> Many economists are not intrinsically apt to take a broad view. They can take too narrow a view. I remember [a University of Chicago professor] running around arguing that there should be no rule against insider trading. . . . But there are forms of insider trading that the country is not going to put up with, like the owner of a business who sells [his stock] short because he has some information on the company, and then reaps the benefits. . . . Economists tend to stop short of a full calculus, whereas lawyers tend to take the full value into account. They are more trained to take into account the big picture—of which economics is an important part.

More fundamental than the type of policy that economists might support, or the range of variables they might consider relevant, many former and current SEC attorneys view the use of economic analysis as a threat to the agency's entire enforcement approach to regulation. Chapter 4 cited a lawyer who argued that economic analysis had nothing to do with fraud. Similar sentiments were expressed in many interviews. For example, a former SEC official argued:

> [The Directorate of Economic and Policy Analysis staff] were always talking about free market issues that had nothing to do with the commis-

sion's work. [But] they did not ever have much say in the commission's decision making, and I don't think that has changed.... It was partly political. People [in the SEC] don't go for the free market ideas. But it is a regulatory agency. Theoretical economics has very little to do with the commission's work. The SEC deals with investor confidence, and economic theory has nothing to do with investor confidence.

And the comments of another former staff attorney reiterate what many see as the irrelevant application of economic analysis in an agency charged with enforcing disclosure—regardless of the costs: "Why, if I'm a lawyer, would I care if it costs the industry more to disclose "X" instead of "X − 1"? If there are costs, tough nuggies. Lawyers view economics as irrelevant to their statutory mandate."

Commissioners and chairmen have tried to incorporate economic analysis to bolster or substantiate policy, and they have reorganized existing economic staff, or created a new office and brought in new economists, to do so. Based on his experience as head of the president's deregulatory task force, Roderick Hills established the Directorate of Economic and Policy Analysis to bring to bear what he saw as additional and necessary information on the agency's decision making—or to "temper the lawyers' urge to regulate relentlessly." Yet, again, because economic analysis is viewed as a threat to the preeminence of legal decision making in general, and to the agency's disclosure-enforcement framework in particular, the DEPA engendered tremendous animosity among the legal staff, and its influence was random, at best. A former member of the economics staff recalled commission meetings in which a senior SEC staffer was always quick to correct anyone who spoke of the *directorate* as equivalent to a regulatory *division*.

Indeed, the kind of commission work that became routine for DEPA reflected its somewhat second-class status. Eventually, DEPA's primary activity was the perfunctory performance of "flex regs"—statistical analyses of an SEC rule to determine its impact on small businesses (SEC, *Annual Report* 1976, 167). A former member of the economic staff recalled that DEPA would occasionally be brought into a commission debate when its positions were appropriate or "lined up" with the position of one division director over another's. However, the comments by a former economic staffer indicate that research and analyses done by DEPA was, for the most part, kept outside the rule-making process: "[We did] mostly mundane things, publishing monthly statistical rules, reviewing rules recommended by other divisions to study the economic effect on regulated entities. Wherever possible, we tried to get in earlier, before [an SEC] rule was recommended."

In an effort to counter the experience of DEPA, Chairman Shad set out to make the new Office of the Chief Economist (OCE) an integral part of commission decision making, as Hills had intended to do with DEPA. Shad hired Charles Cox, a University of Chicago Ph.D., to head the office, as well as two professional research staffers. In his 1983 confirmation hearing (to be discussed later), Cox noted the differences between what had become the work of the directorate and what Chairman Shad was trying to achieve with the OCE:

> I would describe it as follows: the Office of the Chief Economist is organized to bring economists with the latest and most technical training in economics to work on Commission projects. The other division, the Directorate of Economic and Policy Analysis, . . . has a number of tasks of a statistical nature, of ongoing monitoring of a sort different from concentrated research on specific commission issues. (*Cox's Confirmation Hearing* 1983, 10)

Despite the research orientation of the new office, as well as Shad's efforts to hire economists with the "latest and most technical training," the Office of the Chief Economist initially contributed little to agency decision making for three basic reasons. First, according to staff members who were with the SEC at the time, agency personnel assumed that there was no clear difference between DEPA and the new office. Because DEPA's work was typically seen as irrelevant to the role of the commission, the agency's legal staff also assumed that the OCE would not provide useful or pertinent analyses. Second, the OCE was a very small operation within the SEC. At first, it consisted only of the chief economist, two additional professional staff members, and two support staff. Touching on both of these points, one staff member described the legal staff's resistance to the OCE:

> There was the lawyers' hostility toward economists [in general]. Also, [lawyers] have not received good quality advice over the long run. There are several hundred attorneys. They could go to the elite group

[the OCE] without enough staff, or they could get junk from DEPA. The result was the staff wasn't getting economic analysis that was good.

As this staffer indicated, the third—and perhaps most important—reason for the OEC's initial lack of influence was the lawyers' obvious hostility toward economics as a source of policy advice, regardless of the quality of the research. A former member of the economic staff described that antagonism and the reluctance of attorneys to come to OCE for consultation:

> People could walk in the door and ask for information, but I don't remember anyone doing that. . . . There was this sense, better not to get too involved with the economists [because] they might start asking questions people didn't want to answer. [The legal staff wanted] to keep the economists from changing the rules. . . . Economists were viewed as people to cause trouble.

Despite opposition, however, John Shad encouraged and supported the research of the OCE. Further, in interviews, several of Shad's fellow commissioners acknowledged using OCE research in their decision making—although not necessarily to the extent that Shad would have preferred. Though many of the agency's former and current personnel continued to speak of the irrelevance of economic analysis for an enforcement agency, members of the economic staff and several attorneys interviewed believed that Shad's efforts did result in carving out a new role for economics within the SEC. One member of the economic staff described Shad's support of the office and its incorporation into decision making:

> Particularly under John Shad, we had power and influence out of proportion to our numbers. Something could be turned around by a memo [from our office]. A rule [wouldn't] even come up if everyone knew five commissioners [were] going to vote against it. The commission was extremely receptive to arguments we made, even if controversial. [Disagreement] was encouraged, even at the staff level. The [legal] staff [of a division] would present a unified front for "more regulation," but if another office [was] opposed . . . the commissioner [had] something to hang his hat on. Controversy was encouraged under Shad.

In later years, the more aggressive and professional OCE staff also took on controversial issues that the commission had not ad-

dressed in the past. Of particular concern to the legislative committees were its analyses of corporate takeovers and the multiple trading of options contracts—investment instruments that give the
buyer the right, but not the obligation, to buy or sell securities at a
specified price in the future (see Teweles and Bradley 1987, 504).
The former issue pitted the targets of takeover attempts, such as the
Fortune 500 firms, against financiers and corporate "raiders."[3] The
latter issue pitted against each other stock and options exchanges
that would have to compete under multiple trading. At the time,
options contracts on any given security or index were traded exclusively on one exchange as allocated by the SEC.

Economic analysis supported the idea of liberalizing corporate
takeovers as well as the multiple listing of options. As a result, the
role of economists in the SEC became a point of contention not
only for the agency's legal staff, but also for members of the legislative committees whose constituents were associated with Fortune
500 firms and markets holding a monopoly on the trading of a
particular options contract.[4] The SEC's enforcement campaign during the 1970s was also highly controversial for the businesses under
the agency's scrutiny. However, in the 1970s both the SEC and the
Democratic majority on the legislative committees gained from that
agenda, whereas in the 1980s, the preferences of both were somewhat frustrated by Shad and the OCE staff.

Efforts to incorporate economic research in SEC decision making and Shad's new disclosure and enforcement policies were facilitated somewhat by the chairman's willingness to depart from the
norm in his nominations to fill two key SEC positions. In both
instances, the candidates faced harsh congressional scrutiny.

Changes in Agency Personnel

During the 1970s, the SEC career staff was well represented on the
commission. For example, commissioners Philip Loomis and Irving
Pollack, both former SEC career staffers, served from 1971 to 1981
and from 1974 to 1980, respectively. Both were staunch defenders
of staff initiatives during their tenure, particularly the activities of
the Enforcement Division (*New York Times* 12/11/81, D 2; ibid.
5/30/80, IV 2). The opening of a commissionership in 1982, as well
as the departure of Stanley Sporkin, director of enforcement, left

strategic gaps for Shad and the White House to fill. However, they broke with what had become convention—a tradition critical for the maintenance of disclosure-enforcement—for the agency and its legislative committees in the selection process.

From Stanley Sporkin to John Fedders

In 1981 Stanley Sporkin, director of enforcement since 1974, announced he was leaving the SEC to become general counsel of the CIA.[5] The activities of the Enforcement Division under Sporkin were criticized in the transition team's report. Specifically, the report recommended replacing Sporkin, scaling back the director's authority, and reducing the resources of the division (*SRLR*, 1/21/81, K-7–9).

As director, Sporkin spearheaded the agency's program monitoring questionable corporate payments. He was also visibly connected with Democratic leaders on the legislative committees who supported the agency's enforcement agenda.[6] Therefore, perhaps more than any other representative of the agency, Sporkin had been closely identified with SEC activism throughout the 1970s (*New York Times* 6/16/81, D 1). Former members of the SEC staff referred to the 1970s as the era of "Sporkinism." One even commented that under Sporkin "the enforcement staff was very—I don't want to say religious—but very committed." It was that activism, or sense of mission, that the Reagan administration opposed.

If Shad had followed agency precedent, a logical replacement for Sporkin would have been Theodore Levine, one of the division's associate directors. Sporkin had himself been an associate director under Irving Pollack before the latter was nominated to the commission (SEC, *Annual Report* 1973, v), and this pattern of succession had existed within the division for years.[7] In addition to precedent, there was pressure from the Senate Banking Committee to choose a director who would carry on the enforcement practices established under Sporkin (*Washington Post* 4/22/81, E 1, e).

But Shad was interested in changing agency precedent. He hired John Fedders from the Washington law firm of Arnold and Porter (*SRLR* 7/1/81, A 1). Fedders was a controversial choice within the agency and the legislative committees for two reasons. First, as an "outsider," his nomination broke with the old pattern of succession. Second, Fedders was a corporate lawyer specializing in economic crimes, and in his practice he defended several corporations against charges under the Foreign Corrupt Practices Act (*New York Times* 6/30/81, IV 1). The conflict was obvious: Fedders was replacing the initiator of the questionable payments program, endorsed by Congress, while he himself had previously worked to prevent the government from bringing charges of corrupt payments against clients.

The Nomination of Charles Cox

In another break with precedent, John Shad pushed for the nomination of Charles Cox, the agency's chief economist, to the commission. The choice was controversial among members of the legislative committees and within the SEC because Cox did not fit the profile of a securities law expert.

Democratic members of the Senate Banking Committee used Cox's qualifications—his training as an economist rather than a lawyer—as a reason to oppose his candidacy (*Cox's Confirmation Hearing* 1983, 6–10). They were joined in public opposition by SEC commissioners James Treadway, Bevis Longstreth, and Barbara Thomas, who argued that the job required technical and legal expertise that Cox lacked (ibid., 6; *SRLR* 11/11/83, 2065). (Not surprisingly, each of the commissioners did fit the "expert" profile: they had all practiced securities law before their nomination; all had affiliations with prestigious New York and Washington firms and served on ABA committees; all had experience with the agency's regulatory procedures; and none had obvious political connections to the White House.)[8] As a former member of the economic staff put it, they wanted "to keep economists from changing the rules." Members of the Senate and the commissioners were also concerned about how Cox might vote: given Shad's endorsement, he would be expected to push the chairman's deregulatory agenda (*Washington Post* 7/14/83, A 13). As a former SEC official and participant in the debate recalled, "[Cox] was not well liked on the Hill because he was viewed as a Reagan ideologue, as extremely inflexible."

Throughout the 1970s, most of the agency's commissioners had a securities law background.[9] One exception was John Evans, who served for ten years (1973–1983) after serving as a minority staff member on the Senate Banking Committee. Interestingly, Evans was not a lawyer, but had an undergraduate degree in economics before joining the Senate Banking staff (SEC, *Annual Report* 1982, xiii). Yet he received bipartisan endorsements for his nomination in 1973 and his renomination in 1978 (*New York Times* 5/5/83, IV 1). Apparently, the fact that he was a former staff member whose regulatory preferences and priorities were well known overrode any Senate concerns about his lack of a securities law background. Further, Evans's ten-year voting record no doubt allayed apprehensions within the agency about having an economist, rather than a lawyer, on the commission. A former enforcement official called him a "great" commissioner because he supported the Enforcement Division: "Evans was sensational. He was an economist, but he was supportive of enforcement."

And when asked if Evans used economic analysis in his decision making, a former member of the agency's economic staff said that Evans was "less likely" than other commissioners to do so, adding, "On a number of occasions, he would even oppose the [DEPA]. He was very much a regulator."

The nomination of Cox, on the other hand, signaled a different direction in agency policy that was opposed by Democratic members of the legislative committees and the SEC staff. A former SEC attorney discussed the Cox nomination in terms of the potential "harm" he might have done to the agency: "As a member of the securities bar, Cox's appointment was seen as an attempt to jettison someone [John Evans] who had ten years of experience [with the agency]. It was seen as harm to the agency. Cox was a lightning rod."

From the time Shad established the OCE, the incorporation of economic data in agency decision making usually worked in favor of deregulating the securities industry. For example, a 1982 OCE study contributed to commission support of "shelf registration," or SEC rule 415 (see chapter 4). Basically, large corporations were allowed to register a new issue of stock with the agency, but to distribute the issue in pieces (without reregistration) when market conditions were most favorable. The rule released corporations from some of the SEC's registration and disclosure requirements that had multiplied during the previous decade. But the potential consequences of deregulation riled important members of the legislative committees and their constituents—such as the investment bankers whose syndicate operations were threatened by shelf registration and the smaller regional firms who participated in the new issue market through the syndicate distribution system (*Wall Street Journal* 2/22/82, 16).[10] The nomination of Cox—a professional economist—was seen by committee Democrats and SEC staffers as

a guarantee that economic data would play an increasingly important role in commission decisions.

Implications for Disclosure-Enforcement

The Reagan administration set out a series of objectives for regulating securities that challenged established SEC strategies. However,
rather than try to work within the rules of the disclosure-enforcement framework to change the SEC's behavior, the administration
tried to change or undermine many of the rules themselves.

The nomination of John Shad was the first cut at the framework.
Shad's White House and Wall Street connections challenged the
expectation that the nominees would be politically independent of
the administration as well as the industry. Through Shad, the administration hoped to bring about some of the changes outlined in the
transition team's report. For example, rather than having the SEC
continue in its traditional role as policeman of the securities markets, the administration proposed, and Shad endorsed the idea, that
it should promote capital accumulation. The agency's enforcement
campaign of the 1970s had enhanced the SEC's independence, and
its investigations were popular with Democrats in Congress. The
new role proposed for the SEC, therefore, directly contradicted the
incentives driving the SEC staff and the expectations of its legislative committees.

A second cut at the disclosure-enforcement framework was the
incorporation of economic data in agency decision making by Chairman Shad, who sought to advance his deregulatory agenda by creat-
ing the Office of the Chief Economist. Studies produced by the
office were often controversial because they supported changes
that threatened the economic status of key congressional constituents: OCE support for liberalizing corporate takeovers threatened
the status of Fortune 500 firms; OCE support for multiple trading of
options threatened the incomes of regional exchanges; and OCE
support for shelf registration threatened the standing of investment
bankers.

A third assault on the framework was the choice of Cox for
commissioner. This again broke with the tradition, reinforced in the
1970s, that commission nominees should have a securities law back-

ground and consequently work within the disclosure-enforcement framework. Opposition to Cox focused on his credentials as well as his anticipated voting behavior and likely support of Shad's deregulatory policies.

Finally, Shad's selection of Fedders broke with the tradition that a director of enforcement should come from within the agency. Bringing in someone from outside made it more probable that Shad would succeed in shifting enforcement resources away from large cases to individual violators of the securities laws. The SEC's enforcement policies in the 1970s were backed by Democrats on the legislative committees, in part, because of the publicity value of its high-profile cases.

The administration's attempt to undermine the informal rules of disclosure-enforcement were facilitated by two significant political changes in the 1980s. Budget deficit politics weakened the connection between the legislative committees and the SEC's resources (crucial to maintaining disclosure-enforcement), and the SEC became a tool in the partisan conflict between congressional Democrats and a Republican administration. This was in contrast to the previous decade when pledges by members of the legislative committees to increase the agency's budget had credence and the agency cooperated with Congress to establish its independence from the White House.

Deficit Concerns

Beginning with John Shad's tenure, SEC funding fell victim to the new federal deficit politics. In the early 1980s, the agency was the target of severe budget cuts proposed by the administration. Given the passage of the Gramm-Rudman-Hollings Deficit Reduction Act in 1985, the agency had to contend with new decision guidelines used by the House and Senate appropriations subcommittees having jurisdiction over the SEC: according to committee staff members, there was a shift toward across-the-board spending cuts and less consideration of parochial requests. As a result, the SEC's authorization—passed by the legislative committees—became a less powerful means of congressional influence over of the agency and its enforcement framework.

Doing "More With Less"

Early efforts by the Reagan administration to cut the SEC's budget were strenuously opposed by a majority of the agency's commissioners. In a 1981 *Washington Post* editorial (10/16/81, A 27), Commissioner Barbara Thomas argued against a proposed 12 percent reduction in the agency's 1983 fiscal budget and presented evidence that agency resources were already thinly stretched:

> The SEC already is operating with a very lean staff. The entire commission today numbers only 1,930, a mere 15 percent larger than it was in 1941. . . . Indeed, the staff today is actually slightly smaller than it was in 1975, despite the fact that Congress that year amended the securities laws to increase substantially the commission's responsibilities in a number of areas.

Thomas proceeded to list how a 12 percent reduction would effect the work of the agency. She projected closing several regional and branch offices of the SEC; significantly reducing the agency's enforcement staff at a time when, because of Shad's deregulatory efforts, a strong police effort was essential; and cutting the quality and quantity of the agency's oversight of disclosure.

In testimony before the House appropriations subcommittee that oversees the SEC budget, Thomas was joined in opposition by Commissioner Evans and, surprisingly, by Chairman Shad (ibid. 10/28/81, D 8). However, by 1983, there was a clear division between Chairman Shad and the other four commissioners as to the agency's resource needs. For FY 1984, Shad supported a 3 percent increase in the agency's budget over the previous year, but this actually meant a 6 percent reduction in SEC personnel because the number of staff years allocated to the agency would be reduced from a high of 1,982 to 1,795 (ibid. 2/8/83, D-9). The latter figure represented the benchmark set by the OMB for the year. Shad argued that improvements in the agency's efficiency allowed the SEC to cut these positions without jeopardizing its oversight or enforcement responsibilities (ibid.; Senate Banking Committee, *SEC Reauthorization Hearing* 1983, 106–07).

Shad's optimistic assessment of the agency's ability to operate under budget constraints was not shared by commissioners Thomas, Treadway, Longstreth, and Evans. Their view of the agency's needs had an ally in the House Energy and Commerce Committee. In a letter to Chairman Timothy Wirth (D-Colo.) of the House Subcommittee on Finance and Communications, the four commissioners argued that a 4 percent *increase* in the number of staff positions was necessary to boost the agency's staff years to 2,099. They wrote:

> We have concluded that a 6 percent cut in staff positions would make it exceedingly difficult to maintain a satisfactory presence in each of the important areas of our responsibility ... At the present funding level, we are stretched thin—so thin, in fact, that we have concluded it is the minimum responsible staffing level. (*Washington Post* 3/22/83, C 7)

Shad's endorsement of a staff reduction, and the opposition by a commission majority to that cut, created a furor among Democrats on the House Energy and Commerce Committee. Wirth, in particular, accused Shad of "deregulation through attrition" (*New York Times* 11/7/83, IV 1) and charged that his proposed cuts reflected a shift in the agency's determination to police the securities markets (*Washington Post* 4/22/83, C 7). Representative Wirth noted that such slacking threatened investor confidence during a market downturn (ibid. 3/14/83, WB 3).

These same concerns for preserving the agency's enforcement efforts were expressed by Democrats and Republicans alike on the Senate Banking Committee. In a 1983 hearing to authorize funding for the agency, senators questioned Shad on the agency's ability to enforce its mandate with the amount of resources requested. For example, Senator Paul Sarbanes (D-Md.) stated that the purpose of the reauthorization hearing was twofold:

> First, is the commission performing properly and effectively its essential responsibilities to protect the investors and insure the integrity of our capital markets? ... Second, what authorization is needed to enable the [SEC] to do its job responsibly and effectively? Now that job includes, among other things, compelling full and fair disclosure to investors of all the material facts ... [and] correcting unfair practices in the securities market, including the prevention and suppression of fraud. (Senate Banking Committee, *SEC Reauthorization Hearing* 1983, 113)

Sarbanes then pointed out that the other four commissioners opposed Shad on resources and called for an increase in the commission's budget to serve the public interest. Referring to Shad's budget request for the agency, Sarbanes added, "Such a budget, of course, has not been proposed" (ibid.).

In the same hearing, Senator Alfonse D'Amato (R-N.Y.) commended the commission for its gains in efficiency, but was skeptical about the adequacy of Shad's request. After stating that he wanted to ressolve the discrepancies between Shad's projections and those of the other four commissioners, he continued: "We're not going to jeopardize the quality of the SEC at this point in time.... For the lack of $3 or $4 million, I just think we do a terrible disservice to a body that's just too important to the integrity of the industry. The industry doesn't mind tight, tough enforcement. They want it to be fair, tight" (ibid., 120–21). Such bipartisan endorsement of the SEC is important. First, the agency's enforcement efforts provided members with a flow of cases that had tremendous publicity value. Second, by supporting the SEC's Enforcement Division, members could address market fraud and manipulation without altering the regulatory structure. Finally, as indicated in the above comments of Senator D'Amato, the securities industry itself championed strong enforcement efforts.

Wall Street's support for enforcement was substantiated in interviews with industry representatives as well as SEC personnel. For example, a former SEC commissioner and current member of the bar noted, "Most feel that it is in their best interest to have a strong SEC that is well staffed with a good budget." Those sentiments were echoed by another former SEC commissioner, a lawyer, who said, "The SEC is a cop on the beat. It is effective basically because the industry thinks there *should* be a tough cop on the beat." And a current counsel for a major brokerage firm affirmed his company's support for well-policed markets:

> If I put on my business hat here ... and we go to a company to do an underwriting, and we find out two years later that the company's books were fraudulent, that's not good. I want that company to know that there is a tough and vigilant SEC that makes the world [of finance] work.

Members of both the House and Senate committees have used the promise of greater funds and staff positions for the SEC to show their approval of the agency's activities. However, Shad's willingness to work within the parameters set by the OMB attenuated that connection.

Members of the House Energy and Commerce Committee tried to reassert their influence by demonstrating that there was indeed a need for larger budgets. Chairman John Dingell (D-Mich.) of the House Energy and Commerce Committee authorized a General Accounting Office study of the SEC's disclosure and enforcement efforts. Dingell was looking for evidence that a lack of resources was hampering the agency's enforcement of the securities laws. The GAO report, released in 1986, gave him the ammunition he wanted. It reported declines in the SEC's review of disclosure documents filed with the agency and in the number of enforcement actions brought by the SEC in 1985 compared to a similar period in 1978 (*Washington Post* 8/20/86, B 1).

A senior House staff member who recalled Shad's support for staff cuts in 1985 said that Dingell ordered the GAO study because the committee was suspicious of Shad's efficiency claims. In his words, "Shad was always saying they were doing 'more with less,' and Dingell said it was 'less with less.' GAO reports proved it. They looked at how ineffective enforcement was at the time."

Over the loud protests of the House and Senate legislative committees, the agency's final appropriation for FY 1984 was only a $1 million increase over the amount recommended by the OMB. The House Energy and Commerce Committee and the Senate Banking Committee authorized $102 and $99.5 million, respectively (*Congressional Quarterly Almanac* 1983), and the appropriated amount stood at $93 million. That amount could have reflected the appropriations subcommittees' growing concerns about the federal deficit. By the mid-1980s, the constraints of Gramm-Rudman-Hollings increased the likelihood that the appropriations subcommittees would subordinate the parochial concerns of individual authorizing committees—represented by the authorizations they passed.

The SEC Authorization and Across-the-Board Cuts

The 1975 amendments to the Securities Exchange Act contained, for the first time, an authorization for the SEC by the House and Senate legislative committees (*SRLR*, supplement to 5/21/75, 32). The authorization gave the committees some leverage in dealing with the agency through its resources, as well as a way to encourage its enforcement activities.

On the first point, the legislative committees were required to authorize funding before money could be appropriated. This meant that to secure supplemental funding over an authorized amount, the agency had to request it from the legislative committees. The provision also gave the committees a means to increase funding and staff levels for the agency's Enforcement Division. In 1973, for example, members of the House Subcommittee on Finance and Communications (later changed to Telecommunications and Finance) set a goal of doubling the staff over a five-year period (*SRLR* 5/16/73, A 13).

However, the legislative committees' power to influence the SEC's budget through reauthorization faced a formidable and obvious constraint: final action by the House and Senate appropriations subcommittees. Between 1977 and 1980, final appropriations for the SEC decreased significantly from what the House and Senate authorized. For FY 1977, the House Interstate and Foreign Commerce Committee and the Senate Banking Committee each authorized $56.5 million, but the final appropriation was $53 million. Though the Senate authorization for 1978 coincided with the agency's final appropriation at $58.3 million, the House had authorized $63.7 for the year. In 1979, the discrepancy between House and Senate authorizations and the ultimate appropriation was nearly $6 million, and for FY 1980 the difference exceeded $10 million (*Congressional Quarterly Almanac* 1976–1979).

Throughout the early 1980s, the predominant concern of the Reagan administration (and, in later years, of Congress) to reduce government spending further mitigated the influence of the authorization. Working under the constraints of Gramm-Rudman-Hollings, members of the appropriations committees became more willing to consider across-the-board cuts that would have been less likely in the 1970s. Consequently, whereas the authorization might once have been a prominent part of the information considered in an appropriations decision, its significance was overwhelmed by larger considerations. This complicated the connection between the legislative committees and the SEC, and consequently weakened their mutual support of disclosure-enforcement.

The prominence of such macro-level concerns was described by a staff member on the Senate Appropriations Subcommittee for Commerce, State, Justice, the Judiciary, and Related Agencies, who noted the difficulty of restoring programs cut by the OMB during a decade of fiscal restraint. He contrasted the work of the committee in the 1980s to that of the previous decade:

> In the 1970s, the appropriations subcommittee gave the SEC more than the OMB did. One or two times we increased the official SEC budget [the OMB version]. During the eighties [however], we have had these cuts, and we have had to trim everything else to put back in [other] cut programs.

A staff member of the House Appropriations Subcommittee, with similar jurisdiction, also observed a change in the role of the Senate Appropriations subcommittee during the 1980s. Contrasting the two subcommittees, he said: "In the past . . . the Senate Appropriations Committee served more as an appeals body for agencies, but in recent years it has changed its role. It's more similar to what we do."

If, as the Senate staff member noted, it was easier to restore cuts by the administration during the 1970s, that also gave that subcommittee more opportunity to act as an appeals court for parochial concerns. According to the House staffer just cited, tight budgets also made it less practical for members of the House Appropriations Committee to consider SEC policies when making allocations. When asked if the committee's decision making were driven by policy factors or budget constraints, he replied: "To some extent, both. [But] during the 1980s, we have been faced with tight allocations, so budget constraints have driven a lot of things."

A recent round of the budget process showed the continuing force of those constraints: specifically, the need to reduce overall government expenditures prevented the committee from fulfilling individual agency requests. Again, in his words, "[This last year] was the tightest we had seen and it was getting tighter and tighter. Under the circumstances, where we are not going to give *everyone* some help, we are more likely to pare back." To avoid implementing cuts mandated under Gramm-Rudman-Hollings, Congress and the administration negotiated spending cuts in budget summits during the 1980s. These sessions restricted the flexibility of the appropriations process. House and Senate appropriations committee members were encouraged to stick to negotiated spending levels and were discouraged from considering individual requests. For example, in the 1987 budget summit between the administration and Congress, negotia-tors agreed to a 2 percent across-the-board increase for non–defense-related expenditures. According to a member of the Senate staff, the increase accounted only for a federal pay raise. The compro-mise neglected expenditures such as the capital necessary to make a new federal prison project operational, for the national census, and for replacing weather satellites: "Then, to also put back in what the administration had cut, we ended up giving every agency 1 percent. That's what we originally gave the SEC," he remarked.

The impact of Gramm-Rudman-Hollings altered the SEC's rela-tionship with its authorizing and appropriating committees. For example, the SEC's Executive Director's Office had traditionally been the contact point for the House and Senate appropriations subcommittees. As of 1974, the director of Congressional Relations (now the Office of Legislative Affairs, or OLA) was created to handle all other contacts with the Congress.[11] However, Gramm-Rudman-Hollings complicated this arrangement: agency leaders began to assert that, given the appropriations subcommittees' power to un-dercut the agency with across-the-board reductions, the OLA and commissioners should cultivate a more substantial relationship with members of those committees. A senior member of the SEC staff commented, "I have a lot of contact with the authorization committees. . . . It's the lack of contact with the appropriations com-mittees that is our failing at the SEC. It's schizophrenic, just like Congress has a schizophrenic approach to dealing with the SEC budget," referring to the separate authorization and appropriations processes. "The budget process is handled out of the Executive Director's Office. They are not politicians," he concluded.

The OLA plays a mixed role. It is the eyes and ears of the SEC vis-à-vis Congress, an advocate, and a clearinghouse for information. Apparently, this staff member did not think the budget personnel in the Executive Director's Office were equipped to carry out all these tasks.

However, by the end of the decade the commission began to bridge this gap by making a few direct contacts with the appropria-tions subcommittees in addition to those contacts made through the Executive Director's Office. In 1988 SEC Chairman Ruder went di-rectly to the Senate Appropriations Subcommittee to lobby for in-creased funds. In spite of an authorization of $172 million for FY 1989, the SEC's projected appropriation (determined by budget negotiations between the Congress and the administration) threatened to reduce that amount by $30 million. Given the severity of the budget cut, the SEC chairman decided to plead the agency's case directly. One SEC senior staffer expressed the general frustration when he said that the authorizing committees dealt with "funny money," because "you can't spend it. . . . It's the appropriations committees that control the money."

Congressional staffers indicated that this kind of direct dealing by the chairman had helped the SEC secure additional funds over the past few years and that Chairman Ruder's lobbying efforts got the agency an additional $13 million for FY 1989. That "success" prompted agency leaders to make further adjustments in their relations with the appropriations committees. One SEC official commented:

> Contact is fairly limited. The staff of the Executive Director's Office is in close contact with the staff of the subcommittee for our appropriations. We are a comparatively small agency, so we have to make judgments about how pesky to be [in Congress]. . . . The judgment has been that the benefits from a lot of direct contact [with Appropriations] would not be great. I saw the head of the subcommittee twice in two years, and it was clear that there wasn't a lot of give in the budget process, not a lot of flexibility. [However,] I would like to make contact with Appropriations more of a priority.

To recapitulate, the new budgetary restrictions reduced the authorization committees' control over agency resources. Gross spending targets, rather than legislative committee justifications for authorized funds, dominated the appropriations process. In the case of the budget summit outcomes, a minuscule across-the-board increase of 1 percent was drastic enough to force the SEC chairman to break with precedent and to negotiate directly, while the authorizing committees were insignificant participants in the process.

Partisan Politics

The Reagan administration's efforts to alter the disclosure-enforcement framework were also facilitated by an increase in partisan politics that frustrated the lines of communication and trust between the SEC and its legislative committees. A senior SEC staff member, with the agency since the mid-1970s, discussed the agency's relationship with Congress over the last fourteen years: "It's much more political, much more partisan. In the late seventies, we had a Democratic administration and Democratic Congress. Now we have a Republican administration and Democratic Congress. It's set up to be more partisan, more politicized."When asked to elaborate, he continued: "The Congress says, 'What can we do to make an agency, with a chairman appointed by a Republican president, look bad?' " For Democratic members of the House Energy and Commerce Committee, he said, the SEC became a vehicle for opposing the Republican administration.

Another senior official noted a similar change in relations between both House and Senate Democrats and the agency. She said that in the course of regular contact with the SEC, members of the House and Senate committees used to try to embarrass the OMB and the administration. Recalling reauthorization hearings during John Shad's tenure in which Democrats used the SEC's budget requests as a point of contention, she described how Representative Dingell and Senator Riegle (D-Mich.) demanded of SEC officials, "Why don't you ask for more money?" as a way of getting to the OMB.

The use of the SEC as a focal point for partisan politics contributed to the increasingly contentious relationship between the agency and Democratic committee members. In interviews, both SEC and Capitol Hill staffers were quick to attribute this swelling in hostile relations to the partisanship of particular individuals. For example, on the influence of House Energy and Commerce members over the nomination of commissioners, a senior congressional staffer indicated the degree of conflict between committee chairman Dingell and the Reagan White House. She said, "Sometimes, if Dingell doesn't like someone, that's enough to get them nominated!" A senior SEC staff member agreed: "If John Dingell says it's Monday, then by definition it is Tuesday at the Reagan White House!" Both saw that the conflict between Dingell and the administration had consequences for the SEC.

In another example, a House staffer with previous experience in the SEC attributed the changed relationship between Congress and the SEC to the partisan leanings of John Shad. When he was with the agency, "the Commission operated with much less political influence" from the White House. However, when Harold Williams (1977–1981) was replaced by Shad, "it was a whole new ball game. It was because Shad was chair, not something directed from the Hill or the White House." During the 1970s, contacts with the executive branch had been discouraged and deemphasized following the Nixon administration's attempts to interfere with ongoing SEC investigations. Apparently, it was Shad's willingness to work with the White House agenda that made his tenure somewhat unique. White House and congressional pressures always exist for the agency, according to this staff member, but Shad's Republican sentiments made him a source of administration influence over agency policy.[12]

An SEC staff member also identified Shad's partisanship as the source of conflict between House Democrats and the SEC: "A lot of the increase [in partisan politics] was that tension between those two men, [John] Dingell and [John] Shad. . . . Part of the blame goes to the administration and Shad. While he was independent, he made no secret he would keep the budget down to please the White House."

However, others saw the partisanship of individuals—Shad and Dingell, in particular—as reflecting a broader pattern. Specifically, Democrats on the House Energy and Commerce Committee and on the Senate Banking Committee opposed the deregulatory agenda of the Republican Reagan administration. A former staffer from the Senate Banking Committee described Democratic members' apprehension regarding the trend toward sweeping deregulation that was affecting many different policy areas. He referred to a hearing in which an administration witness said, while testifying before the Banking Committee on housing deregulation: "If you really want the housing industry to take off, don't require them to build sewers." As he recalled, the senators "wanted to throw tomatoes at him! Senators were very concerned."

John Shad was closely allied to the executive branch. As indicated in an earlier quote, "He made no secret he would keep the budget down to please the White House." He also made no secret about his compatibility with the White House in promoting deregulation. The SEC was therefore an obvious focus for Democrats who were "concerned" about the administration's broader agenda. A senior House staffer described an early confrontation between Representative Dingell and Chairman Shad. Apparently, Dingell used the committee's authority to oversee the SEC, and the close alliance between the administration and Shad, to drive home the Democratic position:

> Early in 1981, Dingell had a meeting with Shad and Wirth [then chairman of the Finance and Commerce Subcommittee]. Shad was coming over to do the "glad-handing." Dingell laid the letter out to him. He expected him to enforce the securities laws, and he said [the SEC should be] independent of the executive and the OMB. He expressed this in no uncertain terms to Shad.

Again, to the degree that partisan politicking frustrated relations between the SEC and its legislative committees, the barriers to disclosure-enforcement were perhaps made more vulnerable for the administration.

Summary Remarks

The Reagan administration set out to reduce the regulation of securities by breaking the rules of the game. They challenged disclosure-enforcement by departing from the norms that had maintained the framework. Their efforts were facilitated by the destabilization of congressional-SEC relations brought on by budget deficit politics and partisan disputes. Whether or not the administration succeeded in altering the framework, even temporarily, is debatable, and the question will be pursued in chapter 7. What is important here is that the administration caused sufficient trauma between the SEC and its legislative committees to throw the direction of securities policy temporarily into dispute.

7 Expertise and Legislating for Control: The SEC and Congress

*P*erhaps the best way to assess the independent impact of an agency in determining policy outcomes is to examine conflicts between the "experts" and their political overseers. When there is disagreement between an agency and its legislative committees, who wins, and why? Obviously, strategic preferences and posturing by various political actors make it difficult to assess true priorities (Miller and Moe 1983; Bendor, Taylor, and van Gaalen 1987; Ferejohn and Shipan 1988). But, when there is conflict, the revealed preferences of bureaucrats and elected officials that contrast with policy outcomes can be very enlightening.

Federal securities policy was put into play following efforts by the Reagan administration to change the way the SEC did business, by several years of budget deficit politics, and by partisan bickering that sent shock waves through the relationship between the SEC and its legislative committees. Several commissioners appointed by the Reagan administration worked to diminish federal regulations regarding the disclosure of material information, corporate takeovers, the trading of options contracts, and the enforcement emphasis of the agency. Their proposals threatened the economic interests of powerful congressional constituents in the securities industry and corporate America; they posed a threat to the supply of enforcement cases that committee members traditionally supported by promising funding increases; and, at times, they were a menace for career staff attorneys who opposed decision making that veered from the predominant legal format.

However, despite the modifications in the agency's composition and the conflict between attorneys and economists, the agency's strong role as a political participant in the policy process remained intact. In addition, by the mid- to late-1980s, it was apparent that the disclosure-enforcement framework was also intact and that the administration was, at a minimum, respecting that framework once again. Specifically, despite the controversial nominations of Shad and Cox, seven of the ten Reagan nominees to the SEC fit the profile of a securities law "expert," or a nonpolitical nominee, to be discussed later.

There were three primary reasons for both developments. First, the balance between expertise and political control throughout the SEC's history still held. Specifically, when an issue involved technical or sensitive aspects of securities regulation, when the affected industry groups were seriously divided, and when the SEC's enforcement agenda was at issue, the SEC was a significant, independent player in determining policy outcomes.

Second, SEC decision making patterns remained untouched throughout this period. Though attorneys and economists jousted over policy, the latter made room for themselves in a decision-making hierarchy still very much dominated by attorneys. Economic analysis contributed to agency decision making, but still in a support and advisory capacity. Further, the analysis supplied by SEC economists became a tacit part of the agency's capital market expertise, as seen in the debates over corporate takeovers.

Finally, toward the end of the decade the SEC made significant efforts to normalize its relations with Congress in order to preempt the disruptions caused by congressional oversight and investigation carried out in a charged political environment. For example, the agency became more conscientious about how it presented findings and proposals to its legislative committees; it established procedures for dealing with General Accounting Office investigations instigated by Congress, particularly those involving ongoing enforcement activities; and it centralized contacts with Congress in its Office of Legislative Affairs to better coordinate and control the flow of information.[1]

This chapter examines disputes between the SEC and its legislative committees over the direction of securities policy before any significant normalization of relations. My objective is to assess the impact of each on the ultimate outcomes of the disputes and to establish which one succeeded. Although the legislative committees can try to hold the SEC accountable by many means—such as oversight, investigations, confirmation of appointees—I focus here on their power to reauthorize the SEC for its annual appropriation. Two examples will illustrate why, without the agency's cooperation, the congressional committees cannot alter the performance of its "expert" responsibilities or micro-manage the agency's decision making.

Legislating, or a "Love-Hate Relationship"

When asked to describe the SEC's relationship with Congress as a whole, but particularly the House and Senate legislative committees, an SEC staffer with several years' experience on the Hill observed: "It's a symbiotic process. We need [Congress] for appropriations and legislation, and they need us for advice, technical expertise. It's pretty much a love-hate relationship."

In other words, despite the congressional committees' formal authority to pass legislation affecting the SEC, the agency shares in the crafting of securities laws. Consequently, in a conflict, the committees' use of their statutory authority over the SEC's mandate to control or influence the agency could be mitigated by the fact that the agency's cooperation is often essential in drafting and endorsing securities legislation.

Consider the Senate's interest in constraining corporate takeovers. Throughout the mid-1980s many bills were introduced in both houses aimed at halting or restricting corporate takeovers.[2] In 1987 and 1988, Senate Banking Chairman William Proxmire and ranking member Jake Garn (R-Utah) introduced legislation that supporters claimed would make the takeover process more equitable. However, upon closer examination, the bill would have restricted the options available to corporate raiders for purchasing a company, but did little to restrict questionable defensive strategies practiced by company managers (*Congressional Quarterly Weekly* 6/4/88, 1509).

The commission was also concerned about takeovers and the rights of shareholders, but it did not take a concise position on the issue until the middle of the decade, when it opposed restrictions on the practice of takeovers—that is, supported the status quo. In part, the commission did not endorse takeover legislation because of early differences within the agency. There was strong opposition to takeover restrictions by the Office of the Chief Economist (to be discussed later); there was also support for some type of shareholder protections among the regulatory divisions, and the commissioners' views were mixed. However, following the 1985 nomination of Joseph Grundfest to the commission, a firm three-to-two majority opposed legislative changes in the takeover laws, making this position clearly representative of the SEC. Grundfest joined Chairman Shad and Commissioner Cox in backing the legislative status quo (*Washington Post* 1/10/86: E-1; ibid. 2/8/89).

The commission's refusal to endorse legislation aimed at the practice of takeovers[3] was maintained into the chairmanship of David Ruder, nominated by Reagan in 1987. In addition, the agency's 1988 ruling on "one-share, one-vote" was an agency endorsement of shareholder rights in opposition to antitakeover tactics. The SEC did not endorse the Proxmire and Garn legislation when it was proposed in June 1988, and the bill never reached consideration by both chambers before Proxmire's retirement.

Though there was also opposition to takeover restrictions in Congress, according to many persons I interviewed, endorsement of the takeover restrictions by the SEC would have provided the necessary push for legislation. When asked if the agency's opposition helped to maintain the legislative status quo on takeovers, a former member of the Senate Banking Committee replied, "I think it did. If the agency had come down hard and fast in favor of the legislation, it would have made a difference. The legislation would have passed."

An SEC insider agreed with the view that SEC support for takeover restrictions could have turned the tide: "The debate over takeovers was one in which Congress was sharply split. It was not an esoteric issue related to securities legislation. . . . But if the SEC did support the legislation, it would have had a better chance of passing."

Finally, a former member of the SEC's staff with close connections to the legislative process commented on Congress's inability to secure takeover (tender offer) legislation without SEC endorsement:

> In addressing whether there should be federal regulation of tender offers, the commission said to leave it alone. There must have been about a hundred bills in the hopper to try and do something about tender offers—Proxmire's, [William] Armstrong's [R-Colo.], but in the end, Congress couldn't pass the bill without the SEC's initiative.

There were similar legislative stalemates over leveraged buy-outs and the commercial banks' ability to enter the securities business. In a leveraged buyout, a group of investors—typically, the management of a company—buy up public shares of a company by borrowing against the company's assets. To pay back the debt, the owners of the now "private" corporation sell, or "spin off," company assets. The resulting high levels of corporate debt drew congressional attention in 1985, and again in 1988—particularly following the leveraged buyout of RJR Nabisco for $25 billion. Numerous congressional proposals surfaced to limit the practice, but the SEC endorsed none of them. Instead, the agency's position was to rely on its rule-making authority. In reports of pending leveraged buyout legislation, the lack of agency endorsement was cited as a reason for inadequate congressional support to restrain the practice (*Securities Regulation and Law Report* 1/20/89, 130–31).

The practices of commercial banks in the securities business are restricted by the Glass-Steagall Act of 1933. As in the case of takeover restrictions, Senator Proxmire was a strong advocate of repealing the legislation (*Congressional Quarterly Weekly* 3/5/88, 566–68). The Proxmire proposal was opposed early on by the SEC because it failed to address the agency's authority over the securities activities of banks once the legislative barriers were removed (*SRLR* 12/4/87, 1835). Despite Democratic support in Congress and the support of the Reagan administration (ibid., 1837), the legislation failed to pass before Proxmire's retirement in 1988.

Both public and private takeovers and the securities powers of banks are issues that have powerful constituents on both sides. Members of Congress may want to capitalize on these issues by favoring their constituents' interests. The strength of polarized interests alone is no doubt capable of bringing the legislative process to a stalemate. However, in the case of tender offer reform, leveraged buyouts, and the Glass-Steagall repeal, agency and congressional participants saw the lack of SEC endorsement as crucial to their failure to get through. A bill that passed with the SEC's endorsement also illustrates the point.

In 1987 members of the House Energy and Commerce Committee initiated a bill to encourage international cooperation in cases of securities fraud, particularly for insider trading offenses. At the time, neither the SEC nor Congress indicated any significant support. According to a House staff member, when the SEC eventually did endorse the concept, the fate of the legislation was turned around: "When the commission came out with a similar draft—more polished but the same effect—it was all of the sudden motherhood and apple pie. With the commission imprimatur, [the legislation] sailed through."

The SEC draft was part of the Insider Trading Sanctions Bill, which granted increased authority and gave the SEC more sanctions for prosecuting insider trading. In this case, not only was the SEC's endorsement of the international cooperation provision apparently key to getting the bill through committee, but also its ongoing enforcement efforts were said to give the legislation its final push through the House. Following the widely publicized announcement by the SEC of its civil complaint against the investment banking firm Drexel Burnham Lambert, the legislation passed the House by a vote of 410 to zero (*Congressional Quarterly Weekly* 9/17/88, 2580–81). The publicity surrounding the agency's case—the largest insider trading case in the history of the agency—apparently gave all House lawmakers a chance to take a popular stand against Wall Street excess and investment fraud.

As indicated earlier, the drafting of securities legislation is a symbiotic process. These few examples seem to support that contention. Neither the agency or members of the congressional committees can unilaterally control the timing and content of a new securities bill. For example, agency control over the legislative agenda is obviously checked by the committees' own interests and their willingness to commit resources to any issue raised by the SEC. On the other hand, congressional control of the legislative agenda may be limited by its reliance on SEC expertise.

Former and current members of the SEC and committee staffs argued that the SEC had the most influence over the legislative agenda when it wanted to prevent a bill from passing. When asked about the importance of the SEC's backing for passage of securities legislation, a former SEC commissioner, now a securities lawyer, replied:

> It is just short of being decisive.... It almost totally has a veto on securities legislation that it opposes.... When [legislation] passes, it is always satisfactory to the commission. Part of it is the agency's expertise.... It is also that the commission is seen as a responsible, prudent commission. Congress gives a great deal of weight to its opinion. Of course, it is more effective on vetoing legislation that it opposes than in always getting what it wants.

Another former SEC member made the same observation: "If the SEC is strongly opposed to something, they can kill it. They can dig their heels in." He added, however, that typically the agency will not just refuse to act; rather, "They will try to work with the committees towards compromise." This willingness to redraft bills that it opposes or finds unworkable was also pointed out by a former commissioner. He argued that if there is apparently broad support for a particular measure, such as the insider trading bill, the commission might "draft a copy itself, and tell the committees what we don't like about it and how it could be changed." He went on to say that the committees "are very receptive to that approach" primarily "because they hold the commission in tremendous esteem."

As these opinions indicate, the SEC's ability to halt bills that it does not support, as well as to redraft legislative proposals, is closely connected to its reputation on the Hill—both in the legislative committees as well as in the broader Congress. To that must be added congressional reluctance to pass legislation that might hurt the markets and the technical nature of securities law in general. How these conditions work together for the SEC is well summarized by a former SEC staffer who worked closely with the legislative committees:

> A lot of [Congress's deference] is believing that the commission is being honest and straightforward. Part of it is that the SEC holds so many marbles;... one [congressional] staff person can't duplicate the SEC's expertise.... There is a trusting about the SEC.... The SEC is not political, and there is excessive respect for the agency. And the fact that securities legislation is very complicated, and consequential; no one wants to screw up.

The SEC's power to block legislation, or to redraft bills that it opposes, does not rule out the fact that the SEC can also influence the agenda by initiating legislation. When asked if the committees could realistically alter the SEC's mandate over the agency's objections, a former SEC staff member said that not only would the threat lack viability, but also the committees would typically rely on the SEC to start the process. Most legislative committee members, he continued, "have no idea what is going on.... It's not a realistic threat to pass legislation.... There is a lack of an understanding or an ability to do anything.... If motive and inventiveness doesn't come from the SEC, it doesn't get done."

Another former SEC staffer agreed: "There is a close relationship between the oversight staff and the SEC staff in drafting laws. Securities law is arcane stuff, so the committees need commission expertise to do the job." And a current staff member indicated that the SEC does more than provide the "motive and inventiveness" for legislation. When a regulatory division proposes a new law, she said, "We draft [it] and send it out as a package. We even say, 'This bill shall be called such and such.' "

Congressional regard for the SEC's expertise and the agency's ability to veto legislation it opposes was also confirmed in interviews. A former member of the Senate committee said that because of the agency's "considerable expertise and judgment," its legislative recommendations "were highly regarded by members of Congress." Another former member of the House committee concluded that "if the SEC had a strong opinion, it was given a great deal of consideration. The SEC was held in high regard by members of the Congress." On the agency as a veto point, several persons confirmed the view of a former member of the House staff who argued that the SEC is a "respected" regulatory agency and that "it has a good track record" in Congress. "On that alone, if the SEC doesn't support something, it's very hard to get it passed."

As previously mentioned, the SEC's influence through expertise also has its limits. The simple fact remains that Congress must have an interest in a bill if it is to be considered. The SEC can propose legislation all year long but cannot secure it without action by the legislative committees. Given this mutually dependent relationship for passing new securities laws, the statutory process may be an awkward or cumbersome method to exert congressional influence over agency activities when the two are at odds—as they were for most of the 1980s.

EDGAR and the Power of a Reauthorization

When a company offers a new issue of securities for public sale, a prospectus must be filed with the SEC disclosing what the agency deems "material" information relevant to an investment. In addition, when a company's securities are traded in the public markets, it must comply with continual reporting requirements to disclose updated information. As a result, more than 10 million pages are filed annually with the SEC by more than 13,500 companies under the Securities Act and the Securities Exchange Act (*Investment Dealers' Digest* 4/4/88, 17). It costs companies a lot of money to complete the documents and to file them with the agency, and it costs the SEC even more to review, file, and transfer them to microfilm.

When John Shad became chairman in 1981, he wanted to cut the costs of disclosure compliance for businesses filing with the SEC. First, he wanted to reduce the content required in a disclosure document. His efforts to integrate the reporting requirements under the 1933 and 1934 securities acts, as in the case of rule 415, partly achieved this. Second, he wanted to reduce the costs involved with the actual process of disclosure.

To achieve this second objective, Shad initiated a program called Electronic Data Gathering and Retrieval, or EDGAR, that would allow firms to make disclosures electronically through a computer to the SEC. Not only would the disclosure process be cheaper and smoother for the filing companies and the SEC, but also the Shad plan would shift the costs for building EDGAR to the private sector; EDGAR was to be financed with only a few million federal dollars. The private project contractor would pay for the rest, but would then be able to sell the electronically disclosed data to the public—primarily professional investors—at a profit (ibid. 4/4/88, 18).

Two major sources of criticism of the project included the financial data printers industry, represented by the Information Industry Association (IIA, a trade organization for information publishers and service organizations), and state securities regulators. Several of these firms had a stake in repackaging the information in SEC documents for sale to professional and public investors. Too rapid implementation of EDGAR would make it difficult for them to adjust to electronic (rather than conventional hard-copy) disclosure (House Energy and Commerce Committee, *Oversight of the EDGAR System* 1985, 11–28). State regulators, on the other hand, objected to the system's inability to accept numerous disclosure demands not required by the federal government.

These critics took their concerns to the House Energy and Commerce Committee, and committee Democrats decided to put brakes on the project. Committee Chairman John Dingell sent in the General Accounting Office to find flaws in the implementation of EDGAR, and he held hearings on the GAO report in 1985. These hearings culminated in the 1987 SEC authorization, or the "EDGAR Control Act of 1987," as it was less affectionately called by SEC staff members. In the most basic sense, the reauthorizing legislation restricted the agency's realization of the project by limiting how the SEC spent money for EDGAR and by controlling the procedures and pace of implementation.

Congressional Preferences

Testimony given at the House hearing and interviews with people who participated in the EDGAR debates indicate that committee members preferred the regulatory status quo—hard-copy disclosure financed through the public sector—or at least favored delaying the transition to an electronic system. First, the financial data printers and state regulators, primary participants in the hearings, preferred waiting, or slowing, the implementation of EDGAR, and it is not unreasonable to attribute these concerns to the committee members themselves. A staff member of the SEC made this connection when giving his interpretation of why Congress held the EDGAR hearings, as well as the SEC's surprise at the intensity of constituents' concerns:

> Microfiche providers saw EDGAR as a real threat to the need for micro-fiche, same with companies that get [financial] information out fast. . . . They got Congress's ear, persuaded Congress to get a hold of it. The commission was naive about it all. EDGAR was seen as such an obviously good idea. It underestimated these [constituent] concerns. [The SEC] was accused of rushing in too fast, of being out of control. It was said we wanted to exert control and be the czars of industry. . . . It doesn't hold water, but it sounds good.

Second, according to congressional staffers, some members were concerned that money spent on EDGAR would be taken away from the agency's enforcement program, and therefore committee members preferred the status quo for agency expenditures. One former staffer noted:

> There was a lot of interest in the resources allocated to enforcement, especially during the Reagan years. With the deregulatory agenda, enforcement resources were not given to the Enforcement Division. Shad was running around spending money on EDGAR. . . . The Congress

wanted steps taken to protect the enforcement division. . . . That was a strong motivation behind the EDGAR hearings [that funds were not diverted from Enforcement to finance EDGAR].

Finally, committee members were particularly opposed to the agency's plan to finance the project privately. The success of the project would mean the loss of a congressional check on disclosure. Further, companies that were required to disclose information to the SEC could eventually reduce their compliance costs by filing electronically. Without the need for authorized funds, the committee's authority over EDGAR's implementation was remote, and the control over public documents by a private contractor removed another means of accountability. One SEC official who watched the battle firsthand described this legislative concern and how it diminished as the project was later brought on budget:

> The main objection was to the proposal to finance [EDGAR]. . . . A standard government contract was wanted [by the committees]. . . . It was getting more and more tax financed, now maybe 75 if not 80 percent tax financed. The more it goes in that direction, the less heat [the SEC] gets from Congress. They don't want it outside the budget process.

These concerns for accountability and rapid implementation were not entirely unfounded. Before 1987, contracting for and implementation of EDGAR was the responsibility of the SEC's Executive Director's Office. The office acted, and continues to act, primarily as the administrative hub of the agency with responsibility for agency personnel practices, information handling, consumer and public affairs, the agency's budget, and data processing. Following congressional review and criticisms of EDGAR, the agency set up the Office of EDGAR Management to focus attention on the project. A staff member affiliated with this new office described the agency's initial haste and the role of the Executive Director's Office, and argued that the legislative controls on the project may have given it some stability that was previously lacking:

> Things would happen without consultation, [but] it would get done, and the pilot exists [today] because of it. . . . It was haste, in part [that the House objected to]. [The Executive Director's Office] didn't answer

[congressional] questions. Congress sent in the GAO to investigate, and
they hauled the project in.... Now there's regulation, procedures, a
consultative attitude. Before, they were going 100 miles an hour, Congress was not in charge, and [SEC Chairman] Shad had a drive to get this
done on a timetable.

The regulations and procedures that now guide the project
were spelled out in the 1987 reauthorization for the agency. The
law requires the director of the Office of EDGAR Management to
submit a report to the legislative committees every six months on
the status of the project, giving details about the agency's adherence to legislative specifications (SEC, *EDGAR, A Status Report*
1988). These include, for example, use of public-comment rule-
making proceedings for advancing the operational EDGAR system
and contracting with an independent external corporation to perform cost-benefit analyses of the ongoing pilot project. Continuation of the project is contingent on the SEC's compliance with the
biannual reporting requirements.

The Outcome

EDGAR's status as of 1990 represented a successful effort by the
legislative committees to influence the behavior of the SEC through
its statutory authority. Without congressional intervention, the SEC
would have pushed to have EDGAR up and running at full capacity
and financed primarily by the private sector. However, congressional preferences have prevailed. First, as of 1990, EDGAR was still
in the pilot phase, though the number of filings received through
EDGAR and processed by the SEC and the number of participating
companies continued to grow at a steady rate. Second, a significant
portion of the funding for the project came through the authorization and appropriation processes in Congress, which gave the legislative committees close oversight of the project. Third, as discussed
earlier, the SEC created an office of EDGAR management to oversee
its contracting and gradual implementation and to report every six
months on the status of the project. Finally, with the delays, the
financial data industry and state regulators were given adequate
time to prepare for the transition to the new technology.

The acceptability of the EDGAR pilot, once its financing was
brought under congressional scrutiny, was reflected in comments

by a senior House staff member: "Most of our concerns were taken care of when the legislation passed. The adequate controls were put in place. . . . [Committee Chairman] Dingell just wants to make sure that the government is getting a good system for the money."

Despite Congress's "victory," the SEC's ability to influence the outcome was not altogether negligible. There was a strong consensus among members of the SEC staff that the gradual transition to electronic disclosure, and its numerous public benefits, would not exist had it not been for the agency's initiation of the project. When asked who supported EDGAR, staff members involved in the project promptly replied: the agency itself. This was primarily why committee Democrats did not face any organized constituent opposition to their intervention, and perhaps why members considered it safe to take the SEC to task. SEC support for the project continues to be straightforward: when EDGAR becomes fully operational, the agency will realize efficiency gains under electronic disclosure and will benefit from enhanced oversight and enforcement.

Further, from the SEC's perspective, the efficiencies and benefits would not be limited to the agency. Corporate issuers, securities lawyers, and the investing public would all profit from computerized access to market information (Spencer 1983, 1990; Perritt 1989). Yet it was necessary for the SEC to initiate the transition before these potential social benefits could come about. One former staff member said that there were no organized private-sector interests promoting the project primarily because it was not in any particular group's best interests to incur the costs of organization and lobbying for it. Corporate issuers, for example, had sunk costs in their compliance process for paper disclosure; electronic disclosure, though more efficient in the long run, would require changes in their standard operating procedures. This individual presented the SEC's EDGAR project, instead, as a public interest initiative, and contrasted it with agency policy on fixed commissions in 1975. Whereas members of the IIA and state regulators stood to lose a great deal under electronic disclosure, investors and issuers would be making, for the most part, only marginal savings. Yet those individual marginal savings added up to a much more efficient outcome for the general public:[4]

> You need an agency to referee in a correct fashion, to get away from the tendency to make policy for the "squeaky wheel." . . . It was the same

way for fixed commissions. Negotiated versus fixed rates meant pennies to everyone else, but it was everything to the New York Stock Exchange. . . . But the commission pushed for the policy in which society benefits, and you achieve some greater efficiency.

An Assessment

Nevertheless, in the absence of a technical and uncertain issue that required deference to agency expertise, the agency could not combat congressional efforts to pass legislation that affected it directly. In the case of EDGAR, the dispute was over spending agency resources for computer hardware. The constraining legislation (reauthorization) passed without SEC endorsement primarily because other members of Congress considered the computerization of an agency to be a legitimate concern of the oversight committees and a rightful part of the reauthorization.

Further, there was no need to defer to SEC decision making because of diverse preferences among the interests involved. The printers of financial data and state regulators were united in their opposition. On the other hand, corporate issuers—beneficiaries of electronic disclosure—faced the classic collective action problem described by Mancur Olson (1965): though they all might have been better off in the long run with EDGAR in place, the cost of organization for that particular collective good exceeded any immediate individual benefits, given the sunk costs in existing operations.

Finally, concern about maintaining the SEC's strong enforcement efforts motivated legislators to pass the bill. As discussed above, committee members were concerned about the diversion of SEC money from the Enforcement Division to EDGAR.

In contrast to the debate over EDGAR, the conflict over the Office of the Chief Economist (OCE) and its role in developing a policy on corporate takeovers turned on the influence of the SEC. As in the EDGAR debate, legislators attempted to use their formal authority over the agency's mandate to—in this case—shut down the OCE. However, for the Congress as a whole, the attempt was seen as tampering with the SEC's expertise in order to affect policy in a highly technical area—corporate takeovers. In addition, there were tense and deep divisions between congressional constituents over the issue. The efficacy of corporate takeovers was debated within the securities industry as well as between potential takeover targets and the financiers of takeovers. This factor, too, prevented the legislative committees from unilaterally passing legislation that would have had a negative impact on the SEC.

The OCE and Takeovers

In 1987, both the House Energy and Commerce Committee and the Senate Banking Committee attempted to eliminate the SEC's ability to perform economic analysis by refusing to authorize funds for salaries and expenses of the agency's economists. Chairman Dingell of the full House committee, and Chairman Markey (D-Mass.) of the House Subcommittee on Telecommunications and Finance detailed the restrictions in a 1987 joint statement:

> Finally, the bill would provide that none of the funds appropriated may be extended for salaries or expenses of the office referred to as the "Directorate of Economic and Policy Analysis." This provision is proposed as a vehicle for review of the use of the Office of the Chief Economist and the work of the SEC economists to undermine the Commission's enforcement program. (*Joint Statement* 1987, 2)

The Democratic majority of the Senate Banking Committee took the reauthorizing restrictions one step further. As in the House reauthorization, the Senate restricted expenditures for the economic unit: "The subcommittee does not intend that any of the additional funds authorized by the bill beyond the SEC request should be allocated to the operation of Economic and Policy Analysis." But the Senate version also specified necessary changes— restrictions—in how the economic staff performed its research. Specifically, the committee majority wrote:

> The Commission should begin providing advance public notice of its staff's intention to undertake economic studies relating to particular Commission policies or regulatory issues and should solicit public comment on their design before they proceed. Such notices should describe in detail, and should encourage interested members to comment on, such matters as the relevance of the study to the policy or issue being examined, the reliability and completeness of the data to be

examined, and the appropriateness of the analytical techniques to be employed (Senate Banking Committee, *Report on SEC Authorization* 1987, 12–13).

Before the agency's 1988–1989 reauthorization, the research conducted by the Office of the Chief Economist (OCE) endorsed lifting certain restrictions on the controversial practice of corporate takeovers. Research indicated that the takeover of a company was an efficient way to reallocate capital investments and that shareholders from the targeted company profited from the boost given to stock prices during a takeover. The practice, it was argued, therefore benefited the economy and shareholders alike.[5]

These findings clashed with the views of members of Congress who wanted to limit takeovers. Large corporations that felt threatened by the wave of takeovers in the mid-1980s were lobbying Congress to place some restrictions on the activity. They found support, in particular, among leading Democrats on the Senate Banking Committee. Where the OCE argued for the economic benefits of a takeover, these members promoted the negative aspects of takeovers: they disrupted local communities, brought about unemployment, and promoted high-risk corporate debt (*Congressional Quarterly Weekly* 6/4/88, 1506; Senate Banking Committee, *Hearings on Hostile Takeovers* 1987, esp. March 4, 1987).

Controversy surrounding the OCE research was heightened when the office went public in its opposition to some of the agency's most visible enforcement activities: investigations of alleged inside trading activity by risk arbitrageurs. These professional traders invest in certain stocks in anticipation of a takeover. They profit by gambling that the amount a bidder will pay for the stock in a takeover exceeds the current market value of a stock. Amid increasing takeover activity, the SEC's Division of Enforcement took the position that a run-up in the price of a stock prior to the announcement of a takeover could be evidence that professional traders had inside, or private, information on the pending deal. The agency's economists, on the other hand, argued that these professionals were trading in "anticipation" of a takeover, and that to stifle arbitrage with enforcement actions would eliminate a legitimate source of pricing efficiency in the market (*Wall Street Journal* 3/19/87, 34). Its position placed the OCE in conflict with the agency's enforcement staff, as well as with congressional opponents of takeovers and supporters of the division's highly publicized cases against insider trading.

OCE researchers were addressing topics, producing results, and taking positions that contradicted what the Democratic majorities of the House and Senate (and their constituents) wanted to hear. Referring to the authorization for 1988–1989, one member of the SEC succinctly characterized the effort to cut off OCE funding: "They didn't like the results [of the studies]. If they don't like the results, they try to legislate us out of existence. That's the way it is." Another SEC official gave a similar response to the congressional action: "The OCE was studying tender offers and corporate take-overs. . . . There were powerful interests involved with the negative attention. [The OCE] disagreed with powerful members of Congress."

Legislative Restrictions that Backfire

This congressional attempt to micro-manage the SEC through legislation proved to be something of an embarrassment. The provision was a knee-jerk response to the results of SEC decision making (the agency still had not endorsed legislation to restrict takeovers) and showed the legislative committees to be incapable of intervening knowledgeably in the internal operations of the agency. Specifically, the legislation targeted the Division of Economic and Policy Analysis (DEPA) for the budget cut. Apparently, DEPA was assumed to be interchangeable with the Office of the Chief Economist, but the two were quite distinct.

As I discussed in chapter 6, the DEPA was created in 1975 to enhance the agency's use of economics in its decision making (SEC, *Annual Report* 1975, 167). However, despite efforts by the economic staff to provide economic analysis on a wide variety of topics (much of which clashed with the opinions of the SEC's legal staff), DEPA's contribution to SEC decision making was limited to performing regulatory flexibility analyses. "Flex regs," as they are called, are a congressionally mandated function under the Small Business Innovation Act of 1980. The agency is required to analyze proposed regulatory rules to determine their economic impact on small businesses (CIS, *Abstract* 11 [1980], 555). According to economic staff members, the work of DEPA never drew the attention of the legislative committees for two reasons.

First, in keeping with the SEC attorneys' objections to the routine incorporation of economic analysis, the agency apparently had a policy of preventing contact between the DEPA staff and Congress. One former DEPA staff member stated, "There was definitely an attempt made in limiting [economic] staff roles to in-house decisions." According to another former SEC economist, keeping potentially controversial topics addressed by the economic staff away from Congress was something of an informal responsibility of the Office of Legislative Affairs. When asked about any contact the directorate may have had with the Hill, he asserted that the director of OLA "never let [him] get within a thousand yards of Congress." He concluded, "I think they were afraid that Congress would focus in on something we were doing, and we would spend all of our time trying to explain it to them."

Second, DEPA's organizational stability was based on legislative action taken by the small business committees in Congress. With the majority of DEPA's work centered on the performance of "flex regs," the legislative committees that oversaw the SEC took little interest. Initially, Chairman Shad's efforts to create an additional economics unit in 1982 were also obscure or of little interest to Congress. When asked to describe the legislative committees's response to the creation of the office, a former member of OCE said:

> I don't think Congress even knew when it was originally formed. The only way they would ever notice, they could take a look at the budget, if they were really interested. But only totals are reported. I don't recall ever a peep of reaction from Congress. They wouldn't take that close a look.

This indifference was reversed, however, when the new shop of Ph.D. economists began participating in controversial agency policies.[6] The Shad SEC was seen by congressional Democrats as promoting deregulation (backing away from the disclosure-enforcement agenda of the 1970s), and using economic analysis in commission decision making was seen as the fuel. Yet in their efforts to halt the use of economic analysis in the commission, the initial lack of interest with the inner workings of the SEC tripped up the House Energy and Commerce and Senate Banking Committees when writing legislation to restrict expenditures within the OCE. In commenting on the committees' criticism of the OCE, a former member of the OCE described their mistake: "When they were critical of the studies done by OCE, they wrote DEPA [the division] into the bill. They didn't even realize the two were distinct!"

The import of the DEPA-OCE mistake was not lost on the Republican members of the House and Senate. One minority staff member commented, "It was a real embarrassment. We chortled over here." Further, majority staff members also acknowledged the failed effort. One staffer said that the legislative threat was "ineffective" and that it was "an embarrassment for members involved in that legislation."

EDGAR and OCE

The foregoing discussion of the OCE is designed to provide a contrast with the EDGAR project. In both cases, the legislative committees attempted to use their control over the agency's authorization to influence its actions. With respect to EDGAR, members of Energy and Commerce wanted to prevent the rapid implementation of a system that left Congress out of the loop, that appeared to further Chairman Shad's deregulatory agenda, and that might have removed funds from the agency's enforcement program. With respect to the OCE, House and Senate members wanted to prevent the SEC from making policy that could contribute to further deregulation. The office was producing research that supported, for example, easing restraints on takeovers. Consequently, as a former House staff member put it, some committee Democrats saw that office as "an ideological bully pulpit." Yet where the committees successfully practiced micro-management by legislating restrictions on EDGAR, they stumbled in a similar attempt to micro-manage legislatively the type of expertise brought to bear on agency decision making.

A primary difference between the two situations was the committees' inability to oversee the routine operations in the SEC adequately, and therefore to make informed legislative decisions. In the case of EDGAR, the Energy and Commerce Committee sent in the GAO to investigate the program. With results in hand, the committee could hold the project up to intense scrutiny. But in the case of the OCE, the committees had nothing quite so tangible as a GAO report to illuminate the OCE's operations and its relationship to the rest of the agency. It could have been very awkward to send in accountants to audit the work of economists. In both cases, the specifics of inner agency activities were lost on committees that lacked a good grasp of the SEC's internal structure. The GAO filled the gap for EDGAR, but no such solution was apparent for dealing with the OCE. As a result, the committees wrote embarrassing legislation in an attempt to restrict the OCE's methodology, but referenced the wrong group of economists.

A second, and perhaps more significant, difference emerges from the foregoing incident: it involved congressional tampering with the SEC's expertise. In the case of EDGAR, the committees intervened to control the computerization of the agency's disclosure program. The agency worked with outside contractors in its design and development. Further, the issues before Congress were straightforward: how was the project going to be financed, and what would be the pace of implementation? Committee objections to the commission's use of economic data, on the other hand, brought members into the content of SEC decision making. Where legislative restrictions were used successfully to restrict implementation of a large computer project, the committees eventually backed away from trying to restrict the agency's decision making legislatively and removed the provision before the reauthorization was passed. Observers of the incident argued that the agency's reputation and standing in the eyes of the Congress at large, as well as SEC opposition to the move, blocked passage of the provision.

With respect to the SEC's status in Congress, opposition to Democratic efforts to intervene in the agency's decision making was firmly stated by dissenting Senate Banking Republicans in the minority views accompanying the original provision.[7] In addition, a former SEC commissioner who participated extensively in the congressional debate over takeovers described the general perception of the Democratic provision, and Congress's reaction:

> The Congress does not give credence to that kind of petulance. . . .
> There were people on the Hill who were of a different mind on takeovers, and they wanted to pull the teeth of the chief economist. It was a rather small cabal, but they had to pull [the provision] to get [the authorization] approved. Cooler heads prevailed, and there was the feeling that they really should not do that kind of thing to the SEC.

It might well be argued that the committee members who headed up the "cabal" had no intention of going through with the provision and that it was merely congressional posturing to try to get the SEC to change its tone on takeovers. A former Senate staffer made this point. He suggested that the provision was based on the committees' concern that studies coming out of the OCE were biased—they all "echoed a single theme, that the market for corporate control should not be interfered with." The provision, he continued, was the committees' way to "fire a warning shot" indicating that alternative views in the commission should be funded. "To cut off funds entirely was not ever seriously considered." Similarly, a former member of the House staff said, "There is frequently puffing that goes on, and that is part of the jawboning."

The fact that OCE was changing its emphasis on takeovers as the provision was written might indicate that the SEC took the threat seriously. According to a former economic staff official, the chief economist responsible for generating the takeover studies concentrated more than 90 percent of the OCE's resources on this issue. After he left in 1987, his replacement began pursuing a more diversified research agenda. Whether this was indeed an SEC response to a "warning shot" or merely the result of an SEC personnel change is debatable. However, even if the committees intended only to threaten the agency, it strengthens the argument that the SEC's expertise (its decision-making processes) are off-limits to congressional tampering. In an attempt to influence the SEC's policy on takeovers, committee members could assume threatening postures, but they still had to rely upon the SEC to make the internal changes.

Interviews with SEC staff and commissioners made it clear that congressional attempts to intervene in the content of agency decision making was also considered illegitimate within the agency—both intellectually and as a matter of principle. Despite hostility toward economic analysis on the part of attorneys, whether or not the commission chose to incorporate OCE research in its decision making was seen as an independent concern of the commission. For example, a former official referred to the threat as "anti-intellectual book burning." Another reflected the same opinion: "If someone [in Congress] said, 'You've misinterpreted the data,' well then, O.K. But to criticize OCE because Congress doesn't like the results—come on, guys!"

Similarly, with respect to the committees' efforts to dictate agency decision making, a senior staff member commented that, if anything, such threats "strengthened [the commission's] resolve." He described the commissioners' reaction to such intervention: "Who the hell is Congress to tell an independent agency this?"

Finally, a third difference between the debates over EDGAR and OCE was the level of dissent among regulated interests. In the former case, members of the committees faced unified opposition to the project. In the case of the OCE and the SEC's position on corporate takeovers, committee members faced deep divisions between corporate raiders and potential target firms, as well as between the various securities firms that financed takeovers and those who opposed the consequences of takeover financing for the markets and investor confidence. To restrict the SEC legislatively in this conflictual setting was to risk angering constituents and possible retaliation at election time.

As in the case of EDGAR, a significant motivation for the legislative effort was to protect the flow of enforcement cases. In the dispute with the OCE, opposition to the Enforcement Division's pursuit of insider cases was expressed by the OCE and served as a possible threat to a congressionally popular flow of enforcement actions. Whereas the presumed threat to case flow was blocked in the case of EDGAR, the more controversial and technical aspects of shutting down the OCE—tampering with the SEC's expertise and meddling in the area of corporate takeovers—stymied congressional efforts.

Concluding Remarks

The legislative tug and pull between the SEC and its legislative committees reveals the hostile relations between the two in a charged political context. Nevertheless, as I argued in chapter 4, the incentives driving members of the SEC (particularly its career staff) and members of the legislative committees to support the disclosure-enforcement framework are still intact. Conditions during much of the 1980s hampered the SEC and its legislative committees in their attempts to work together, but did not destroy the fundamental regulatory framework. Indeed, despite the bickering, efforts were made throughout the decade by both the SEC professional staff and the legislative committee members to maintain the disclosure-enforcement system.

The appointments considered "nonpolitical"—those receiving the backing of agency staff and legislative committee members throughout the decade—serve as primary evidence. By the end of Reagan's second term, seven of the ten commission nominations made during his tenure fitted the profile of a securities law "expert."[8] This is perhaps proof that Reagan's attempts to break the rules maintaining the disclosure-enforcement framework came at a cost. In the nomination of Charles Cox, Reagan faced the opposition of three SEC commissioners—two of whom he had appointed himself—Democrats and several Republicans on the Senate Banking Committee, and representatives of the securities bar and the securities industry. Given the liabilities of confrontation (the expense of political capital on the Hill and the time required to get the nomination through the Senate), adherence to the disclosure-enforcement profile again became the norm by the mid-1980s.

Regardless of the conflict between the SEC and its legislative committees on various issues, the incentives to support the disclosure-enforcement framework were still very much intact under Reagan. The president, once a potentially destabilizing force, backed off and began playing by the rules.

8 An Unusual Institution

If I were ever to write a book about the SEC I would call it the "peculiar institution." It really is. Most who work there don't know it. They don't have experience anywhere else in government. It's amazingly well insulated from politics, even with the scandals of the Nixon administration. The moral of those incidents is you can't fix the SEC. . . . It has a high-quality staff, and there are some people there who really have a sense of mission. The government would be better off if it could infuse that spirit elsewhere in the government.

These comments by a longtime staff member of the SEC reflect the views expressed in interviews by agency representatives, members of Congress, and even individuals in the securities industry. This is not to say that the SEC is without its critics, but preponderantly, those interviewed invoked phrases such as "tremendous integrity," "highly dedicated," "nonpolitical," "independent," and "professional" to describe the SEC. In an era where "bureau bashing" has been recognized as a popular pastime for politicians and academicians alike (Gormley 1989), these perceptions of the SEC are an interesting and unusual twist.

Yet, these claims to the contrary, the SEC—like any agency—is indeed a very political organization. First, its control of the securities markets is built upon the stability of a set of formal and informal rules that dictate the distribution of costs and benefits associated with the government regulation of securities. Second, and more important, these rules are derived from a balance between the accountability of the agency to elected officials and those officials' dependence upon the expertise of the SEC. Given that dependence, the SEC's professional staff and commissioners are as critical to the definition and maintenance of the rules as are the agency's political overseers. In other words, they have a politically *independent* and *significant* role to play in formulating securities policy.

The Independent Role of an Agency

As a student of public administration, I find it somewhat amazing that the independent significance of the bureaucracy in the policy process requires a defense. Despite the cogent arguments of early scholars of public administration that a bureaucracy could serve a government and its people in a neutral (apolitical) and businesslike fashion (Wilson, 1887; Bruere 1912; Willoughby 1919), the politically important role of the bureaucracy was eventually justified, accepted, and indeed made a moot point by the 1950s (Appleby 1949; Long 1949; Kaufman 1956). Yet recent trends in explaining bureaucratic behavior are reminiscent of these early debates over the division of administration between the bureaucracy and "politics."

Specifically, scholars advancing the rational-choice "principal-agent" theory treat the bureaucracy as an instrument to be controlled by elected officials and their constituents. While some limit their analysis to the control exerted by one institution, such as Congress (Weingast and Moran 1983), others take a more pluralistic approach to the question of who controls the bureaucracy (Moe 1989). Nevertheless, the bureaucracy itself is given no independent role in these explanations for bureaucratic behavior and policy results. Rather, bureaucratic behavior is said to represent the defining structures and incentive systems imposed upon the bureaucracy by actors in the "political" arena—Congress, the president, possibly the courts, and their respective constituencies.

But just as Frank Goodnow (1900) and others had a difficult time maintaining the theoretical boundary between "politics" and administration, the rational-choice "principal-agent" approach is on precarious ground in denying a politically significant and independent role to the bureaucracy. In trying to isolate administration from politics, Goodnow argued that "politics" (or the ability to influence policy through discretion) could be sealed off in the office of a politically appointed executive. But the argument was on a slippery slope. If discretionary decision making could occur in the office of an appointed official within a bureaucracy, then what of the offices filled by that leader, and by their personnel, and so on? In other words, once any political discretion was allowed for within the bureaucracy, it was impossible to separate the political world from the administrative world.

Today, in the rational-choice literature, the problem relates to use of the term *control*.[1] Specifically, how do we recognize it when we see it? Is an agency's personnel under control (not able to exercise their own discretion) if they have room to interpret their mandate within a broadly defined framework—one acceptable to political overseers? Or does control—constraint of such discretion—require a more fine-tuned and limiting framework? Again, without a workable definition of control, it becomes impossible to draw the line between the preferences and demands of political overseers and bureaucratic personnel or to assess the impact of each on policy outcomes.

The principal-agent concept, in particular, has enabled researchers to make many critical contributions to the study of bureaucracy. Perhaps most important, it has challenged the conventional wisdom that bureaucracies are not accountable to their elected officials. Throughout the 1970s, an image of a runaway bureaucracy was prevalent. Some pointed to the lack of congressional oversight (defined as a serious monitoring of bureaucratic actions) as evidence that the bureaucracy lacked guidance and control (Truman 1973; Dodd and Schott 1979). Rational-choice scholars offered a different interpretation of the same phenomenon: a lack of serious oversight simply meant that the bureaucrats were doing exactly what elected officials wanted them to do; in fact, if there were no hearings or investigations in progress, the agency in question was probably under sufficient legislative control (McCubbins and Schwartz 1984). Similarly, while scholars lamented the excessive delegation of authority to the bureaucracy by Congress (Lowi 1979; Friendly 1962), the rational-choice scholars proposed to explain why Congress delegates in the first place (Fiorina 1982, 1986), and why there are varying types of procedural political controls imposed on the bureaucracy within the context of broad delegations of power (McCubbins, Noll, and Weingast 1987).

This scholarship has also called our attention to the importance of bureaucratic design, procedures, and the location of a given bureaucracy in the government. According to the rational-choice tradition, political behavior is best understood in the context of rules that define and motivate goal-oriented individuals. Because the rules are so critical to ultimate outcomes, political actors will care about them and fight over whether to maintain or change them. Consequently, we can think of bureaucratic structure and procedure as representing political preferences for policy outcomes. Just as the rules of baseball determine which team wins a game, an agency's structure and decision making are critical for determining who gets what from government.

What this literature has not dealt with, however, is the often decisive role of bureaucrats themselves in formulating and protecting those rules. Granted, the bureaucracy is not a branch of government with its own constitutional authority. In fact, the Constitution gives but scant attention to the role of an administrative apparatus in the federal government. But just as we recognize the political importance of congressionally delegated powers to the president, we cannot ignore the delegation of authority to agencies. The importance of the Executive Office of the President (and particularly the OMB) is commonly acknowledged and accepted by scholars as an essential means by which the president can attempt to manage, direct, or control bureaucratic behavior (Neustadt 1960; Hess 1976; Heclo 1977; Rockman 1984; Edwards and Wayne 1990). Yet development of the office required a congressional delegation of authority.

The United States' federal bureaucracy was developed to confront the growing problems faced by an increasingly complex nation (Waldo 1948). In designing various administrative institutions, Congress has had to balance the need for accountability (the accessibility of an agency to its political overseers) with, in many cases, the demand and need for specialized skills and expertise. The delegation of authority to an agency may represent calculated "symbolic" choices when conflict is high (Edelman 1964), or may be a response to pressures from powerful interests (Bernstein 1955; Kolko 1965). But it also may reveal the inability of elected officials to make knowledgeable decisions in a particular area.[2] Once authority is delegated, bureaucratic experts not only play a key role in interpreting statutory language—who or what is the "public interest" to be served, and how—but also can become central players in defining future legislation and policy options in their area of expertise (Woll 1977).

Just as the critics of the politics-administration dichotomy so readily point out and many scholars of the bureaucracy continue to accept as a given, bureaucracies are political players with their own sources of power and influence (Kaufman 1990). Given the tremendous increases in congressional oversight throughout the 1980s (Aberbach 1990) and the president's use of the OMB to monitor agency decision making (Eads and Fix 1984; Cooper and West 1988), the bureaucracy is not "out of control." Indeed, many would argue that the U.S. bureaucracy labors under excessive outside control (Gormley 1991). But the degree to which bureaucracies are controlled by external actors is tempered by the need of these same actors to defer to expertise.

As I have argued throughout this study, Congress defers to the expertise of the SEC because of the technical and uncertain nature of securities policy, the diversity of regulated interests, and Congress's dependence on the SEC to enforce the securities laws. The result is a balance between respect for expertise, on the one hand, and the demand for accountability to elected officials, on the other, that gives the SEC and its political overseers mutual and reciprocal influence over the framework, or set of rules, for regulating securities.

Any rigorous modeling of bureaucratic behavior must address the role of expert knowledge and skill in maintaining and amending policy. Expertise is provided for in the institutional design of many agencies; agency staffers, who often have strong opinions about decision making and internal structure, are key participants in developing both; and these institutional arrangements then continue to shape and motivate bureaucratic behavior. The interesting issue is not how well bureaucracies are controlled, but rather the balance between expertise and accountability in different policy areas and the limits or constraints on each. In my examination of the SEC and its political overseers, I have sought to illustrate that balance and to demonstrate the importance of dealing directly with expertise as it is captured in the formal and informal institutional arrangements that guide regulation of the securities markets.

While a great deal of my study concerns the development and maintenance of the disclosure-enforcement framework, the question of destabilization and change remains. Efforts by the Reagan administration to alter the way the SEC regulated the securities markets touched a raw nerve in the agency: they disturbed the domination of the SEC's decision making by securities lawyers. By injecting economic considerations into the SEC through the appointments process, the Reagan administration introduced a competing world view of regulation. By the end of the decade the economists had eventually achieved a more peaceful coexistence with the attorneys, but the latter still "drove the policy wagon"—as a former staff member put it.

Nevertheless, should economic analysis again gain favor within the agency (commissioners may increasingly rely upon economic analysis in their voting actions, for example), this balance may be disturbed and the regulation of the securities markets opened to debate. Perhaps this source of competition is what makes the disclosure-enforcement framework most vulnerable. The following two sections address the tug-of-war between the two professions (law and economics), and the economic and political changes that might advance the status of economics within the SEC.

Economists, Attorneys, and the Institutionalization of Ideas

One characteristic that makes the SEC unusual is the traditional domination of a single professional view—that of the securities lawyer—over agency decision making. The political strength of the SEC is derived from the demand for its expertise, and its ability to deliver that expertise in a professional and coherent manner enhances its position as the securities "expert." Yet securities lawyers are not the only source of the expert knowledge and skill necessary for overseeing the securities markets. Economists have long offered a competing professional approach. At the most basic level, the two groups offer differing interpretations of the public interest to be served, and consequently differ over the efficacy of the disclosure-enforcement framework.

Competing Views of Regulation

Attorneys and economists both inside and outside the SEC disagree over the nature of the public interest, or the investing interests, to be furthered by the regulation of securities.[3] For attorneys, investors' interests are best served by a focus on fraud—specifically, the prevention of fraud through full disclosure and the prosecution of fraud through enforcement. Within this perspective, the cost of regulation for the regulated, or the cost of an enforcement action, is not as relevant as the effectiveness of the action in bringing about "truth in securities" and in stopping or preventing investor fraud (Cohen 1966, 1985; Sommer 1969).

For economists, investors benefit if the securities markets are allowed to operate most productively. Stigler (1975, 88) argues that not only are efficient capital markets "more important than the protection of investors," but also "efficient capital markets are the major protection of investors." Within this perspective, the cost of a new rule or regulation should be considered in terms of its impact on the markets' ability to allocate capital efficiently. For example, an increase in public disclosure is justified only if it enhances the quality of information related to securities, and hence the ability of investors to better separate good from bad investments (Stigler 1975). Similarly, the cost of enforcement, such as the prosecution of insider trading, should be weighed against the loss of valuable information for the efficient pricing of securities (Manne 1969; Manne and Solomon 1974).

These conflicting views of the investors' interests were debated within the SEC during the later 1980s. For example, whereas SEC attorneys view the sudden rise in the price of a stock prior to a takeover as evidence of possible illegal insider trading, economists in the commission see the run-up as evidence that the market is effectively ferreting out information related to the targeted company based upon research (and perhaps guesswork) by arbitrageurs (*Wall Street Journal* 3/19/87, 34). In the lawyers' view, an elevated stock price suggests that some investors had nondisclosed information that others did not—information to which all investors should have equal access. Anything but equal access is considered fraudulent. For economists, information that helps the market allocate investor capital more efficiently is seen as the best means of protecting investors' interests.

The competition between attorneys and economists is hardly unique to the SEC. In 1984, for example, the entire spring issue of the *Antitrust Bulletin* (published by the Department of Justice) was devoted to the question of integrating law and economics in the Antitrust Divison. An Economic Policy Office was established within the division in 1973, but by 1984 there were still questions, conflicts, and irritations between the two professions as to the appropriate role of economics in a traditional law enforcement agency (Kauper 1984). Nevertheless, despite some verbal jousting, economic ideas had obviously become a significant influence over the Antitrust Division's work, and the task for the division was to achieve an acceptable balance between the sway of economists and that of the legal profession.

Later I will discuss a similar infiltration of economic thought in the 1970s in the Federal Trade Commission, the Interstate Commerce Commission (ICC), and the now defunct Civil Aeronautics Board (CAB).[4] Just as economic arguments were used to encourage and support John Shad's deregulatory efforts in the SEC (such as the implementation of shelf registration, or rule 415), the deregulation of the trucking and the airline industries has also been attributed, in part, to the political acceptability of economic ideas within the ICC and the CAB, and throughout the federal government (Derthick and Quirk 1985; Quirk 1988).

Controlling Differences Through Hierarchy

In the SEC, unlike other government agencies, problems that could arise because of these differing views of regulation have been controlled by the agency's formal structure and decision making patterns. The SEC is divided into four regulatory divisions: Corporation Finance, Market Regulation, Investment Management, and Enforcement. These divisions can initiate regulatory actions that must be approved by the full commission. The stability of this structure represents the degree to which attorneys, as the "elite" profession, have captured the core of the agency (Mosher 1982). In other words, attorneys make up the primary staff of those divisions in which the prestige and authority of the agency are concentrated.

The economists, on the other hand, serve in the Office of Economic Analysis (formerly the Office of the Chief Economist). "Offices" in the SEC, such as the Office of the General Counsel, serve in a support and advisory capacity and cannot initiate regulatory actions. Consequently, their impact must come in the form of advice to the attorneys before a regulatory initiative is made, or advice to the commissioners before a vote is taken. Until, or if, the position of economists in the formal hierarchy is changed, the professionally potent ideas inside the SEC will likely remain those articulated by the legal staff.

This dominance of one profession stands in stark contrast to the institutionalized competition between attorneys and economists who deal with antitrust cases at the Federal Trade Commission (FTC). In the FTC a Bureau of Competition, staffed by attorneys, operates in conjunction with a Bureau of Economics. Because both have bureau status (the equivalent of a division in the SEC), each has a formal and equal role to play in the case selection process.

The regulatory environments of the FTC and the SEC are very similar. Policy making by the FTC (particularly related to antitrust) is technical and outcomes are uncertain; its constituent base is diverse, and the agency pursues a tangible enforcement agenda that—during the 1970s, at least—meshed well with the consumer-interest policies of members of Congress. Yet the institutionalized differences between economists and attorneys in the FTC might make the FTC less of an "expert" and more vulnerable to intervention by outside elected officials.

If elected officials can exploit the differences between economists and attorneys in the FTC, they can cause regulatory stalemate, thereby diminishing the technical expertise the agency might otherwise bring to shaping federal antitrust and trade policy. For example, in his study of the FTC, Robert Katzmann writes about a division between agency attorneys and economists over an FTC investigation of the natural gas industry. Professional differences between the two groups were made public by a House subcommittee in order to support the committee chairman's opposition to the deregulation of natural gas. Exposure of the division not only pushed the FTC toward inaction, but also threatened agency lines of communication with the natural gas companies and others that were promised confidentiality for their cooperation (1980, 149–54).

The internal disagreements in this case reflect more generalized differences between the FTC's economists and lawyers in terms of the agency's overall enforcement profile—what Katzmann calls a "proactive" versus a "reactive" approach (1980, 27–35). Whereas the Bureau of Economics prefers enforcement actions intended to restructure and reallocate market power (enhancing market efficiency), the Bureau of Competition prefers enforcement actions taken in response to complaints of illegal practices received by the agency (pursuing fraud). If the agency does not have a clear preference for one type of case over another, the ability of Congress to intervene in the agency's decision making, as in the case of the natural gas investigation, is possibly enhanced.

A similar institutionalized competition exists in the SEC's sister agency, the Commodity Futures Trading Commission (CFTC), in which economists again play a prominent role. The premise for an economic presence is statutory: whereas the SEC's mandate focuses on disclosure and the prosecution of fraud, the mandate of the CFTC requires the agency to apply regulatory economic benefit analyses to decision making. This difference is reflected in the regulatory divisions of each agency, and it parallels differences between the FTC and the SEC. In the SEC economists play a support role for the four regulatory divisions and are housed in the Office of Economic Analysis. CFTC economists are based in the Division of Economic Analysis, which is institutionally on a level with that agency's Division of Enforcement and the Division of Trading and Markets.

As in the FTC, internal divisions might lead to a reduction in perceived expertise, and consequently a loss in the CFTC's political clout—in its ability to influence federal futures policy. The CFTC has never received the kind of deference that Congress accords the SEC, and indeed has been forced to defend its existence in several reauthorization battles (*Congressional Quarterly Almanac* 1978, 450). A significant portion of the criticism launched against the agency can be traced to a powerful and often unified opposition in the futures industry to strong regulation (*National Journal* 12/5/87, 3091–93; ibid. 6/25/88, 1670–74). Further, the fact that the industry is typically a unified constituency before Congress also diminishes the necessity of an "expert" mediator between interests, similar to the role played by the SEC. Nevertheless, the lack of a dominant profession (and consequently, a dominant regulatory perspective) in the agency has no doubt reduced its ability to maneuver in the political arena.

In the SEC the presence of economists has increased the level of debate and drawn the attention (and wrath) of Congress, but the attorneys' determination to dominate the formal decision-making hierarchy has enabled the agency to articulate a unified concept of regulation. The SEC's current structure mutes differences between economists and attorneys and allows what an SEC staff member called a team spirit to flourish. When asked how differences within the agency affected the SEC's position as the expert in securities policy, this same staffer argued that when differences existed between and within the regulatory divisions, there was a "tremendous esprit de corps among staff at the commission" and that division directors acted as "team players" promoting a more unified viewpoint before the press and the agency's political overseers. Yet this team approach is in part possible only because, without a competing regulatory division of economists to challenge the lawyers' " expertise," economic analysis can be ignored by division directors.

The lack of a competing regulatory division has also promoted a rare level of formality and secrecy in the agency's activities. As discussed in chapter 4, there is strong support in all of the regulatory divisions for disclosure-based enforcement. Though SEC economists have at times questioned the efficacy of the agency's enforcement activities (such as those relating to insider trading) and disclosure demands, the divisions do not waver. A belief in the importance of the agency's regulatory role, combined with the staff's esprit de corps, has created what many see as an impenetrable decision-making procedure in matters of enforcement and disclosure. A former member of the SEC staff characterized the relationship among SEC attorneys in the agency:

> There is a formality for going about its business that you don't find elsewhere. The SEC does not go about its business loosey goosey. . . .
> I've since lobbied the SEC from time to time, and it's tough to get any information from them. You learn right away not to try to find out things you are not supposed to. The potential of disclosing nonpublic information is immense. . . . There is a need to know that the SEC will not change its behavior willy nilly. The SEC is fundamentally a disclosure agency, and there is a need to know that the information is fair.

This team approach to policy making, and the formality and secrecy surrounding the agency's disclosure and enforcement activities, would not be maintained if another regulatory division could routinely challenge studies, recommendations, and decisions made by the other legal divisions.[5] This unity and formality, in turn, solidifies the role of the SEC as the securities expert in the broader political arena.

John Kingdon makes a similar argument regarding the impact of more broadly defined "policy communities"—groups of specialists including bureaucrats, interest group analysts, congressional staffers, and academics—on policy making. He argues that when a policy community (such as health care specialists) shares a "common paradigm," that unity prevents "fragmentation" of the community and instead promotes "integration" (1984, 126). Because an approach to policy must "both sweep a community and endure" in order to take hold (ibid., 137), the integrated community would seem to have a better chance of affecting the policy process than the fragmented community.

The argument applies to the SEC at both the agency level and the policy community level. First, the agency itself maintains a high degree of integration (it prevents fragmentation) due to the institutionalization of a single regulatory perspective. Second, the policy community of securities law specialists (including the private bar) also adheres to a "common paradigm" that has endured, and that promotes reliance upon disclosure-enforcement as the accepted approach to securities regulation.[6]

Sources of Change

Of course, the SEC and its professional legal staff are not impervious to change. Martha Derthick and Paul Quirk (1985) make a compelling argument for the significance of "ideas" in the transformation of regulatory policy. They trace the evolution of the "economic" idea as applied to regulation and argue that its political acceptability (within agencies, Congress, the presidency, the courts, and a variety of interested groups) was critical to the eventual deregulation of various industries (see also Quirk 1988). Ideas are important to elected officials because they promote definitions of the public interest to be served by any given policy, and consequently the distribution of costs and benefits to be borne by society. But they are also critical to the personnel of an agency whose professional stature depends on the efficacy and institutionalization of one particular idea. To challenge that idea is to challenge the political potency of agency personnel in the policy process.

Nevertheless, economic and political change promote a constant rethinking of the ideas that guide (and rationalize) the policy process. When ideas are widely accepted, agencies can, and as Derthick and Quirk (1985) argue, do adapt. This final section addresses economic and political pressures that might alter the domination of securities law within the SEC and make room for the competing economic approach to investors' interests.

Changing Economic Conditions

The stock index future has developed as a popular and prominent investment instrument. Yet questions surrounding its regulation could be a source of instability in the SEC's regulatory environment. Basically, a stock index future allows an investor to hedge investments in the stock market by betting what the price of an index of stocks (such as the Standard and Poor 500) will be at some future time. Though no actual stocks trade hands when the contract expires (all contracts are settled in cash), the instrument is traded on futures exchanges, just like any other futures contract on any given commodity. However, because the value of the contract is tied to the purchase and sale of stocks, the product explicitly links activities in the futures and stock markets.

Currently, these investment products are regulated as futures contracts by the CFTC and trade exclusively on futures exchanges. But following the stock market crashes of 1987 and 1989, the SEC and representatives of the securities industry began advocating a change (*National Journal* 12/5/87, 3091–93). It has been argued that the loose regulation of these products under the CFTC causes extreme market volatility in the stock markets and that the SEC should assume jurisdiction over the products to better prevent fraud, abuse, and further market disruptions.[7]

One recommendation advocated by the SEC and its supporters is to merge the CFTC and the SEC. Given that the markets are so closely linked, a single regulator could rationalize the regulation of the capital markets. The boost in jurisdiction for the SEC might be attractive. However, if the Commodities Exchange Act remains the statute governing trades in stock index futures, the SEC will have to incorporate economic benefit analyses when making decisions about these investment products, as is currently done by the CFTC. This direct elevation of economic analysis could fuel the already strained relationship between economists and lawyers in the SEC, weaken the staff's esprit de corps, and, if the two groups were routinely divided, perhaps reduce the agency's power of advocacy before Congress.

Additional overlaps with the U.S. securities markets are developing both domestically (such as with the U.S. markets for futures)
and internationally. These developments could also alter the kind of
expertise required by the SEC, or the kind of expertise perceived as
necessary for dealing with the changes. For example, the U.S. securities markets increasingly overlap with securities markets in places
such as Tokyo, London, Paris, and Singapore. Multinational corporations list their securities with exchanges around the world and
investors in any given country have access to markets in a variety of
other countries. As the markets have become global, the SEC has
made an effort to establish an enforcement presence through cooperative agreements with regulators in other countries, as well as
to "harmonize" the levels of disclosure required for foreign corporations that sell stock in U.S. markets, and U.S. corporations that sell
stock abroad (*National Journal* 1986, 2244–50; *Institutional Investor* 1990, 118–20). The effort is very much within the bounds of
the SEC's disclosure-enforcement effort in this country.

Yet a strong argument might be made that regulating the connections between international markets may require a different "idea"—
something other than a focus on enforcement and prevention of
fraud. In particular, it might require greater sensitivity to economic
concerns. For example, to increase disclosure requirements for multinational corporations or to subject foreign investors to the enforcement powers of the SEC might be to scare away foreign investment in
this country. Consequently, if the United States is to be a thriving
participant in global markets, a greater understanding of (and sensitivity to) the economic impact of regulation could be regarded as
essential.

A similar argument can be made about the increasing overlap
between commercial and investment banking. The Glass-Steagall
Act of 1933 currently prohibits commercial banks from underwriting corporate securities. However, through a loophole in the law
the Federal Reserve Board has allowed bank holding companies to
operate a securities unit under limited conditions (*New York Times*
1/16/91). Unless the securities activities of banks are brought under
SEC jurisdiction (*Economist* 1/6/90, 73–74), the intermixing of
industries could also bring a clash of ideas about regulation that
might diminish the role of securities law experts in defining policy.

Francis Rourke argues that the political clout of a professional group within an agency is most potent when it commands a "highly technical body of knowledge that the layman cannot readily master" and when it can "produce tangible achievements that the average citizen can easily recognize" (1984, 94). He points to NASA's ability to send rockets and astronauts into space as an example. Yet, as Rourke acknowledges, (and as the recent difficulties of NASA demonstrate), failure to produce at some point a "tangible achievement" or to cope with change challenges the professional expertise in an agency.

As the markets for banking, securities, and futures continue to overlap, and as events in Tokyo continue to rock the New York markets, the expertise of the SEC may be tested. If the disclosure-enforcement approach is seen as limiting the competitiveness of U.S. industries or as inadequate to deal with increasingly complex financial markets, elected officials may begin to seek a change. Specifically, they may turn toward economic ideas to promote deregulation or toward reducing international market barriers. Moreover, mergers of various markets (such as banking and securities) may create several large financial institutions that deal in commercial and investment banking, and consequently reduce the number of competing interests in the securities markets. Similarly, an international trend may force economic interests to seek policies that benefit U.S. markets in general, rather than policies that benefit the New York markets versus the regional exchanges or the over-the-counter markets. This homogenization of interests may lessen the need of a professional mediator and increase the likelihood of direct legislative policies.

On the other hand, if the uncertainty surrounding the regulation of the financial markets persists, elected officials may become more dependent upon a trusted expert to address such complexities. Further, just as there is political capital to be gleaned from enforcement actions in the U.S. markets, there is surely much to be gained from international enforcement efforts. Finally, rather than reduce the need for a mediator, economic interests may require an even more adept mediator—one knowledgeable about the international market. The SEC's success in developing enforcement accords with several nations has brought the agency international prestige. In other words, rather than challenge the ideas of disclosure-enforcement, the changes may indeed reinforce the framework.

Political Pressures for Change

I have argued throughout this study that the SEC's legislative oversight committees have been stalwart supporters of disclosure-enforcement and have typically opposed a formal role for economic analysis. Until securities policy becomes a predictable business, until the securities industry is unified in its opposition to disclosure-enforcement, and until enforcement is no longer a popular public policy, there will be little incentive to turn against disclosure-enforcement.

Nevertheless, like the experts who wield them, elected officials use ideas as political weapons. Despite general bipartisan support for the disclosure-enforcement framework, members of the committees most supportive of the framework have at times been on the same side as the SEC economists on particular issues. Recall the dispute over the one-share, one-vote decision. Senator Proxmire's opposition to any rule that appeared to facilitate takeovers placed him in the same camp as the SEC economists who opposed intervening in decision making at the corporate level. Members of Congress respond to constituent demands, and as those demands change, so does their support for policies and the ideas upon which they are premised. It is not unthinkable to imagine a shift in constituent preferences under changing market conditions, and consequently a shift in congressional support for the premise of disclosure-enforcement.

Just as committee support for a policy does not guarantee its maintenance, however, a shift in congressional support for disclosure-enforcement would not necessarily lead to a wholesale revision of the SEC's regulatory approach. Again, a dependence upon expertise given the still technical and uncertain nature of the policy may limit the extent to which politicians are willing and able to restructure and incorporate new ideas. Further, even if the committees are willing to legislate change based on their own constituent concerns, the broader Congress may still turn to a known expert, the SEC, for its cue in any legislative voting that tampers with the agency's expertise (see chapter 7).

Presidents, on the other hand, are a more potent source of destabilization. Presidents respond to a wider constituency than members of the legislative committees, and they often have broad economic agendas that might include changes in the regulation of finance. Given demands from the larger business community to ease SEC regulations, President Reagan sought to shift the role of the SEC from that of a prosecuting regulator to a facilitator of capital accumulation. A significant, and to some degree successful, part of that effort included injecting economic analysis into the SEC through the nominations of John Shad and Charles Cox, and the chairman's subsequent selection of personnel and establishment of the Office of the Chief Economist (OCE).

Similarly, the appointment of Caspar Weinberger by Richard Nixon in 1970 served to reinvigorate an institutionalized role for economic analysis in the FTC. Before 1970 the Bureau of Economics played a minor role in agency decision making, despite a formal position in the agency's hierarchy, largely because few of the economists held Ph.D.s. Consequently, they were not necessarily motivated to challenge the attorneys by pushing for an "efficient market" agenda, as they might have done if driven by a professional research orientation. It was perhaps that obscurity that brought the bureau poor funding (Katzmann 1980, 38). But two reports highly critical of the agency, as well as the president's interest in capitalizing on consumer sentiment, provided the seeds of change. In 1969 a group headed by Ralph Nader released a report criticizing the FTC for not sufficiently protecting the rights of consumers. That same year the American Bar Association released another attack aimed at enhancing the quality of work coming out of the FTC—both legal and economic (Clarkson and Muris 1981, 2).

With the consumer movement and the American Bar Association pressing for reform, Nixon made the FTC a priority and, one can argue, made a strategic move. He appointed Caspar Weinberger FTC chairman with a mandate to reorganize the agency (Clarkson and Muris 1981, 3). The reorganization included revitalizing the Bureau of Competition (formerly the Bureau of Restraint of Trade), as well as reinvigorating the Bureau of Economics. Whereas previous economists did not have the professional drive to challenge the attorneys over antitrust policy, the new economists did. One could assert that the Bureau of Economics was intentionally strengthened (given more money and a new staff of Ph.D.s with research backgrounds) to place a check on the aggressive prosecution of cases by a recharged Bureau of Competition. Consequently, consumer interests would be addressed by the new Bureau of Competition, while business interests would be served by a potential sticking point in the selection of cases—the Bureau of Economics.

It is interesting to note the essential synchronization of ideas with institutions in this example. Before the FTC's reorganization, the economic staff had the means (a place in the formal structure) but not the professional drive to challenge the legal profession. Following the revitalization of the Bureau of Economics, economists with an academic orientation had a motive to pursue an efficient market, and they used the formal hierarchy to do so. Similarly, consider the SEC. Without an institutionalized role in the SEC's formal decision making, the agency's economists have reasons but not the capacity to formulate their own initiatives. Institutional design does matter, but the incentives that institutions create do not guarantee particular behavior. Nixon's ability (through Weinberger) to place economists in the FTC able to use the power of the formal structure was pivotal to the transformation of that agency's approach to antitrust policy.

Other presidential appointees have been credited with making dramatic changes in an agency's direction and performance. For example, the appointment of an economist, Alfred Kahn, to the CAB was cited as critical to the deregulation of the airlines (McCraw 1984). Similarly, the appointment of economists as ICC commissioners has been related to the eventual deregulation of the trucking industry (Weidenbaum 1990; Alexis 1983).

Under the right conditions, the appointment of an SEC chairman, like Shad, who was interested in utilizing economic analysis might serve to elevate the institutional role of economists in the agency. A chairman with majority support on the commission could make the funding and staffing of the economic staff a prime objective. Further, with majority support, the chairman could count on fellow commissioners to incorporate economic analysis into their decision making—perhaps as readily as commissioners currently rely upon the Office of the General Counsel or the Office of the Chief Accountant. The ICC chairman was backed by a majority in his campaign to deregulate trucking (Derthick and Quirk 1985, 89), just as Kahn, and the chairman before him, had majority support in the CAB for his agenda (McCraw 1984; Behrman 1980).

The creation of a commission majority that supported a more formal role for economic analysis would require a long and concentrated effort by the president and would no doubt be costly. Until the SEC, the securities industry, the congressional legislative committees, and securities lawyers cease insisting that nominees fit the securities law profile, unpalatable candidates will be hotly contested. The Reagan administration had a strong mandate from the business community to reduce the burdens of SEC regulations during an economic downturn in 1980. Yet judging from the majority of its nominees, the administration ran out of steam, or interest, in its efforts to name commissioners who significantly broke with tradition. It is likely that other presidents might have the same experience.

Nevertheless, as the markets continue to change, so might the demand for securities market expertise in the agency. To maintain their status as the securities experts, SEC staff and commissioners may find it prudent to incorporate economic analysis in their decision making more routinely. The agency took one such step in 1988 when Chairman David Ruder merged the OCE and DEPA to form the Office of Economic Analysis (OEA) and authorized the hiring of additional economists with Ph.D.s. In interviews, several staff members argued that the merger was largely a response to the 1987 stock market crash. Recall that following the crash, a presidential commission identified the Federal Reserve Board as the primary source of economic expertise in dealing with the financial markets. Consequently, the move by the SEC was an attempt to preempt criticisms of the agency's ability to adapt to, and deal with, changing market conditions (such as increased volatility). In the meantime, the economic staff was brought one step closer to playing a more integral part of agency decision making.

Concluding Remarks

If one believes the popular press, any agency that is celebrated for its commitment, persistence, and sense of mission is indeed an unusual phenomenon today. Within the SEC, that sense of mission is derived from broad support for its disclosure-based enforcement policies and is reinforced by the dominance of securities lawyers within the agency. If those factors were altered, a more "political" agency (one susceptible to outside intervention), or one with less significance as a political player in the policy process, might be the result.

The fact that the securities law profession has been preeminent for so long, however, can be attributed partly to the role of the SEC professional staff and commissioners in upholding the disclosure-enforcement system. Institutions do matter! And the SEC personnel are aware of the significance of their internal rules for maintaining disclosure-enforcement, and consequently for protecting their role in the policy process. To change the internal structure of the SEC would be to fundamentally alter the balance of power within the institution, and consequently the agency's pursuit of the public interest.

Whether or not such stability is good or bad, and of course whether or not such stability indeed represents the public interest, is debatable. Robert Reich and colleagues argue that in a democratic society the role of policy makers and analysts should be to present a variety of ideas in order to stimulate debate and deliberation. They argue that a preformed definition of the public interest, such as the maximization of some social net benefit, inevitably defines the politics surrounding an issue. How a problem is defined determines what groups form to oppose or support it, places value on particular social and material goods, and directs the dialogue of debate. If, however, policy makers, such as public managers, make an effort to place issues before the people and encourage public debate, the public interest can be fostered through a deliberative approach to making policy (Reich et al. 1988, 123–56).

While the SEC does take a deliberative approach to rule making, it does so within a set paradigm dominated by the securities law profession. To challenge that paradigm (as economists and those seeking to loosen the disclosure-enforcement framework did throughout the 1980s) would be to throw risk and uncertainty into the equation for SEC professionals, competing interests in the securities industry, and their representatives in Congress. Further, SEC decision making premised on a new paradigm would face the uncertainty of judicial review. Institutionalized procedure and practice are the expression of political concerns, and they act to protect (and perhaps lock in) the choices and priorities of the primary participants. Such is the case for the institutionalization of disclosure-based enforcement.

Appendixes
Notes
Bibliography
Government Documents
Index

Appendix 1

Research Methods and Study Design

The nucleus of this study is drawn from over one hundred hours of interviews conducted with members of the following groups: (1) past and present commissioners of the Securities and Exchange Commission, (2) past and present staff members of the Securities and Exchange Commission; (3) past and present staff members of the House Energy and Commerce Committee and subcommittees, the Senate Banking, Housing and Urban Affairs Committee and subcommittees, the House Appropriations Subcommittee on Commerce, State, Justice, and Related Agencies, and the Senate Appropriations Subcommittee on Commerce, State, Justice, and Related Agencies; (4) past members of the Senate Banking Committee and of the House Energy and Commerce Committee; and (5) representatives of the securities industry. I conducted these interviews in Washington, D.C., in October 1988, January 1989, throughout the fall of 1989, and the first few months of 1990.

The interviews were conducted with a loosely structured question format. I addressed specific issues in each interview, but questions were designed to glean as much information as possible about the SEC and its relationship with (1) its political overseers, and (2) the regulated industry. Therefore, even though a line of questioning was prepared in advance, the open-ended nature of the questions meant that certain topics were covered in greater detail in some interviews than in others.

Initially, the questions were designed to test directly the question of control of the bureaucracy. Specifically, what were the limits (if any) of legislative control, in particular, and presidential control, in general? Questions referred to the legislative committees' use of their reauthorization power, their oversight mechanisms (hearings, investigations, and other more informal contacts with the agency), legislation, and the Senate's approval of nominees as ways of attempting to influence the agency, and asked about the relative success of those efforts. Questions also addressed the president's power to appoint SEC chairmen and its impact on agency behavior. Similarly, I asked interviewees about the strengths of the agency in dealing with its legislative committees and the White House, and what (if any) characteristics of the SEC might counter the influence of the agency's political overseers.

Interpretation of the interview data was an exercise in qualitative methodology. I proceeded in roughly the following manner. Following the first round of interviews, conducted exclusively with SEC personnel, I combed through responses in search of trends or similar comments. Based upon that initial review, I made several "first cut" conjectures about the dynamics of the SEC's relationship with its political overseers, mainly Congress, and the influence of each side on policy outcomes. Without refining the initial format, I conducted the second round of interviews primarily with congressional personnel.[1] Again, I sought trends or similarities in comments and made a few surmises about the relationship between the SEC and Congress from the predominantly congressional perspective. I then analyzed the two rounds of interview data simultaneously to identify trends common to both sets.

Throughout this later process, patterns emerged that confirmed or contradicted my initial conjectures regarding the influence of the committees and the SEC in determining policy outcomes. For example, interviewees repeatedly pointed to the upper hand of the SEC vis-à-vis Congress when a particular issue was highly technical or had direct implications for the market; when there were diverse interests involved; and when enforcement issues were at stake. I then focused more directly on these themes in the final rounds of interviews conducted with former and current SEC personnel, former and current congressional staff members, former members of the legislative committees, and representatives of the securities industry. At this point, I also shifted the focus of my documentary research to assess these themes with respect to SEC rules and pieces of securities legislation. Several secondary themes emerged from the combined analysis of the first two rounds, such as the relationship between economists and attorneys on the SEC staff, the relationship between SEC attorneys and the securities bar, the role of "experts" on the congressional staffs, and the importance of a "professional" SEC to the securities industry. I traced these themes in later interviews and examined them more closely in my ongoing documentary research.

In general, interviews were conducted in government offices and law firms, most of them in Washington, D.C. However, I conducted several interviews over the telephone. I learned and developed my interview technique on the job. I took handwritten notes at each meeting and eventually developed a sort of shorthand that allowed me to record significant portions of the interviews. Immediately after each interview, I sat down to fill in gaps while my memory was fresh. My notes were then rewritten by hand within one or two hours after the interview and shortly thereafter typed.

Tape recording my conversations was out of the question for several reasons. First, I began the interview process at a very critical time for the SEC. The Dow Jones industrial average had fallen by 508 points in October

1987, one year before I began my interviews. Everyone on Capitol Hill (and even in the White House) wanted to know what happened, why, and how to prevent it from happening again, and the SEC was the logical place to turn. From the 1987 crash to October 1988 (when I held my first round of interviews), the SEC was on the Hill to testify more than twenty-five times with approximately seven different committees. In response to the crash, SEC Chairman David Ruder requested a study of the events of October. The agency's Division of Market Regulation performed the study, at great cost to its own resources and its ongoing oversight activities. In addition to holding numerous hearings, Congress was very interested to know the results of the SEC study. Overall, the pressures from Congress and the consequent strain on agency resources (related to hearing preparation and the study) made the staff and commissioners careful and discriminating when talking about their relations with Congress.

Second, a great deal of secrecy surrounds the work of the SEC, and the staff and commissioners are alert to the possibility of leaks to Congress that might be used in a public hearing. Because the SEC is both an overseer of the markets and an enforcer of the law, its actions can have a direct impact on capital investment. For example, I was conducting the interviews in the aftermath of the Ivan Boesky and Dennis Levine insider trading convictions and as the agency was preparing its case against the investment banking firm of Drexel Burnham Lambert and Drexel executive Michael Milken. As we have seen, the indictment against Drexel was no doubt a significant factor in the firm's filing for bankruptcy on February 12, 1990, and—given the pivotal role of Milken and Drexel in the junk bond market—the subsequent volatility in the markets for low-grade debt. Members of Congress were very interested in the ongoing investigations, and, as is customary, the SEC staff was very cautious about the possibility of leaks.

Consequently, I think that my interest in the relationship between the SEC and Congress, in particular, made some interviewees initially reluctant to answer my questions. Yet after my assurances that my interest was strictly academic, that I was not interested in particular enforcement actions, and that all responses would be kept anonymous, I was able to secure interviews with even the most hesitant. Many spoke openly and frankly, and I am confident that the fact that I took handwritten notes rather than recording the interviews helped to allay their apprehensions. (I should point out that former SEC staff and commissioners, and former staff and members of the congressional committees, were rarely hesitant about responding.)

Throughout my study I have cited liberally from these interviews to substantiate my arguments. Because of my promise of anonymity I have identified my sources as, for example, a congressional staff member, an SEC official or staff member, a member of the securities bar, or an employee of a brokerage firm. If reference to an individual's position or committee membership is critical to a particular point, and if the quote is also of a noncontroversial nature, the interviewee is identified by professional role (for example, SEC division director, member of the economic staff, or commissioner), by congressional committee, or role in a securities firm. These are of course judgment calls, but I have considered each quote carefully and feel that I have not jeopardized the identity of any interviewee.[2]

The decision to use interview data to study the political context of the SEC was based on my interest in the actual informal and formal processes that lead to policy outcomes, as well as my interest in how participants perceive their strengths and weaknesses in the policy process. To recognize that the legislative committees have tremendous authority over the SEC, for example, or that the SEC has great expertise in dealing with securities legislation is meaningless unless we place both in the broader context of their day-to-day interaction. Similarly, to point out the power of presidential appointment is meaningless unless we consider an appointee in the institutional setting of the SEC. I felt that the best way to get at these concerns was to talk directly with the participants and ask them about the implications of congressional (and to a lesser degree, presidential) oversight of the SEC for policy outcomes. For example, do staff and commissioners actually anticipate congressional sanctions to their rulings? Do members of the Senate Banking Committee use the confirmation process to try to maintain or influence the behavior of the SEC? How are congressional letters and inquiries received by the SEC, and what impact do they have?

The focus of my interviews with members of the securities industry was slightly different. In these cases, I was interested in several things: first, the contact between representatives of the industry and the SEC as well as with the congressional committees and the administration; second, the degree of industry support for SEC activities and whether that support was translated into congressional support for the agency; third, the degree to which the SEC was captured, if at all, by particular segments of the industry; fourth, the source of SEC rule-making and legislative initiatives. In other words, what was the role of the industry's self-regulatory organizations, firms, investment companies, and other professionals in initiating policy versus the role of the SEC as an "independent" regulator?

Many times, interviewees fulfilled dual and even triple roles. Some had experience as SEC staff members, as congressional staff members, and might be currently working in the private sector as securities lawyers. The combinations were numerous. However, in selecting a particular individual for an interview I was typically interested in his or her perspective in a single capacity at a specific time.

My study also draws on several other sources of data. First, I made a comprehensive overview of the *New York Times*, the *Washington Post*, the *Wall Street Journal*, and the *Securities Regulation and Law Reports* for the years 1970–1989. I searched for references to SEC nominations, particular rules passed by the agency, congressional correspondence with the SEC and general congressional reactions to SEC activities, and feature stories on the agency and its staff. Second, I relied heavily on government documentation—primarily congressional oversight, appointment, and legislative hearings and reports. I also relied on the SEC's *Annual Reports*, SEC releases, and specific agency studies. Finally, I drew on numerous articles and books about securities law, economics, accounting, and history for facts about the agency as well as contrasting interpretations and evaluations of its work.

Appendix 2

SEC Commissioners

Roosevelt Appointments:

Joseph P. Kennedy, June 1934–September 1935
George C. Mathews, June 1934–April 1940
James M. Landis, June 1934–September 1935; Chairman, September
    1935–September 1937
Robert E. Healy, June 1934–November 1946
Ferdinand Pecora, June 1934–January 1935
J. D. Ross, October 1935–October 1937
William O. Douglas, January 1936–September 1937; Chairman, September 1937–April 1939
Jerome N. Frank, December 1937–April 1939; Chairman, May 1939–April
    1941
John W. Hanes, January 1938–June 1938
Edward C. Eicher, December 1938–April 1941; Chairman, April 1941–
    January 1942
Leon Henderson, May 1939–July 1941
Sumner T. Pike, June 1940–April 1946
Ganson Purcell, June 1941–January 1942; Chairman, January 1942–June
    1946
Edmund Burke, Jr., July 1941–October 1943
Robert H. O'Brien, February 1942–December 1944
Robert K. McConnaughey, December 1943–June 1949
James J. Caffrey, May 1945–July 1946; Chairman, July 1946–December
    1947

Truman Appointments:

Richard B. McEntire, June 1946–May 1953
Edmond M. Hanrahan, July 1946–May 1948; Chairman, May 1948–
    November 1949

Harry A. McDonald, March 1947–November 1949; Chairman, November 1949–February 1952

Paul R. Rowen, May 1948–June 1955

Donald C. Cook, November 1949–February 1952; Chairman, February 1952–June 1953

Edward T. McCormick, November 1949–March 1951

Robert I. Millonzi, July 1951–June 1952

Clarence H. Adams, May 1952–June 1956

Howard J. Rossbach, August 1952–February 1953

Eisenhower Appointments:

Ralph H. Demmler, June 1953–May 1955

Sinclair J. Armstrong, July 1953–May 1955; Chairman, May 1955–June 1957

Jackson A. Goodwin, July 1953–December 1955

Andrew Downey Orrick, May 1955–July 1960; Acting Chairman, May 1957–August 1957

Harold C. Patterson, August 1955–November 1960

Earl F. Hastings, March 1956–August 1961

James C. Sargent, June 1956–October 1960

Edward N. Gadsby, August 1957–August 1961; Chairman, August 1957–March 1961

Byron Woodside, July 1960–April 1967

Daniel J. McCauley Jr., October 1960–March 1961

Kennedy Appointments:

Allen J. Frear Jr., March 1961–September 1963

William L. Cary, March 1961–August 1964

Manuel F. Cohen, October 1961–August 1964; Chairman, August 1964–February 1969

Jack M. Whitney II, November 1961–June 1964

Johnson Appointments:

Hugh F. Owens, March 1964–November 1973

Hamer H. Budge, July 1964–February 1969; Chairman, February 1969–January 1971

Francis M. Wheat, October 1964–September 1969
Richard B. Smith, May 1967–July 1971

Nixon Appointments:

James J. Needham, July 1969–July 1972
A. Sydney Herlong, Jr., October 1969–June 1973
William J. Casey, April 1971–February 1973
Philip A. Loomis Jr., August 1971–1982; Acting Chairman, April 1981–May 1981 *
Bradford G. Cook, March 1973–May 1973
John R. Evans, March 1973–December 1983
Ray Garrett, Jr., August 1973–October 1975
A. A. Sommer, Jr., August 1973–June 1976
Irving M. Pollack, February 1974–June 1980

Ford Appointments:

Roderick M. Hills, October 1975–June 1977

Carter Appointments:

Harold M. Williams, April 1977–April 1981
Roberta S. Karmel, September 1977–February 1980
Stephen J. Friedman, April 1980–June 1981
Barbara S. Thomas, October 1980–November 1983

Reagan Appointments:

John S. R. Shad, May 1981–March 1987
Bevis Longstreth, July 1981–June 1984
James C. Treadway, September 1982–April 1985
Charles C. Cox, December 1983–September 1989; Acting Chairman, June 1987–July 1987
Charles L. Marinaccio, May 1984–July 1985
Aulana L. Peters, June 1984–July 1988
Joseph A. Grundfest, October 1985–January 1990
Edward H. Fleischman, January 1986–present

David S. Ruder, August 1987–May 1989
Mary L. Schapiro, September 1988–present

Bush Appointments:

Richard C. Breeden, October 1989–present
Philip R. Lochner Jr., February 1990–present
Richard Y. Roberts, September 1990–present

Note: Italicized names indicate service on the commission as a chairman.

Notes

Chapter 1. Introduction

1. Throughout this study, the term *formal institutions* will be used to refer to explicit structures and procedures that are provided for constitutionally or through statute. *Informal institutions* refer primarily to procedures that become standard through consensus and use and act as rules guiding behavior. This distinction is also made below.

2. Terry Moe (1988, 1989) deals explicitly with the question of control as it relates to professionals. However, his work does not allow for an "independent" role for professionals. Rather, he argues that professional groups are intentionally selected by elected officials and their constituents as a predictable set of decision makers; by making decisions according to their professional standards, these bureaucrats will be meeting the priorities of interested groups and politicians. In other words, professionals may think they are acting independently, but they are really agents of the outside principals who selected them.

3. Briefly, a stock index future is a product whose value is based upon the price of stocks that make up a stock index—such as the Standard and Poor 500. The purchaser of an index future has an obligation to receive or deliver a cash amount equal to the difference between the price of the index stated in the contract, and the value of the contract on that future date. It is used as an instrument to hedge, or avert risk, in stock market purchases.

4. See testimony of SEC Chairman Richard Breeden in Senate Committee on Banking, Housing, and Urban Affairs 1990, *Hearing Concerning Intermarket Regulation*; see testimony of Federal Reserve Board Chairman Alan Greenspan, Treasury Undersecretary Robert Glauber, SEC Chairman Richard Breeden, and CFTC Chairwoman Wendy Gramm, before the Senate Agriculture, Nutrition, and Forestry Committee 1990, *Hearing Concerning Intermarket Regulation*.

5. See testimony of John Shad in Senate Banking Committee 1984, *Hearings on Tender Offer Practices and Corporate Director Responsibilities*; see testimony of Charles Cox in Senate Finance Committee 1985,

Hearings on Tax Treatment of Hostile Takeovers; and *Wall Street Journal* 6/24/87, 12; and see testimony of David Ruder in House Energy and Commerce Committee 1987, *Tender Offer Reform*, pt. 2.

6. Gormley (1986) makes a similar argument with respect to the complexity and salience of an issue area. When issues are highly complex *and* salient, Gormley argues that the role of the professional (the bureaucratic expert) in determining outcomes is increased, primarily because politicians are "repelled by complexity." However, in contrast to the argument made here, he also argues that the lower the salience of an issue the greater the likelihood that professionals will be less influential because of the behind-the-scenes strength of powerful business interests.

7. This is the first of many quotes taken from interviews conducted with former and present staff and commissioners of the SEC, former and present staff members of the House and Senate, former members of the committees, and representatives of the securities industry. Throughout the text, quotations without a direct citation are taken from these interviews. (See Appendix 1.)

8. Scher (1960) describes the willingness of committee members with jurisdiction over the National Labor Relations Board to intervene in the decision making of the agency when their constituent support came from either the solid labor or solid business side of the debate. At the time of his study, members rarely had constituents on both sides. Consequently, for each member, there was a unified constituent position.

9. The argument made here concerning the role of an agency in the policy process is similar to the argument that Congress will initially delegate authority to an agency in order to "shift the blame" when conflict is high (Fiorina 1982). However, that decision (to delegate) has ongoing implications for an agency's ability to influence the policy process (Woll 1977; Wilson 1980). Regardless of the decision to delegate to an agency, it is argued here that there is power in the role of mediator between competing interests.

10. In an interview, a Senate staff member contested this point. Following the 1987 stock market crash, several congressional staff members participated in the Presidential Task Force (the Brady Commission) study of the crash by interviewing market participants. During the interviews, managers for investment funds were asked why they did not lobby against, or object to, the high commission rates paid to specialists on the NYSE to execute their trades. According to this staff member, some large-block traders view the high commissions as an insurance premium paid to guarantee the immediate execution of their trades in the event of a market slide— such as the 1987 crash.

11. Briefly, unlike a stock exchange, the over-the-counter market is not bound by physical location. Instead, the market is as vast as the number of

OTC dealers across the country. Trading of securities takes place through a network of telephones, telegraphs, and computers, as opposed to the floor of a stock exchange. An extensive discussion of the OTC market and the exchanges is provided in chapter 3.

12. Weaver (1980) makes a similar argument with respect to the lack of congressional intervention in the activities of the Antitrust Division of the Department of Justice.

13. Appendix 1 explains the interview methodology used in this study. A list of SEC chairmen and commissioners is provided in Appendix 2.

Chapter 2. A Regulatory Framework

1. When a company's stock is "listed" on a stock exchange, that company has applied and met the qualifications of the stock exchange to have its securities traded in that market. The qualifications include standards for the company's earnings; a minimum market value for currently held public securities; a minimum level of net tangible assets; a minimum amount of shares; and a minimum level of share distribution—the number of investors holding stock in the company. These requirements vary from exchange to exchange, the New York Stock Exchange having the most demanding requirements (See Teweles and Bradley 1987, 112–22).

2. See House Interstate and Foreign Commerce Committee 1934, *Hearings on Stock Exchange Regulation*; and Senate Banking and Currency Committee 1934, *Hearings on Stock Exchange Practices*, pts. 15–16.

3. It should be noted that critics of the SEC have charged the agency with excessive use of its rule-making authority in the area of disclosure (See Kripke 1979). However, these rules tend to pertain to the quantity and kind of information companies must disclose to the SEC, rather than to the standards for how financial data is reported.

Chapter 3. Expansion, Delineation, and Institutionalization

1. For an extended discussion of the OTC and exchange markets, see Tyler (1965) and Robbins (1966). Crossland and Sehr (1968) provide an excellent review of the exchange specialist system and its relationship to the "third market"—where exchange listed securities are traded over the counter.

2. It should not be assumed that the roles of brokers and dealers are mutually exclusive. A specialist acts as both a broker and a dealer. Here, I have differentiated the two based on their role in "making a market." How-

ever, when executing trades for brokers, the specialist is a broker's broker. When specialists buy and sell from their own account—to maintain continuity and liquidity in the market—they are a dealer (see Rice 1975, for a more detailed differentiation between brokers and dealers).

3. In 1941 the SEC, in response to a request from the House Interstate and Foreign Commerce Committee, submitted proposals to amend the Securities Exchange Act that dealt with the regulation of proxy solicitations under section 14 of the act, and the governance of trading by corporate insiders in section 16. World War II began during hearings on the proposals, and the hearings were postponed. In 1949, 1950, and 1957, the agency again proposed the legislative extension of disclosure requirements to companies whose securities were traded OTC (SEC, *Annual Report* 1945, 8; ibid. 1949, iv–xv; ibid. 1957, 10–17).

4. This argument is in stark contrast to that offered by Weingast (1984), who argues that the SEC was interested in new legislation during this period but that the gap in legislative action represented a lack of congressional interest. He holds that this was due to the lack of a sufficient political benefit for committee members to be derived from dealing with securities law at the time.

5. The legislation contained a phase-in provision to gradually drop the number of shareholders to 500.

6. The legislation did, however, contain several provisions that prohibited certain investment transactions, as well as provisions governing the structure of investment companies.

7. For SEC recommendations, see SEC, *Annual Report* 1972, 5–6. For committee acceptance of SEC recommendations, see House Subcommittee on Commerce and Finance, *Securities Industry Study* 1972, esp. 15–17. The compatibility between the SEC and the committees on this point was also noted in interviews with former members of the SEC staff who worked closely on the development and passage of the amendments with the congressional legislative committees.

8. Senate Banking, Housing, and Urban Affairs Committee 1975, *Summary of the Principal Provisions of the Securities Acts Amendments of 1975*, 9; Conference Committee 1975, *Report on Securities Acts Amendments of 1975*, 49, 73.

9. See Subcommittee on Oversight and Investigations and the Subcommittee on Consumer Protection and Finance 1977, *Oversight of the Functioning and Administration of the Securities Acts Amendments of 1975*; and House Interstate and Foreign Commerce Committee 1980, *National Market System: Five Year Status Report*.

10. See SEC, *Securities Exchange Act Release*, no. 11942, 1975; ibid., no. 13662, 1977; and ibid., no. 15679, 1979.

11. In 1987, 1,523 different stocks were registered to trade through

ITS, with an average volume of 8,781,600 shares traded daily (SEC, *The October 1987 Market Break* 1988, 7/41–42.

12. Senate Banking Committee, *Summary of Principal Provisions of the Securities Acts Amendments of 1975*, May 1975, 94th Cong., 9; Conference Report, *Securities Acts Amendments of 1975*, May 1975, 94th Cong., 49, 73.

13. The debate over "fairness" has since extended beyond the Investment Company Act. For example, during the late 1970s the SEC proposed rule 13e-2 for "going private" transactions. When a company goes private the buyers force a majority of the shareholders out. The SEC wanted to include a provision that the squeeze out had to be "fair" to the other shareholders. The provision, however, was excluded in the final release (*Securities Exchange Act Release*, no. 16075, August 2, 1979). Ultimately, the fairness issue is a federal question. State law prohibits unfairness; therefore, any federal law is supplementary.

Chapter 4. Maintaining Disclosure-Enforcement

1. All of this is not to say that the SEC does not make rules. For example, throughout this chapter the SEC's July 1987 one-share, one-vote rule is discussed. The rule addressed the controversial issues of corporate governance and voting rights associated with common stock (*Washington Post* 7/8/88, G1), and the agency stepped in to make a ruling after SEC supervised negotiations between the New York Stock Exchange (NYSE), the American Stock Exchange (AMEX), and the National Association of Securities Dealers (NASD) broke down (*Wall Street Journal* 6/5/87, 2; *Investment Dealers' Digest* 2/23/87, 56; ibid. 4/20/87, 8). The point here is that issues that divide participants in the securities industry, such as the one share issue, have at times been mediated by an SEC rule initiative.

2. The importance of ideological predisposition and the policy preferences of bureaucratic personnel has been demonstrated by Aberbach and Rockman (1976), and by Rothman and Lichter (1983). The topic is also discussed by Kaufman (1960) as it relates to forest service personnel.

3. It should be noted that this statutory base was drafted, in large part, by Landis, one of the agency's first commissioners and second chairman. Further, expansions of the agency's disclosure mandate were typically premised on SEC proposals.

4. I estimated this on the basis of a background review of the SEC's commissioners from 1934 to the present, as provided by the biographical sketches of commissioners in the SEC *Annual Reports* and various historical and journalistic accounts of the appointments process.

5. Robert Katzmann (1980) makes a similar argument with respect to

the professional incentives of the attorneys in the Federal Trade Commission. Chapter 8 deals with this issue in a comparative context.

6. McCraw (1984) and Chatov (1975) disagree on this last point. Chatov argues that the failure of the SEC to impose or require accounting standards has left control over accounting practices with the corporate financial community. McCraw argues that the agency's "enlistment" of accountants has given the profession a tremendous boost toward independence.

7. This point has been disputed by several economists. See Stigler (1975) and Manne and Solomon (1974).

8. This argument is similar to the prisoner's dilemma argument in the provision of a collective good (Rapoport and Chammah 1965; Rapoport 1982). The dilemma, it is argued, is that the pursuit of individual self interest (individually "rational" behavior) will often produce outcomes that are inferior for the collective whole. In other words, the group might be better off if each individual took a different action other than pursuing immediate self-interest, but without any enforcement mechanism or alternative incentive the group will not achieve that better outcome. See also Mancur Olson (1965) for a discussion of the incentives facing individuals to participate in collective activities.

9. The exact number of additional staff positions or the amount of money intended by the legislative committees for enforcement efforts has not been determined. However, in 1987 there was bipartisan support in the Senate Banking Committee for these increases, particularly in the wake of the Levine and Boesky cases (*Wall Street Journal* 2/25/87, 5; *Washington Post* 2/4/87, G-1).

10. The extent to which the authorization can influence the amount appropriated for the agency is debatable and will be discussed in greater detail in chapter 6. At this point it is assumed that the committees' authority to set agency authorizations is significant for the resources that are actually appropriated.

11. For criticisms of this practice, see Freedman (1975), and Jenkins (1978). The agency takes this action under its "Rules of Practice and Rules Relating to Investigations," issued in 1960, and updated periodically. For example, recently the SEC ruled that its Rule 2(e) hearings, dealing with disbarment, be made public (*Securities Regulation and Law Report* 12/23/88, 1959).

12. Senate Banking, Housing, and Urban Affairs Committee 1983, *Report on Amending the Securities Exchange Act of 1934*, 3; House Energy and Commerce Committee 1983, *Report on the Authorization of Appropriations for the SEC*, 5, 16; House Energy and Commerce Committee 1985, *Report on Securities and Exchange Commission Authorization of Appropriations*, 5; *Wall Street Journal* 2/25/87, 5.

Chapter 5. A Decade of Activism

1. The total dollar volume traded on the American Stock Exchange (AMEX) rose from $9.02 billion, in 1965, to $31 billion, in 1969. Several of the regional exchange markets experienced similar increases in dollar volume. For example, the Pacific Coast Stock Exchange dollar volume jumped from $2.2 billion in 1965, to $5.5 billion, in 1969; the Philadelphia-Baltimore-Washington Stock Exchange dollar volume increased from slightly more than $1 billion to $2.5 billion during the same period (SEC, *Annual Report* 1966, 162; ibid. 1970, 220).

2. Under the Securities Exchange Act, the SEC has authority to set minimum net capital requirements for brokers and dealers and to limit the amount of indebtedness they may incur. A standard formula is used to calculate a broker's net capital, and the ratio of "aggregate indebtedness" to net capital cannot exceed an SEC specified level. In 1969, aggregate indebtedness could not be more than 20 times a broker's net capital (SEC, *Annual Report* 1969, 85).

3. Senate Governmental Affairs Committee 1977,*Study on Federal Regulation*, vol. 2. The nine agencies were the Civil Aeronautics Board, the Consumer Product Safety Commission, the Federal Communications Commission, the Federal Maritime Commission, the Federal Power Commission, the Federal Trade Commission, the Interstate Commerce Commission, the Nuclear Regulatory Commission, and the SEC (*SRLR* 2/16/77, A-1).

4. In 1988 the SEC reported that, on average, attorneys in the GS-11, GS-12, and GS-13 grades stayed with the agency for .5, 1.17, and 2.92 years, respectively. The turnover rate slowed for GS-14 to 3.67 years and for GS-15 to 8.83 years. The higher grades reflect career staff status (SEC, *Self-Funding Study* 1988, A-1).

5. See Bernstein (1958) and Thompson (1961) for discussions of the conflict between authority and expertise in bureaucratic organizations. See Kaufman (1981) on the limits of leadership and the significance of agency staff in the definition of agency agendas.

6. The connection to the Progressive and New Deal eras is strong with respect to the argument that professionals can best represent the "public interest" because they do not represent the interests of narrow economic concerns (Landis 1938; McCraw 1984).

7. Fowlkes (1971b) discusses the the Wall Street lobbying effort during the hearings.

8. It is interesting to note that one year after leaving the commission, Sommer joined the critics of the agency's expanded disclosure program (see, for example, *New York Times* 7/23/77, III-1).

Chapter 6. Breaking the Rules

1. Congressional scrutiny of the agency's enforcement agenda did not visibly ease until 1986 when the SEC went public with its insider trading cases against investment banker Dennis Levine and arbitrageur Ivan Boesky. Both provided members of Congress with high-profile cases that drew attention to what were, according to some, Wall Street's excesses under a Republican administration (*Congressional Quarterly Weekly* 12/13/86, 3074).

2. Participation of the economic staff is documented in a series of analytical memoranda issued by the Office of Economic Research and the chief economist throughout the commission rate debates. See, for example, "Comment on Antitrust and the NYSE—The Issue—Minimum Brokerage Commission," 10/28/71; "NYSE 1971 Commission Rate Proposal," 9/16/71; "Additional Percent of Commission Revenue and percent of Total Revenue from Orders in Excess of $100,000," 12/1/70; "Draft Commission Rate Material," September 1970.

3. *Raider* is a term that describes the leader of a corporate takeover. Takeovers can be friendly—in that there is some form of cooperation between the target company and the takeover group—or hostile.

4. For the position of the OCE on corporate takeovers, as well as congressional reactions, consult hearings before the Senate Securities Subcommittee in Senate Banking, Housing, and Urban Affairs Committee 1985, *Hearings on the Impact of Corporate Takeovers*, esp. 365–443. For the position of the OCE on multiple trading, see *Staff Studies of Multiple Trading of Options*, November 1986. For congressional reactions to MTOs, see *SRLR* 9/4/87, 1358–59).

5. Sporkin was offered the position by the director of the CIA, William Casey. It was reported that when Casey was chairman of the SEC (1971–1972), Sporkin saved him from being implicated in a White House scandal. When the Nixon administration attempted to delay an SEC investigation of New Jersey financier Robert Vesco, Sporkin advised Casey to let the investigation continue (*Washington Post* 4/22/81, E-1). Vesco, a contributor to the Nixon presidential campaign, was later indicted for defrauding mutual fund investors.

6. For example, during an SEC appropriations hearing in 1974, Senator William Proxmire (D-Wis.) made SEC Chairman Garrett promise, on the public record, to maintain a particular level of funding for Stanley Sporkin's enforcement efforts.

7. For example, Irving Pollack was named director of the Division of Trading and Markets (split into the Division of Enforcement, and the Division of Market Regulations in 1972) in 1966. Before his appointment, Pollack served as the associate director of the division under Ralph Saul

(SEC, *Annual Report* 1964, xi). Saul, in turn, was an associate director of the division from 1958 until 1960 (SEC, *Annual Report* 1960, xii). Philip Loomis was the division's director from 1955 to 1963, and served as an associate director of the division in 1954 (SEC, *Annual Report* 1955, xii).

8. SEC, *Annual Report* 1983; *New York Times* 10/22/80, IV-1; ibid. 6/22/81, D-2; *Wall Street Journal* 4/27/82, 7).

9. Of the five chairmen who served between 1971 and 1980, all practiced law before their appointment, and three had extensive experience in securities law. Two of the five were former members of the SEC staff. Of the seven other commissioners that served in that same period, five had a law degree, and four of the five had extensive experience in securities law. Two were former members of the SEC staff (SEC, *Annual Report* 1971–1980).

10. Chairman John Dingell (D-Mich.) of the House Energy and Commerce Committee undertook an investigation of Shad's financial dealings with investment bank Morgan Stanley prior to the SEC vote on rule 415. Dingell was looking for a conflict of interest between Shad's participation in the SEC deliberations and the lobbying efforts of Morgan Stanley in opposition to the rule. It should be noted that the committee found no wrongdoing and that Chairman Shad voted in support of the rule (*New York Times* 3/18/82, IV-1; ibid. 11/23/82, IV-1).

11. Position Description, filed by the SEC with the Civil Service Commission, 1/31/74.

12. It is interesting that this staff member distinguished between the political influence brought to bear on the commissioners versus the greater independence of the agency's staff. Even under Shad, he said, "I thought the staff had a fair degree of autonomy to take the correct approach. I still think the commission can do an awful lot of work without interference," because of that staff autonomy.

Chapter 7. The SEC and Congress

1. These changes were cited and discussed in interviews with the staff and commissioners of the SEC.

2. See House Energy and Commerce Committee 1987, *Hearings on Tender Offer Reform*, pts. 1–2; House Energy and Commerce Committee 1985, *Hearings on Corporate Takeovers*, pt. 2; House Energy and Commerce Committee 1984, *Hearings on Takeover Tactics and Public Policy*. Senate Banking, Housing, and Urban Affairs Committee 1987, *Hearings on Hostile Takeovers*; Senate Banking Committee 1987, *Hearings on Regulating Hostile Takeovers*; Senate Banking Committee 1984, *Hearings on Tender Offer Practices and Corporate Director Responsibilities*; Senate Banking Committee 1985, *Hearings on Impact of Corporate Takeovers, April 3,*

4, June 6, 12, 1985; Senate Finance Committee 1985, *Hearings on Tax Treatment of Hostile Takeovers.*

3. One exception was the commission's endorsement of a proposal to narrow or close the ten-day window. Once a purchaser (such as a corporate raider) acquires 5 percent of a company's outstanding stock, the buyer has ten days to disclose the purchase to the SEC. The proposal was intended to make takeover attempts a more public process.

4. Noll and Owen (1983) make a similar argument about the potential for a regulatory agency to see beyond the interests articulated by dominant economic groups in order to better serve a "public" interest that is perhaps unrepresented.

5. See, for example, SEC, Office of the Chief Economist, *Economics of Any-or-All, Partial and Two-Tier Tender Offers*, April 1985; *Impact of Targeted Share Repurchases (Greenmail) on Stock Prices*, September 1984; *Shark Repellents and Stock Prices: The Effects of Antitakeover Amendments Since 1980*, July 1985; *Noninvestment Grade Debt as a source of Tender Offer Financing*, June 1986; *Motivations for Hostile Tender Offers and the Market for Political Exchange*, September 1985; and *Washington Post* 8/3/83, DC-13.

6. For example, in early 1983 the OCE chief economist stood in opposition to a rule that would have slowed the pace of a tender offer so that shareholders could absorb the information concerning the proposed purchase. The OCE argued that the change would slow down the rate of takeovers at a greater net social loss than any benefit that would accrue to shareholders (*Wall Street Journal* 7/8/83, 9; *Washington Post* 8/3/85, DC-13).

7. See the minority views on the report on SEC reauthorization in Senate Banking, Housing, and Urban Affairs Committee 1987, *Securities and Exchange Commission Authorization of Appropriations and Technical Amendments to the Securities Laws, Report together with additional views to accompany S. 1452*, 42–43. Republican support for preserving the SEC's independent expertise must be tempered by the fact that there was also support among these members for the SEC's position on takeovers.

8. In addition to Shad and Cox, the third "political" nomination by the Reagan administration was Mary Schapiro. Schapiro was nominated during a congressional recess, allowing her to serve for one year without confirmation. Prior to her appointment Schapiro served as an executive assistant to Chairwoman Susan Phillips of the Commodity Futures Trading Commission, and then as top lawyer and senior vice-president of the Futures Industry Association—a trade group representing the futures industry (*Wall Street Journal* 9/13/88, 44). Despite her credentials as an attorney and regulator, interests in the SEC as well as in the securities industry believed Schapiro was representative of the Reagan administration's stance against

additional regulation of the commodity markets following the 1987 market crash. The Securities Industry Association (representing primarily regional and small brokerage firms) supported tighter regulation of stock index futures as a means to prevent volatile markets and, therefore, to boost the confidence of the individual investor in the markets. In the SEC there was (and is) strong consensus for a greater agency role in the regulation of stock index futures. Schapiro's connections to the "enemy," as some saw it, made her a threat to agency and industry policy, and provoked comments by industry representatives such as, "Schapiro has no business being there." Had Schapiro been a general counsel for the SIA, regardless of her capabilities as an attorney, there would have no doubt been a presumption that her decision making would follow agency precedent and procedure. It should be noted that these initial fears must have been allayed when Schapiro (reappointed by the Bush administration and confirmed by the Senate) came out in favor of a full merger of the CFTC into the SEC (*Wall Street Journal* 3/21/90, C-1).

Commissioner Grundfest's background as general counsel and senior economist of the Council of Economic Advisors made his appointment in 1985 somewhat controversial. But his solid legal background in securities law (he was with the Washington law firm of Wilmer, Cutler, and Pickering prior to service on the CEA) apparently attenuated criticisms (Senate Banking, Housing, and Urban Affairs Committee 1985, *Hearing before the Committee on Banking, Housing and Urban Affairs on the nomination of Joseph Grundfest, to be a Commissioner on the Securities and Exchange Commission; SRLR* 10/4/85, 1749).

Chapter 8. An Unusual Institution

1. Authors within the principal-agent literature have acknowledged the problems associated with a definition for "control" of the bureaucracy. See, for example, Moe (1987).

2. Indeed, as I argued in chapter 2, a future SEC commissioner, James Landis, played a central role in drafting the legislation that delegated the authority to the SEC in the first place.

3. It is not my intention to categorically identify all the economists within or outside of the SEC as representative of one perspective, and all the attorneys as representative of another. Obviously, individual economists and attorneys adopt perspectives that are representative of a blend of concerns. However, for purposes of the discussion, this categorical distinction is reasonably made.

4. Competition between attorneys and economists also took hold in an executive branch regulatory agency, the Environmental Protection Agency

(EPA). Melnick (1983) offers vivid accounts of the conflict between the EPA's attorneys and economists, as well as between the agency's engineers in the Office of Air Quality Planning and Standards, and the agency's attorneys in the General Counsel's Office and the Office of Enforcement.

5. Jenkins-Smith and Weimer (1985) make a similar argument related to the use of policy analysis as a means to blunt or reverse policy initiatives that are not compatible with the institutionalized perspective of an agency. They argue that analyses generated by a predominant, institutionalized "perspective" can serve to veto or undermine alternative views within an agency.

6. For years the Forest Service was also able to maintain a high level of integration within the agency and in the broader policy community. According to Kaufman (1960), this was due largely to the institutionalization of a single professional perspective—that of the professionally trained forest ranger. However, increasing concern for the environment and the political power of organized environmental constituencies has created professional fragmentation in the broader policy community that has reached the agency, as well (Tipple and Wellman 1991; Culhane 1981; Le Master 1984).

7. See testimony of SEC Chairman Richard Breeden before the Senate Banking Committee's Subcommittee on Securities: Senate Committee on Banking, Housing, and Urban Affairs 1990, *Concerning Intermarket Regulation*; *National Journal* 12/5/87, 3091–93.

Appendix 1. Research Methods and Study Design

1. During this trip to Washington I also conducted a few interviews with former SEC staff and commissioners.

2. In one case an interviewee is identified directly because of the importance of identification for the argument. Explicit permission was given.

Bibliography

Aberbach, Joel D. 1990. *Keeping a Watchful Eye: The Politics of Congressional Oversight*. Washington, D.C.: Brookings.

Aberbach, Joel D., and Bert A. Rockman. 1976. "Clashing Beliefs Within the Executive Branch: The Nixon Administration." *American Political Science Review* 70: 446–68.

Alexis, Marcus. 1983. "The Political Economy of Federal Regulation of Surface Transportation." In *The Political Economy of Deregulation: Interest Groups in the Regulatory Process*, ed. Noll and Owen. Washington, D.C.: American Enterprise Institute.

Allison, Graham T. 1971. *Essence of Decision: Explaining the Cuban Missile Crisis*. New York: Scott, Foresman.

Appleby, Paul H. 1949. *Policy and Administration*. University, Ala.: University of Alabama Press.

Armstrong, J. 1959. "Congress and the SEC." *Virginia Law Review* 45: 795–816.

Baruch, Hurd. 1971. *Wall Street: Security Risk*. Washington, D.C.: Acropolis Books.

Baxter, William F. 1970. "NYSE Fixed Commission Rates: A Price Cartel Goes Public." *Standford Law Review* 22: 669.

Bendor, Jonathan, Serge Taylor, and Roland van Gaalen. 1987. "Politicians, Bureaucrats, and Asymmetric Information." *American Journal of Political Science* 31: 796–828.

Behrman, Bradley. 1980. "Civil Aeronautics Board." In *The Politics of Regulation*, ed. Wilson. New York: Basic Books.

Bernheim, Alfred, and Margaret Grant Schneider, eds. 1935. *The Securities Markets: Findings and Recommendations of a Special Staff of the Twentieth Century Fund*. New York: Twentieth Century Fund.

Bernstein, Marver. 1955. *Regulating Business by Independent Commission*. Princeton, N.J.: Princeton University Press.

———. 1958. *The Job of the Federal Executive*. Washington, D.C.: Brookings.

Brooks, John. 1987. *The Takeover Game*. A Twentieth Century Fund Book. New York: E. P. Dutton.

Bruere, Henry. 1912. "Efficiency in City Government." *Annals of the American Academy of Political Science* 42 (May): 3–5.

Bullock, Hugh. 1959. *The Story of Investment Companies.* New York: Columbia University Press.

Calvert, Randall, Mathew McCubbins, and Barry Weingast. 1989. "A Theory of Political Control and Agency Discretion." *American Journal of Political Science* 33 (August): 588–611.

Calvert, Randall, Mark Moran, and Barry Weingast. 1987. "Congressional Influence Over Policy Making: The Case of the FTC." In *Congress: Structure and Policy,* ed. McCubbins and Sullivan. Cambridge: Cambridge University Press.

Cary, William L. 1967. *Politics and the Regulatory Agencies.* New York: McGraw-Hill.

———. 1964. "Administrative Agencies and the Securities and Exchange Commission." *Law and Contemporary Problems* 29: 653–62.

Chatov, Robert. 1975. *Corporate Financial Reporting: Public or Private Control?* New York: Free Press.

Chubb, John. 1983. *Interest Groups and the Bureaucracy: The Politics of Energy.* Stanford, Calif.: Stanford University Press.

Clarkson, Kenneth, and Timothy Muris. 1981. *The Federal Trade Commission Since 1970: Economic Regulation and Bureaucratic Behavior.* Cambridge: Cambridge University Press.

Cohen, Milton H. 1985. "The Integrated Disclosure System—Unfinished Business." *Business Lawyer* 40 (May): 987–95.

———. 1966. " 'Truth in Securities' Revisited." *Harvard Law Review* 79: 1340–1408.

Cooper, Joseph, and William West. 1988. "Presidential Power and Republican Government: The Theory and Practice of OMB Review of Agency Rules." *Journal of Politics* 50: 864–95.

Crossland, Hugh J., and Robert James Sehr, Jr. 1968. "The Gods of the Marketplace: An Examination of the Regulation of the Securities Business." *Boston University Law Review* 48: 515–58.

Culhane, Paul. 1981. *Public Lands Politics: Interest Group Influence on the Forest Service and the Bureau of Land Management.* Baltimore, Md.: Johns Hopkins University Press.

Dahl, Robert A. 1947. "The Science of Public Administration: Three Problems." *Public Administration Review* 7: 1–11.

de Bedts, Ralph F. 1964. *The New Deal's SEC: The Formative Years.* New York: Columbia University Press.

Derthick, Martha. 1990. *Agency Under Stress: The Social Security Administration in American Government.* Washington, D.C.: Brookings.

Derthick, Martha, and Paul Quirk. 1985. *The Politics of Deregulation.* Washington, D.C.: Brookings.

Dexter, Lewis Anthony. 1970. *Elite and Specialized Interviewing.* Northwestern University Press.

Dexter, Lewis Anthony. 1969. "Congressmen and the Making of Military Policy." In *New Perspectives on the House of Representatives*, ed. Peabody and Polsby. Chicago: Rand McNally.

Dodd, Lawrence, and Richard Schott. 1979. *Congress and the Administrative State.* New York: Wiley.

Eads, George C., and Michael Fix, eds. 1984. *Relief or Reform? Reagan's Deregulatory Dilemma.* Washington, D.C.: Urban Institute.

Edelman, Murray. 1964. *The Symbolic Uses of Politics.* Urbana: University of Illinois Press.

Edwards, George C., III, and Stephen J. Wayne. 1990. *Presidential Leadership: Politics and Policy Making.* 2d ed. New York: St. Martin's Press.

Eisenhower, Dwight D. 1960. *Public Papers of the Presidents of the United States*, vol. 1 (1953). Washington, D.C.: U.S. Government Printing Office.

Eisenstadt, Samuel N. 1965. "Bureaucracy and Bureaucratization." In *Essays on Comparative Institutions.* New York: John Wiley.

Fenno, Richard. 1973. *Congressmen in Committees.* Boston: Little, Brown.

Ferejohn, John. 1987. "The Structure of Agency Decision Processes." In *Congress: Structure and Policy*, ed. McCubbins and Sullivan. Cambridge: Cambridge University Press.

Ferejohn, John, and Charles Shipan. 1988. "Congressional Influence on Administrative Agencies: A Case Study of Telecommunications Policy." In *Congress Reconsidered*, 4th ed., ed. Dodd and Oppenheimer. Washington, D.C.: Congressional Quarterly Press.

Fiorina, Morris. 1986. "Legislative Uncertainty, Legislative Control, and the Delegation of Legislative Power." *Journal of Law, Economics, and Organization* 2 (Spring): 33–51.

———. 1982. "Legislative Choice of Regulatory Forms: Legal Process or Administrative Process?" *Public Choice* 39 (September): 33–66.

———. 1977. *Congress: Keystone of the Washington Establishment.* New Haven, Conn.: Yale University Press.

Fiorina, Morris, and Roger Noll. 1978. "Voters, Bureaucrats, and Legislators: A Rational Choice Perspective on the Growth of Bureaucracy." *Journal of Public Economics* 9 (June): 239–54.

Fowlkes, Frank V. 1971a. "Economic Report/New Studies Set Stage for Expanded Federal Regulation of Securities Industry." *National Journal* (December 25): 2518–24.

Fowlkes, Frank V. 1971b. "Agency Report/Congress Prods SEC to Get Firmer Grip on Nation's Securities Industry." *National Journal* (February 20): 373–88.

Freedman, Monroe H. 1975. *Lawyers' Ethics in an Adversarial System*. Indianapolis: Bobbs-Merrill.

Freeman, Milton. 1976. "The Legality of the SEC's Management Fraud Program." *Business Lawyer* 31 (March): 1295–1303.

Friendly, Henry J. 1962. *The Federal Administrative Agencies*. Cambridge, Mass.: Harvard University Press.

Garrett, Ray, Jr. 1974. "New Directions in Professional Responsibility." *Business Lawyer* 29: 7–13.

Giannelli, Paul C. 1970. "The New York Stock Exchange Minimum Commission Rate Structure: Antitrust on Wall Street." *Securities Law Review* 2: 496–528.

Glass, Andrew J. 1973. "Economic Report/Wall Street, Beleaguered and Divided, Tries to Shape Congressional Pressure for Reform." *National Journal* (May 18): 709–18.

Goldberg, Lawrence G., and Lawrence J. White, eds. 1979. *The Deregulation of the Banking and Securities Industries*. Lexington, Mass.: Lexington Books.

Goodnow, Frank J. 1900. *Politics and Administration*. New York: Macmillan.

Goodsell, Charles. 1985. *The Case for the Bureaucracy: A Public Administration Polemic*. 2d ed. Chatham, N.J.: Chatham House.

Gormley, William T., Jr. 1991. "The Bureaucracy and Its Masters: The New Madisonian System in the U.S." *Governance* 4 (January): 1–18.

———. 1989. *Taming the Bureaucracy: Muscles, Prayers and Other Strategies*. Princeton, N.J.: Princeton University Press.

———. 1986. "Regulatory Issue Networks in a Federal System." *Polity* 7: 595–620.

Grundfest, Joseph A. 1989. "Management Buyouts and Leveraged Buyouts: Are the Critics Right?" In *Leveraged Management Buyouts: Causes and Consequences*, ed. Amihud. Homewood, Ill.: Dow Jones–Irwin.

Gujarati, Damodar. 1984. *Government and Business*. New York: McGraw-Hill.

Hammond, Thomas, Jeffrey Hill, and Gary Miller. 1986. "Presidents, Congress, and the 'Congressional Control of Administration' Hypothesis." Presented at the annual meeting of the American Political Science Association, Washington, D.C., August 30.

Hammond, Thomas H., and Jack H. Knott. 1988. "A Formal Model of Subgovernment Power in the Policymaking Process." Presented at the annual meeting of the Midwest Political Science Association, April 14–16.

Hardy, Timothy. 1971. "Informal Bargaining Process: An Analysis of the SEC's Regulation of the New York Stock Exchange." *Yale Law Review* 80: 81.

Heclo, Hugh. 1977. *A Government of Strangers: Executive Politics in Washington.* Washington, D.C.: Brookings.

Hensley, Dennis C. 1969. "The Application of Antitrust Laws to the Securities Industry." *Securities Law Review* 1: 476–510.

Hess, Stephen. 1976. *Organizing the Presidency.* Washington, D.C.: Brookings.

Hill, Jeffrey. 1987. "Oversight, Agency Latitude, and Congressional Control of the Federal Energy Commission." Presented at the annual meeting of the Southern Political Science Association, Charlotte, N.C., November 5–7.

———. 1985. "Why So Much Stability? The Role of Agency Determined Stability." *Public Choice* 46: 275–87.

Hyneman, C. 1950. *Bureaucracy in a Democracy.* New York: Harper.

Janowitz, Morris. 1960. *The Professional Soldier.* New York: Free Press.

Jarrell, Gregg A. 1984. "Change at the Exchange: The Causes and Effects of Deregulation." *Journal of Law and Economics* 27 (October): 273–314.

Jenkins, John A. 1978. "Such Good Friends: The SEC and Securities Lawyers." *Washington Monthly* (February): 53–57.

Jenkins-Smith, Hank, and David Weimer. 1985. "Analysis as Retrograde Action." *Public Administration Review* 45: 485–94.

Jennings, Richard. 1964. "Self-Regulation in the Securities Industry: The Role of the SEC." *Law and Contemporary Problems* 29: 663–90.

Jones, Charles O. 1961. "Representation in Congress: The Case of the House Agriculture Committee." *American Political Science Review* (June): 358–67.

Karmel, Roberta S. 1981. *Regulation by Prosecution.* New York: Simon and Schuster.

Katzmann, Robert. 1980. *Regulatory Bureaucracy: The Federal Trade Commission and Antitrust Policy.* Cambridge, Mass.: MIT Press.

Kaufman, Herbert. 1990. "The End of an Alliance: Public Administration in the Eighties." In *Public Administration: The State of the Discipline,* ed. Lynn and Wildavsky. Chatham, N.J.: Chatham House.

———. 1981. *The Administrative Behavior of Federal Bureau Chiefs.* Washington, D.C.: Brookings.

———. 1960. *The Forest Ranger: A Study in Administrative Behavior.* Baltimore, Md.: Johns Hopkins Press.

———. 1956. "Emerging Conflicts in the Doctrines of Public Administration." *American Political Science Review* 50: 1057–73.

Kauper, Thomas E. 1984. "The Role of Economic Analysis in the Antitrust Division Before and After the Establishment of the Economic Policy Office: A Lawyer's View." *Antitrust Bulletin* (Spring): 111–32.

Kingdon, John W. 1984. *Agendas, Alternatives, and Public Policies.* Boston: Little, Brown.

Knott, Jack H., and Gary J. Miller. 1987. *Reforming Bureaucracy: The Politics of Institutional Choice*. New York: Prentice-Hall.

Kohlmeier, Louis M., Jr. 1969. *The Regulators: Watchdog Agencies and the Public Interest*. New York: Harper and Row.

Kolko, Gabriel. 1965. *Railroads and Regulation, 1877–1916*. New York: Norton.

Kripke, Homer. 1979. *The SEC and Corporate Disclosure: Regulation in Search of a Purpose*. New York: Permissions, Law & Business, Inc.

Landis, James. 1938. *The Administrative Process*. New Haven, Conn.: Yale University Press.

Le Master, Dennis C. 1984. *Decade of Change: The Remaking of Forest Service Statutory Authority During the 1970's*. Westport, Conn.: Greenwood Press.

Levine, Theodore. 1978. "How the SEC Will Continue to Use Consent Decrees." *Legal Times of Washington* 1 (June 5): 16–17.

Levinthal, Daniel. 1988. "A Survey of Agency Models of Organizations." *Journal of Economic Behavior and Organization* 9: 153–85.

Lipsky, Michael. 1980. *Street-Level Bureaucracy: Dilemmas of the Individual in Public Service*. Beverly Hills, Calif.: Sage Publications.

Lipton, David A. 1982. "Best Execution: The National Market System's Missing Ingredient." *Notre Dame Lawyer* 57: 447–509.

Long, Norton E. 1949. "Power and Administration." *Public Administration Review* 9: 257–64.

Loomis, Carol. 1970. "Wall Street on the Ropes." *Fortune* 6 (December): 62.
———. 1969. "They're Tearing Up Wall Street." *Fortune* 80 (August): 88.
———. 1968. "Big Board, Big Volume, Big Trouble." *Fortune* 77 (May): 146.
———. 1967. "The SEC Has a Little List." *Fortune* (January): 110.

Lowi, Theodore. 1979. *The End of Liberalism: The Second Republic of the United States*. 2d ed. New York: Norton.

McCraw, Thomas K. 1984. *The Prophets of Regulation*. Cambridge, Mass.: Belknap Press of Harvard University Press.

McCubbins, Mathew, Roger Noll, and Barry Weingast. 1987. "Administrative Procedures as Instruments of Political Control." *Journal of Law, Economics, and Organization* 3: 243–77.

McCubbins, Mathew, and Talbot Page. 1987. "A Theory of Congressional Delegation." In *Congress: Structure and Policy*, ed. McCubbins and Sullivan,. Cambridge: Cambridge University Press.

McCubbins, Mathew, and Thomas Schwartz. 1984. "Congressional Oversight Overlooked: Police Patrols Versus Fire Alarms." *American Journal of Political Science* 28: 165–79.

McCubbins, Mathew, and Terry Sullivan. 1987. *Congress: Structure and Policy*. Cambridge: Cambridge University Press.

McGurn, Patrick S., Sharon Pamepinto, and Adam B. Spector. 1989. *State*

Takeover Laws. Washington, D.C.: Investor Responsibility Research Center, Inc.

Macey, Jonathan R., and David D. Haddock. 1985. "Shirking at the SEC: The Failure of the National Market System." *University of Illinois Law Review* 2: 315-62.

MacKay, Robert J., and Joseph D. Reid, Jr. 1979. "On Understanding the Birth and Evolution of the Securities and Exchange Commission." In *Regulatory Change in an Atmosphere of Crisis*, ed. Walton. New York: Academic Press.

Manne, Henry G., ed. 1969. *Economic Policy and the Regulation of Corporate Securities*. Washington, D.C.: American Enterprise Institute.

Manne, Henry G., and Ezra Solomon. 1974. *Wall Street in Transition: The Emerging System and Its Impact on the Economy*. New York: New York University Press.

March, James, and Johan Olsen. 1989. *Rediscovering Institutions: The Organizational Basis of Politics*. New York: Free Press.

March, James G., and Johan P. Olsen. 1984. "The New Institutionalism: Organizational Factors in Political Life." *American Political Science Review* 78: 734-49.

Mayhew, David R. 1974. *Congress: The Electoral Connection*. New Haven, Conn.: Yale University Press.

Melnick, R. Shep. 1983. *Regulation and the Courts: The Case of the Clean Air Act*. Washington, D.C.: Brookings.

Miller, Gary, and Terry Moe. 1983. "Bureaucrats, Legislators, and the Size of Government." *American Political Science Review* 77: 297–322.

Miller, James C., III. 1989. *The Economist as Reformer: Revamping the FTC, 1981–1985*. Washington, D.C.: American Enterprise Institute.

Moe, Terry. 1989. "The Politics of Bureaucratic Structure." In *Can the Government Govern?* ed. Chubb and Peterson. Washington, D.C.: Brookings.

———. 1988. "Political Control and Professional Autonomy: The Institutional Politics of the NLRB." In *Studies in American Political Development*, vol. 2, ed. Orren and Skowronek. New Haven, Conn.: Yale University Press.

———. 1987. "An Assessment of the Positive Theory of 'Congressional Dominance.'" *Legislative Studies Quarterly* 12 (November): 475–520.

———. 1984. "The New Economics of Organization." *American Journal of Political Science* 28: 739–77.

Mosher, Frederick C. 1982. *Democracy and the Public Service*. New York: Oxford University Press.

Mosher, William, and Donald Kingsley, eds. 1936. *Public Personnel Management*. New York: Harper and Brothers.

Neustadt, Richard E. 1960. *Presidential Power: The Politics of Leadership*. New York: John Wiley.

Niskanen, William. 1975. "Bureaucrats and Politicians." *Journal of Law and Economics* 18: 617–43.

———. 1971. *Bureaucracy and Representative Government*. Chicago: Aldine Publishing.

Noll, Roger, and Bruce Owens, eds. 1983. *The Political Economy of Deregulation: Interest Groups in the Regulatory Process*. Washington, D.C.. American Enterprise Institute.

Olson, Mancur. 1965. *The Logic of Collective Action*. Cambridge, Mass.: Harvard University Press.

Painter, William H. 1973. "An Analysis of Recent Proposals for Reform of Federal Securities Regulation." *Michigan Law Review* 71: 1575.

Parrish, Michael E. 1970. *Securities Regulation and the New Deal*. New Haven, Conn.: Yale University Press.

Patterson, James T. 1967. *Congressional Conservatism and the New Deal*. Lexington: University of Kentucky Press.

Perritt, Henry H. 1989. "Electronic Acquisition and Release of Federal Agency Information: Analysis of Recommendations Adopted by the Administrative Conference of the United States." *Administrative Law Review* 41: 253–314.

Peterson, Mark A. 1990. *Legislating Together: The White House and Capitol Hill From Eisenhower to Reagan*. Cambridge, Mass.: Harvard University Press.

Phillips, Susan M., and J. Richard Zecher. 1981. *The SEC and the Public Interest*. Cambridge, Mass.: MIT Press.

Porter, Kirk H., and Donald Bruce Johnson. 1970. *National Party Platforms 1840–1968*. Urbana: University of Illinois Press.

Poser, Norman. 1981. "Restructuring the Stock Markets: A Critical Look at the SEC's National Market System." *New York University Law Review* 56: 883–958.

Quirk, Paul. 1988. "In Defense of the Politics of Ideas." *Journal of Politics* 50: 31–41.

Rapoport, Anatol. 1982. "Prisoner's Dilemma: Recollections and Observations." In *Rational Man and Irrational Society?* ed. Barry and Hardin. Beverly Hills, Calif.: Sage Publications.

Rapoport, Anatol, and Albert M. Chammah. 1965. *Prisoner's Dilemma: A Study in Conflict and Cooperation*. Ann Arbor: University of Michigan Press.

Ratner, David L. 1970. "Regulation of the Compensation of Securities Dealers." *Securities Law Review* 2: 451–73.

Reich, Robert B., ed.. 1988. *The Power of Public Ideas*. Cambridge, Mass.: Harvard University Press.

Rice, Dennis T. 1975. "The Expanding Requirement for Registration as 'Broker-Dealer' Under the Securities Exchange Act of 1934." *Securities Law Review* 7: 503–19.

Riker, William H. 1987. *The Development of American Federalism*. Boston: Kluwer Academic Publishers.

———. 1982. *Liberalism Against Populism: A Confrontation Between the Theory of Democracy and the Theory of Social Choice*. San Francisco: W. H. Freeman and Co.

Ritchie, Donald A. 1980. *James M. Landis: Dean of the Regulators*. Cambridge, Mass.: Harvard University Press.

———. 1975. "The Pecora Wall Street Expose: 1934." In *Congress Investigates: A Documented History, 1792–1974*, vol. 4, ed. Arthur Schlesinger, Jr., and Roger Bruns, 2555–2731. New York: Chelsea House.

Robbins, Sidney. 1966. *The Securities Markets: Operations and Issues*. New York: The Free Press.

Rockman, Bert A. 1984. *The Leadership Question: The Presidency and the American System*. New York: Praeger.

Roosevelt, Franklin Delano. 1938. *The Public Papers and Addresses of Franklin D. Roosevelt: With a Special Introduction and Explanatory Notes by President Roosevelt*, vols. 1–5. New York: Random House.

Ross, Stephen. 1973. "The Economic Theory of Agency: The Principal's Problem." *American Economic Review* 63: 134–39.

Rothenberg, Lawrence S. 1987. "Presidential Management of the Bureaucracy: The Reform of Motor Carrier Regulation at the ICC." Presented at the annual meeting of the Midwest Political Science Association, Chicago.

Rothman, Stanley, and S. Robert Lichter. 1983. "How Liberal are Bureaucrats?" *Regulation* (November–December): 16–22.

Rourke, Francis E. 1984. *Bureaucracy, Politics, and Public Policy*. 3d ed. Boston: Little, Brown.

Scher, Seymour. 1960. "Congressional Committee Members as Independent Agency Overseers: A Case Study." *American Political Science Review*: 911–20.

Schwartz, Bernard, ed. 1973. *The Economic Regulation of Business and Industry: A Legislative History of U.S. Regulatory Agencies*. New York: Chelsea House.

Seidman, Harold, and Robert Gilmour. 1986. *Politics, Position, and Power: From the Positive to the Regulatory State*. 4th ed. New York: Oxford University Press.

Seligman, Joel. 1985. *The SEC and the Future of Finance*. New York: Praeger.

———. 1982. *The Transformation of Wall Street: A History of the Securi-*

ties and Exchange Commission and Modern Corporate Finance.
Boston: Houghton Mifflin.

Shepsle, Kenneth A. 1978. *The Giant Jigsaw Puzzle*. Chicago: University of Chicago Press.

Simon, Herbert. 1976. *Administrative Behavior*. 3d ed. New York: Free Press.

Skowronek, Stephen. 1982. *Building a New American State: The Expansion of National Administrative Capabilities, 1877–1920*. Cambridge: Cambridge University Press.

Sobel, Robert. 1975. *N.Y.S.E.: A History of the New York Stock Exchange, 1935–1975*. New York: Weybright and Talley.

Sommer, A. A., Jr. 1976. "The Disclosure of Management Fraud." *Business Lawyer* 31 (March) 1283–93.

———. 1969. "Comments on Papers by Professor Demsetz and Professor Benston." In *Economic Policy and the Regulation of Corporate Securities*, ed. Manne. Washington, D.C.: American Enterprise Institute.

Spencer, Lee B., Jr. 1990. *1990 Annual Report and Proxy Rules of the Securities and Exchange Commission*, pp. ii–iv.

———. 1983. "The Electronic Library: Impact on Professionals." *Journal of Accountancy* (August): 74–76.

Stigler, George J. 1975. "Public Regulation of the Securities Market." In *The Citizen and the State*, ed. Stigler. Chicago: University of Chicago Press.

Stoll, Hans R. 1981. "Revolution in the Regulation of Securities Markets: An Examination of the Effects of Increased Competition." In *Case Studies in Regulation: Revolution and Reform*, ed. Weiss and Klass. Boston: Little, Brown.

Teweles, Richard J., and Edward S. Bradley. 1987. *The Stock Market*. 5th ed. New York: John Wiley.

Thompson, Victor A. 1961. *Modern Organization*. New York: Alfred A. Knopf.

Tipple, Terence, and J. Douglas Wellman. 1991. "Herbert Kaufman's Forest Ranger Thirty Years Later: From Simplicity and Homogeneity to Complexity and Diversity." *Public Administration Review* 51 (September–October): 421–28.

Truman, David, ed. 1973. *The Congress and America's Future*. New York: Prentice-Hall.

Tyler, Poyntz, ed. 1965. *Securities, Exchanges, and the SEC*. New York: H. W. Wilson.

Viscusi, W. Kip. 1984. *Regulating Consumer Product Safety*. Washington, D.C.: American Enterprise Institute.

———. 1983. "Presidential Oversight: Controlling the Regulators." *Journal of Policy Analysis and Management* 2: 157–73.

Waldo, Dwight. 1990. "A Theory of Public Administration." In Public Administration: The State of the Discipline, ed. Lynn and Wildavsky. Chatham, N.J.: Chatham House.

———. 1986. Afterword to *A Search for Public Administration*, ed. Brown and Stillman. College Station: Texas A&M University Press.

———. 1948. *The Administrative State: A Study of the Political Theory of American Public Administration*. New York: Ronald Press.

Walter, Ingo, ed. 1985. *Deregulating Wall Street: Commercial Bank Penetration of the Corporate Securities Market*. New York: John Wiley.

Warwick, Donald P. 1975. *A Theory of Public Bureaucracy*. Cambridge, Mass.: Harvard University Press.

Weaver, Suzanne. 1980. "Antitrust Division of the Department of Justice." In *The Politics of Regulation*, ed. Wilson. New York: Basic Books.

Weidenbaum, Murray L. 1990. *Business, Government, and the Public*. 4th ed. New York: Prentice-Hall.

———. 1984. "Regulatory Reform Under the Reagan Administration." In *The Reagan Regulatory Strategy: An Assessment*, ed. Eads and Fix. Washington, D.C.: Urban Institute.

Weingast, Barry R. 1984. "The Congressional-Bureaucratic System: A Principal-Agent Perspective with Applications to the SEC." *Public Choice* 44: 147–91.

Weingast, Barry R., and Mark J. Moran. 1983. "Bureaucratic Discretion or Congressional Control? Regulatory Policymaking by the Federal Trade Commission." *Journal of Political Economy* 91: 765–800.

Weiss, David M. 1986. *After the Trade is Made: Processing Securities Transactions*. New York Institute of Finance.

Welles, Chris. 1975. *The Last Days of the Club*. New York: E. P. Dutton.

Werner, Walter. 1975. "Adventure in Social Control of Finance: The National Market System for Securities." *Columbia Law Review* 75: 1233–98.

Wexler, Bernard. 1975. Memorandum to the Attorneys in the Office of Opinions and Review, "History of the SEC," August 3.

White, Leonard D. 1926. *Introduction to the Study of Public Administration*. New York: Macmillan.

Willoughby, W. F. 1919. *The Government of Modern States*. New York: Century.

Wilson, James Q. 1989. *Bureaucracy: What Government Agencies Do and Why They Do It*. New York: Basic Books.

Wilson, James Q., ed. 1980. *The Politics of Regulation*. New York: Basic Books.

Wilson, Woodrow. 1887. "The Study of Administration." *Political Science Quarterly* 2 (June): 197–222.

Wolfson, Nicholas. 1981. "A Critique of the Securities and Exchange Commission." *Emory Law Journal* 30: 119–67.

Woll, Peter. 1977. *American Bureaucracy*. 2d ed. W. W. Norton.

Government Documents

Congressional Hearings and Committee Reports Cited

Conference Committee

1975   *Report on Securities Acts Amendments of 1975,* S. 249, H. Rpt. 94-229, May 19, 1975, 94th Cong.

House Energy and Commerce Committee

1983   *Hearing before the Subcommittee on Telecommunications, Consumer Protection, and Finance to review SEC programs and FY84–FY86 authorization request,* February 15, 1983, 98th Cong.
   Report on the Authorization of Appropriations for the Securities and Exchange Commission, May 11, 1983, 98th Cong.

1984   *Hearings before the Subcommittee on Telecommunications, Consumer Protection, and Finance, Takeover Tactics and Public Policy,* March 28, May 23, 1984, 98th Cong.

1985   *Hearings before the Subcommittee on Telecommunications, Consumer Protection, and Finance, Corporate Takeovers,* pt. 2, May 23, June 12, October 24, 1985, 99th Cong.
   Report on Securities and Exchange Commission Authorization of Appropriations, June 4, 1985, 99th Cong.
   SEC: Oversight of the EDGAR System, March 14, 1985, 99th Cong.

1987   *Hearings before the Subcommittee on Telecommunications and Finance, Tender Offer Reform,* pt. 1, June 11, July 9, 22, 29, 1987, 100th Cong.
   Hearings before the Subcommittee on Telecommunications and Finance, Tender Offer Reform, pt. 2, September 16, 17, 1987, 100th Cong.

Joint Statement of John D. Dingell, Chairman, Committee on Energy and Commerce, and Edward J. Markey, Chairman, Subcommittee on Telecommunications and Finance, to accompany the introduction of FY1988–FY1990 authorization of the Securities and Exchange Commission, June 4, 1987, 100th Cong.
Report on Securities and Exchange Commission Authorization Act of 1987, September 9, 1987, 100th Cong.

1988　*Hearings on the SEC's Study on Self-Funding*, December 20, 1988, 100th Cong.

1989　*Hearings before the Subcommittee on Telecommunications and Finance on the Stock Market Reform Act of 1989, and Other Related Issues Concerning the Integrity of Our Financial Markets*, September 1989, 101st Cong.

House Interstate and Foreign Commerce Committee

1934　*Hearings on Stock Exchange Regulation*, February 14–16, 20–24, 27, 28, March 2, 6–8, 20–24, 1934, 73d Cong.

1972　*Report of the Subcommittee on Commerce and Finance, Securities Industry Study*, 1972, 92d Cong.

1977　*Report of the Subcommittee on Oversight and Investigations and the Subcommittee on Consumer Protection and Finance, Oversight of the Functioning and Administration of the Securities Acts Amendments of 1975*, June 21–23, July 26–28, 1977, 95th Cong.
Report of the Subcommittee on Oversight and Investigations and the Subcommittee on Consumer Protection and Finance, Oversight of the Functioning and Administration of the Securities Acts Amendments of 1975, November 15, 1977, 95th Cong.

1980　*Report of the Subcommittee on Oversight and Investigations and the Subcommittee on Consumer Protection and Finance, National Market System: Five Year Status Report*, August 1980, 96th Cong.

Senate Agriculture, Nutrition and Forestry Committee

1990   *Hearing on Issues Related to the Jurisdiction of the Commodity Futures Trading Commission and the Securities and Exchange Commission*, May 8, 1990, 101st Cong.

Senate Banking and Currency Committee

1934   *Hearings on Stock Exchange Practices*, pt. 15, February 26–28, March 1, 2, 5–9, 12, 16, 1934; pt. 16, March 23, 24, 27, April 2, 3, 5, 1934, 73d Cong.

1955   *Stock Market Study Report*, 1955, 84th Cong.

Senate Banking, Housing, and Urban Affairs Committee

1971   *Hearing on the Nomination of Philip A. Loomis, Jr., to be a member of the Securities and Exchange Commission*, September 22, 1971, 92d Cong.

1972   *Report of the Subcommittee on Securities, Securities Industry Study*, 1972, 92d Cong.

1973   *Hearing on the Nominations of G. Bradford Cook, Philip A. Loomis, Jr., and John R. Evans to be members of the Securities and Exchange Commission*, February 21, 1973, 93d Cong.
       Hearing on the Nominations of William E. Young, to be a member of the National Credit Union Board; David O. Meeker, Jr., to be Assistant Secretary of Housing and Urban Development; Ray Garrett, Jr. and A. A. Sommer, Jr., to be members of the SEC, July 26, 1973, 93d Cong., pp. 11–25.

1974   *Hearing on the Nominations of Henry C. Wallich, to be a member of the Board of Governors of the Federal Reserve System; Irving M. Pollack, to be a member of the Securities and Exchange Commission, and Jerome W. VanGorkom to be a Director of the Securities Investor Protection Corp.*, February 7, 1974, 93d Cong., pp. 4–16.
       Hearing on the Nominations of Philip A. Loomis, Jr., to be a member of the Securities and Exchange Commission, and Allen Greenspan, to be a member of the Council of Economic Advisors, August 8, 1974, 93d Cong.

1975   *Report on the Securities Acts Amendments of 1975*, April 14, 1975,
        94th Cong.
        *Hearing on the Nomination of Irving M. Pollack to be a member
        of the Securities and Exchange Commission*, July 31, 1975, 94th
        Cong.
        *Hearing on the Nomination of Roderick M. Hills to be SEC Chair-
        man*, October 6, 1975, 94th Cong.
        *Summary of the Principal Provisions of Securities Acts Amend-
        ments of 1975*, S. 249, January 1975, 94th Cong.

1983   *Hearing before the Subcommittee on Securities, SEC Reauthoriza-
        tion Request for Appropriations for FY 1984 through 1986*,
        March 25, 1983, 98th Cong.
        *Hearing on the Nomination of Charles Cox to be Commissioner
        on the Securities and Exchange Commission for a term ending
        June 5, 1988*, November 9, 1983, 98th Cong.
        Report on Amending the Securities Exchange Act of 1934, May 18,
        1983, 98th Cong.

1984   *Hearing on the Nominations of Charles L. Marinaccio, to be a
        Commissioner of the Securities and Exchange Commission for
        the remainder of the term expiring June 5, 1985, and Aulana L.
        Peters to be a Commissioner for a term expiring June 5, 1989*,
        May 16, 1984, 98th Cong.
        *Hearings on Tender Offer Practices and Corporate Director Respon-
        sibilities*, October 2, 1984, 98th Cong.

1985   *Hearing before the Committee on Banking, Housing and Urban
        Affairs on the nomination of Joseph Grundfest, to be a Commis-
        sioner on the Securities and Exchange Commission*, October 2,
        1985, 99th Cong.
        *Hearing before the Subcommittee on Securities to consider S. 919,
        to amend the Securities Exchange Act of 1934 to authorize
        FY86–FY88 appropriations for SEC*, April 17, 1985, 99th Cong.
        *Hearing before the Subcommittee on Securities, Impact of Corpo-
        rate Takeovers*, April 3, 4, June 6, 12, 1985, 99th Cong.

1987   *Hearings on Hostile Takeovers*, January 28, March 4, April 8, 1987,
        100th Cong.
        Hearings on Regulating Hostile Takeovers, June 23–25, 1987,
        100th Cong.
        Securities and Exchange Commission Authorization of Appropria-

tions and Technical Amendments to the Securities Laws, Report together with additional views to accompany S. 1452, July 9, 1987, 100th Cong.

1990 *Joint Hearings before the Subcommittee on Securities and the Committee on Banking, Housing, and Urban Affairs, SEC/CFTC Jurisdiction and Margin,* March 29, July 11, 12, 14, 1990, 101st Cong.

Senate Finance Committee

1985 *Hearings on Tax Treatment of Hostile Takeovers,* April 22, 1985, 99th Cong.

Senate Governmental Affairs Committee

1977 *Reports on the Study on Federal Regulation,* vols. 1–2, January, February, 1977, 95th Cong.

Agency and Task Force Reports and Studies Cited

General Accounting Office

1988 *Report to Congressional Requesters: Financial Markets, Preliminary Observations on the October 1987 Crash,* January 1988.

Presidential Task Force on Market Mechanisms (Brady Commission)

1988 *Report of the Presidential Task Force on Market Mechanisms, submitted to the President of the United States, the Secretary of the Treasury and the Chairman of the Federal Reserve Board,* January 1988.

Securities and Exchange Commission

1963 *Report of Special Study of the Securities Markets of the Securities and Exchange Commission, to the House Interstate and Foreign Commerce Committee,* H. Doc. no. 95, 88th Cong., 1963.

1966   *Public Policy Implications of Investment Company Growth, Referred to House Interstate and Foreign Commerce Committee*, H. Rpt. no. 2337, December 2, 1966, 89th Cong.

1971   *Institutional Investor Study*, H. Doc. no. 92-64, 92d Cong., 1971.

1972   *Rules of Practice and Rules Relating to Investigations and Code of Behavior Governing Ex Parte Communications Between Persons Outside the Commission and Decisional Employees*, effective December 1, 1972.
       Statement on the Future Structure of the Securities Markets, February 1972.

1973   *Policy Statement on the Structure of a Central Market System*, March 1973.

1986   *Staff Studies of Multiple Trading of Options*, November 1986.

1987   *Internationalization of the Securities Markets: A Report of the Staff of the U.S. Securities and Exchange Commission to the Senate Committee on Banking, Housing and Urban Affairs and the House Committee on Energy and Commerce*, July 27, 1987.

1988   *EDGAR: A Status Report*, June 30, 1987. Issued in compliance with the Securities and Exchange Commission Authorization Act of 1987, Pub. Law 100-181 (December 4, 1987).
       The October 1987 Market Break: A Report by the Division of Market Regulation, February 1988.
       Self-Funding Study, September 20, 1988. Submitted in partial response to the request of the Securities Subcommittee of the Senate Committee on Banking, Housing and Urban Affairs (S. Rpt. 100-105), 100th Cong.

1990   Division of Market Regulation, *Trading Analysis of October 13 and 16, 1989*, May 1990.

Index

269

Pitt Series in
Policy and Institutional Studies

BERT A. ROCKMAN, *Editor*

Demographic Change and the American Future
R. Scott Fosler, William Alonso, Jack A. Meyer, and Rosemary Kern

Economic Decline and Political Change: Canada,
Great Britain, and the United States
Harold D. Clarke, Marianne C. Stewart, and Gary Zuk, Editors

Executive Leadership in Anglo-American Systems
Colin Campbell, S.J., and Margaret Jane Wyszomirski, Editors

Extraordinary Measures: The Exercise of
Prerogative Powers in the United States
Daniel P. Franklin

Foreign Policy Motivation: A General Theory and a Case Study
Richard W. Cottam

"He Shall Not Pass This Way Again":
The Legacy of Justice William O. Douglas
Stephen L. Wasby, Editor

History and Context in Comparative Public Policy
Douglas E. Ashford, Editor

Homeward Bound: Explaining Changes in Congressional Behavior
Glenn Parker

How Does Social Science Work? Reflections on Practice
Paul Diesing

Imagery and Ideology in U.S. Policy Toward Libya, 1969–1982
Mahmoud G. ElWarfally

The Impact of Policy Analysis
James M. Rogers

Iran and the United States: A Cold War Case Study
Richard W. Cottam

Japanese Prefectures and Policymaking
Steven R. Reed

Making Regulatory Policy
Keith Hawkins and John M. Thomas, Editors

Managing the Presidency: Carter, Reagan,
and the Search for Executive Harmony
Colin Campbell, S.J.

The Moral Dimensions of Public Policy Choice:
Beyond the Market Paradigm
John Martin Gillroy and Maurice Wade, Editors

Native Americans and Public Policy
Fremont J. Lyden and Lyman H. Legters, Editors

Organizing Governance, Governing Organizations
Colin Campbell, S.J., and B. Guy Peters, Editors

Party Organizations in American Politics
Cornelius P. Cotter et al.

Perceptions and Behavior in Soviet Foreign Policy
Richard K. Herrmann

Pesticides and Politics: The Life Cycle of a Public Issue
Christopher J. Bosso

Policy Analysis by Design
Davis B. Bobrow and John S. Dryzek

The Political Failure of Employment Policy, 1945–1982
Gary Mucciaroni

Political Leadership: A Source Book
Barbara Kellerman, Editor

The Politics of Public Utility Regulation
William T. Gormley, Jr.

The Politics of the U.S. Cabinet: Representation
in the Executive Branch, 1789–1984
Jeffrey E. Cohen

Politics Within the State: Elite Bureaucrats
and Industrial Policy in Authoritarian Brazil
Ben Ross Schneider

The Presidency and Public Policy Making
George C. Edwards III, Steven A. Shull, and Norman C. Thomas, Editors

Private Markets and Public Intervention: A Primer for Policy Designers
Harvey Averch

The Promise and Paradox of Civil Service Reform
Patricia W. Ingraham and David H. Rosenbloom, Editors

Public Policy in Latin America: A Comparative Survey
John W. Sloan

Reluctant Partners: Implementing Federal Policy
Robert P. Stoker